HOW TO BE THE MOST INTERESTING MAN IN THE ROOM

44 Techniques for Mastering Knowledge, Skills, and Charisma to Captivate Any Audience

JAMES RUGGER

Copyright © 2023 by James Rugger

All rights reserved.

No part of this book may be used or reproduced in any form whatsoever without written permission except in the case of brief quotations in critical articles or reviews.

First Edition: April 2023

Table Of Content

More Books From The Author 5
Introduction 1
    Why Being Boring is a Crime 4
    How to Use This Book 5
Chapter 7
One 7
    The Art of Captivating Conversation 7
        How to Charm Your Way Through Any Social Situation 8
        From Small Talk to Big Ideas: Mastering the Art of Conversation 24
        Secrets of Storytelling: How to Leave Your Audience Begging for More 27
        DISCLAIMER!!! 30
Chapter 33
Two 33
    Hacking Your Brain for Maximum Fascination 33
        How to Develop a Magnetic Personality That Draws People In 34
        Mind Hacking 101: Unlocking Your Inner Genius 36
        Secrets of the World's Most Fascinating People 39
Chapter 43
Three 43
    Unlock Your Inner Genius: Mastering Knowledge and Skills 43
        Ignite Your Passion: Unleashing the Power of Curiosity 44
        Skill Up Your Game: Building a Diverse Skillset 46
        Learn Like a Pro: Strategies to Rapidly Absorb New Information & Become Fascinating 48

Chapter 53
Four 53
   Adventures of a Lifetime: Living Your Most
   Interesting Life 53
      How to Make Every Day a New Adventure 56
      The Science of Adventure: Why Taking Risks is
      the Key to Happiness 59

Chapter 63
Five 63
   Making the Most of Your Unique Talents and
   Abilities 63
      Steps to Making the Most of Your Unique
      Talents and Abilities 65
      Standing Out in a World Full of Copycats 67
      People who embraced their unique abilities 69

Chapter 73
Six 73
   Overcoming Obstacles to Fascination 73
      How to Overcome Shyness and Social Anxiety 74
      The Art of Handling Criticism and Rejection with
      Grace 81
      The Science of Confidence: How to Project it,
      Own it, and Love it 84

Conclusion 91
Bonus 95
   7-Day Challenge to Become the Most Interesting Man 95

More Books From The Author

(All available in the Amazon store!)

How to Not Give a Fck Guide: A Down-To-Earth Guide on How to Not Care What Others Think of You and Live Life on Your Own Terms

How to Not Give a Fck Journal: Unleash Your Inner Rebel and Live Authentically with Prompts and Quotes

My Little Request

I need to improve my contents and book creation process to keep satisfying and giving you value and I can only improve through your feedback.

So I'd appreciate your feedback as you go through this book. Leave a review or send me a private email at jamesrugger001@gmail.com.
Thank you.

Introduction

Have you ever found yourself at a social gathering, feeling awkward and out of place?

I know I have. I remember attending a fancy dinner party at a friend's house about 12 years ago.

I was dressed to the nines, but my confidence was shattered. I was surrounded by successful, well-spoken individuals, and I felt like I didn't belong.

That was until a man walked in and changed the entire dynamic of the room. He was charismatic, charming, and incredibly interesting. Everyone gravitated towards him, eager to hear more about his stories and experiences. It was as if he had a magnetic force that drew people in.

As the night went on, I found myself observing him closely, trying to figure out what made him so captivating. Was it his perfectly-tailored suit? His vast knowledge on a range of topics? His ability to make everyone laugh? I couldn't quite put my finger on it.

But what I did know was that I wanted to be like him. I wanted to be the person who could light up a room with just their presence. I wanted to be the most interesting man in the room.

And that took me on a long journey of discovering the secrets of being able to become amazingly charming. Through years of research, trial and error, and personal experience, I've discovered the secrets to becoming the most fascinating person in any social setting, and today, I am nothing compared to myself many years ago. I am a far more interesting person.

At first, I only taught my friends and family those secrets, but to my amazement, my techniques performed wonders. I stretched my borders a little and taught those techniques to strangers who had problems with social situations, and I got the same result.

Soon enough, I discovered that many other individuals had the same issue, and they wanted to go from being shy and not knowing what to say in social situations to becoming a confident, magnetic person who easily connects with people. That is exactly why I put together everything I've learned in my quest to become an interesting man in this book. And I did it in such a way that even a 10-year-old could easily apply them.

These techniques were the perfect solution for my friend Mike and hundreds of other people; they worked for them, and I believe that with a little reading time and practice, they will work for you too.

The truth is, there are other strategies out there that claim to make you socially awesome, but in the end, they only give you shallow-rooted information that may or may not work. Trust me when I tell you, I practically tried almost everything I could lay my hands on before discovering what it takes.
In the pages that follow, you'll find practical tips, techniques, and strategies for unlocking your true potential and captivating anyone you meet. Whether you're a shy introvert or a confident extrovert, this book will help you master the art of social interaction and become the person everyone wants to be around. So, let's get started on your journey to becoming the most interesting man in the room!

Why Being Boring is a Crime

Being boring is a crime. Yes, you read that right. In today's fast-paced and hyper-connected world, where attention spans are dwindling by the second, being boring can have dire consequences. It can mean the difference between landing a job, winning a client, or impressing a potential partner, and falling short.

Think about it: when was the last time you were genuinely captivated by someone who was dull and uninteresting? When was the last time you were intrigued by someone who had nothing exciting to say or lacked passion for anything?

Chances are, you can't remember.

Now, think about the people who have left a lasting impression on you. The ones who had a unique perspective, a captivating story, or an infectious energy. These are the people who grab our attention, inspire us, and leave us wanting more.

The truth is, being boring is not just a personal shortcoming - it can have real-world consequences. It can affect our relationships, our careers, and our overall quality of life. And that's why it's crucial to learn how to become an interesting person.

By cultivating a curious mindset, developing a diverse skillset, and finding our passion, we can break free from the shackles of boredom and unleash our full potential. So, let's make a pact to never settle for mediocrity, to always strive for excellence, and to become the most interesting versions of ourselves. After all, being boring is a crime we can't afford to commit.

How to Use This Book

Welcome to "How to Become the Most Interesting Man in the Room"! This book is designed to help you unlock your full potential and become the most captivating person in any social setting. Here's a quick note on how to use the book:

Read the book from start to finish: The book is divided into chapters that cover various aspects of becoming the most interesting person in the room. I recommend reading the book in order to get a comprehensive understanding of the strategies and techniques covered.

Take notes: As you read the book, take notes on the strategies and techniques that resonate with you. Jot down examples and ideas that you can apply to your own life.

Practice, practice, practice: Becoming the most interesting person in the room requires practice. Try out the techniques and strategies covered in the book in your daily life. Challenge yourself to step outside your comfort zone and apply what you've learned.

Share your journey: Share your progress and experiences with others. Seek feedback and advice from trusted friends or mentors. Engage in meaningful conversations and apply the strategies covered in the book to cultivate deeper connections.

Also, I want you to know that becoming the most interesting person in the room is not an overnight process. It takes time, effort, and commitment. But with the strategies and techniques covered in this book, you can unlock your full potential and become the most captivating version of yourself.

Chapter One

The Art of Captivating Conversation

Welcome to the art of captivating conversation! We've all been there - stuck in a conversation that feels dull and lifeless, desperately searching for a way out. On the other hand, we've also experienced those conversations that leave us feeling energized, inspired, and connected to the person we're speaking with.

The ability to engage in captivating conversation is a valuable skill that can enhance every aspect of our lives. Whether it's in our personal or professional relationships, being able to communicate effectively and connect with others on a deeper level can lead to better outcomes and a more fulfilling life.

In this chapter, we'll explore the secrets to captivating conversation.

From mastering the art of active listening, to knowing how to ask the right questions and deliver engaging stories, we'll cover everything you need to know to become a skilled conversationalist.

You'll learn how to approach any conversation with confidence, connect with others on a deeper level, and leave a lasting impression. So, whether you're an introvert looking to break out of your shell, or an extrovert looking to take your conversation skills to the next level, this book has something for you.

So, let's dive in and discover the art of captivating conversation!

How to Charm Your Way Through Any Social Situation

Charming your way through any social situation is not about being fake or manipulative, but rather about having the ability to connect with others in a genuine and authentic way. Whether you're at a job interview, a networking event, or a social gathering, being able to make a good impression and connect with others can open up doors of opportunity.

So, how do you charm your way through any social situation? Here are a few key strategies:

1. MASTER THE ART OF BODY LANGUAGE:

Did you know that your body language can speak volumes before you even utter a single word? That's right, mastering the art of body language can be a game-changer in your social interactions, whether it's a job interview, a first date, or a networking event. So, let's dive into the fascinating world of body language and explore how you can use it to charm your way through any social situation.

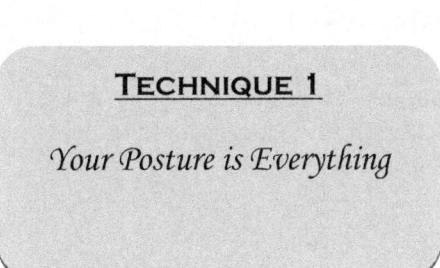

TECHNIQUE 1

Your Posture is Everything

First and foremost, posture is everything. Standing tall with your shoulders back and your head held high conveys confidence and authority. On the other hand, slouching and looking down at the ground can make you appear insecure and unapproachable.

TECHNIQUE 2

Make eye contact

Eye contact is another crucial element of body language. Making eye contact with the person you're speaking with shows that you're engaged and interested in the conversation. Avoiding eye contact can make you seem a bit shifty or untrustworthy. But, be careful not to overdo it - staring too intensely can make the other person uncomfortable.

Gestures can also be an effective way to convey your message and emphasize key points.

Just be careful not to use too many distracting or exaggerated gestures, or you risk coming across as insincere or over-the-top.

TECHNIQUE 3

Copy their body language

Mirroring the other person's body language can also be a powerful tool in establishing rapport and connection. If the other person leans in, you should lean in too. If you see them crossing their arms, you can do the same. This subconsciously tells the other person that you're on the same wavelength and can create a sense of trust and comfort.

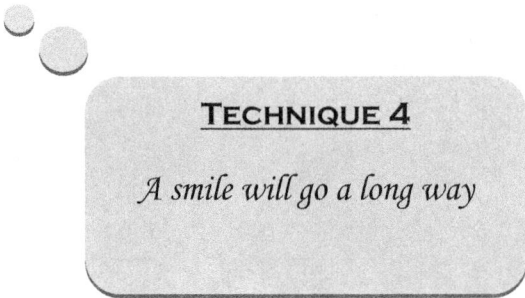

TECHNIQUE 4

A smile will go a long way

Your facial expressions are also crucial in conveying your emotions and interest in the conversation. A smile can go a long way in making you seem approachable and friendly, while a frown or scowl can make you seem unapproachable and unfriendly.

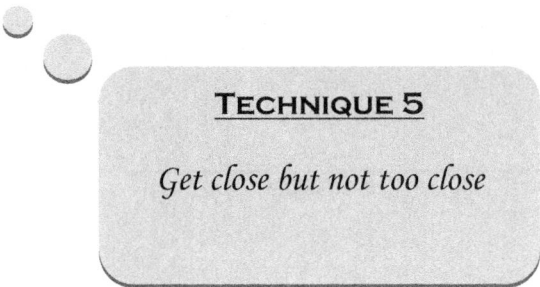

TECHNIQUE 5

Get close but not too close

And finally, be aware of personal space. Invading someone's personal space can really make them feel uncomfortable or even threatened. On the other hand, standing too far away can make you seem distant and uninterested.

By mastering the art of body language, you can communicate more effectively, establish deeper connections, and ultimately charm your way through any social situation. So, start practicing your posture, eye contact, gestures, and facial expressions, and watch how your social interactions improve dramatically!

2. DELIVER A MEMORABLE INTRODUCTION

Delivering a memorable introduction can set the tone for any social or professional interaction. It's your chance to make a great first impression and establish a connection with the other person or group.

Here are some tips for delivering a memorable introduction:

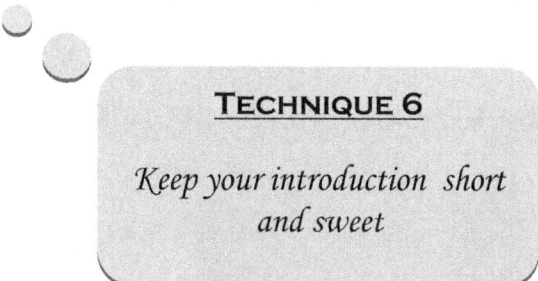

TECHNIQUE 6

Keep your introduction short and sweet

Your introduction should be brief and straight to the point. A long and rambling introduction can make you seem nervous or unprepared.

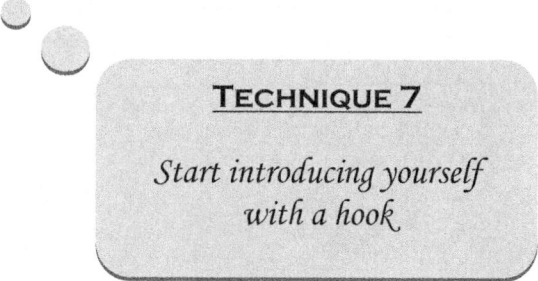

TECHNIQUE 7

Start introducing yourself with a hook

Grab the other person's attention with a catchy opening line or an interesting fact about yourself. This alone will make them more likely to remember you.

TECHNIQUE 8

Approach people with confidence!

Confidence is key when delivering an introduction. Stand up straight, make eye contact, and speak clearly and confidently.

TECHNIQUE 9

Put in full enthusiasm

Demonstrate your enthusiasm for the topic or situation at hand. This will make you seem more approachable and engaging.

TECHNIQUE 10

Just be your respectful self

Don't try to be someone you're not. Be yourself and let your personality shine through.

TECHNIQUE 11

Practice. Practice. Practice!

Practice your introduction beforehand so that you feel comfortable and confident when the time comes.

Remember, the goal of a memorable introduction is to create a connection with the other person or group. By keeping it short and sweet, starting with a hook, being confident and enthusiastic, and staying true to yourself, you can deliver an introduction that will leave a lasting impression.

3. ENGAGE IN MEANINGFUL CONVERSATION:

Engaging in meaningful conversation is a valuable skill that can help you establish deeper connections with others, learn new perspectives, and broaden your horizons. But what does it mean to have a meaningful conversation, and how can you engage in one? Here are some advice to follow and examples to help you out.

TECHNIQUE 12

Give them your full attention

One of the keys to engaging in a meaningful conversation is to actively listen to the other person. This means giving them your full attention, asking questions, and showing that you are genuinely interested in what they have to say. For example, you could ask follow-up questions like "Could you tell me more about that?" or "How did you feel when it happened?"

Share your own experiences: Don't be afraid to share your own experiences and perspectives. This can help the other person understand where you're coming from and can lead to a deeper conversation. For example, if the other person is talking about a recent trip they took, you could share your own travel experiences and ask them for recommendations.

TECHNIQUE 13

Be open-minded in your conversations

Try to approach the conversation with an open mind and a willingness to learn. Don't dismiss the other person's ideas or opinions without considering them first. For example, if the other person has a different political view than you, you could ask them why they believe what they do and try to understand their perspective.

TECHNIQUE 14

Do better than small talk

While small talk can be a good icebreaker, it doesn't usually lead to a meaningful conversation. Instead, try to steer the conversation towards more meaningful topics, such as personal values, goals, or experiences. For example, instead of asking about the weather, you could ask the other person about a recent challenge they overcame.

TECHNIQUE 15

Always stay focused in the conversation

Try to stay focused on the conversation and avoid distractions. Put away your phone, turn off the TV, and give the other person your undivided attention. This shows that you respect their time and are fully engaged in the conversation.

Overall, engaging in meaningful conversation requires active listening, sharing your own experiences, being open-minded, avoiding small talk, and staying focused. By practicing these skills, you can build deeper connections with others and broaden your horizons.

4. USE HUMOR AND POSITIVITY

Using humor and positivity is a powerful tool for building connections with others, defusing tension, and boosting your own mood. Here are some tips and real-life examples of how to use humor and positivity effectively:

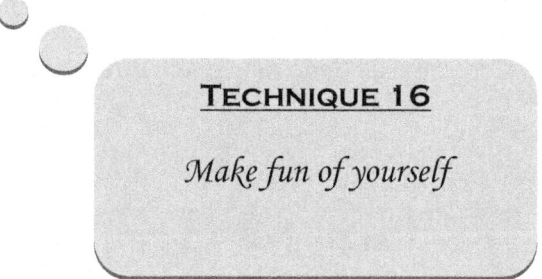

TECHNIQUE 16

Make fun of yourself

One way to use humor is to make fun of yourself. This can help to break the ice and put others at ease. For example, if you spill your coffee in a meeting, you could joke about needing a bib.

Don't take yourself too seriously. If you make a mistake, just laugh it off and move on. This can show others that you're easygoing and approachable. For example, if you trip and fall, you could laugh and say, "I meant to do that!"

If there's tension in a situation, using humor can help to break the tension and make everyone more comfortable. For example, if two colleagues are arguing, you could crack a joke to lighten the mood and help them move past the disagreement.

When things go wrong, try to find the silver lining. This can help you stay positive and focused on solutions. For example, if your flight gets delayed, you could use the extra time to catch up on work or read a book.

TECHNIQUE 17

Share good news with people

Sharing good news with others can help to spread positivity and boost everyone's mood.

For example, if you get a promotion at work, you could share the news with your colleagues and celebrate together.

> **TECHNIQUE 18**
>
> *Speak positive things into your life*

Positive affirmations are statements that reinforce positive beliefs about yourself or others. These can help to boost your mood and build confidence. For example, you could say to yourself, "I am capable and confident" before giving a presentation.

Overall, using humor and positivity can help you build connections with others, defuse tension, and boost your mood. By using self-deprecating humor, looking for the bright side, sharing positive news, using humor to defuse tension, using positive affirmations, and laughing at yourself, you can create a more positive and enjoyable environment for yourself and others.

5. LEAVE A LASTING IMPRESSION

> **TECHNIQUE 19**
>
> *Make your leave memorable*

As the conversation winds down, make sure to leave a lasting impression. Thank the person for their time, exchange contact information if appropriate, and follow up with a thoughtful email or message to solidify the connection.

In conclusion, charming your way through any social situation is a skill that can be learned and refined with practice. By mastering the art of body language, delivering a memorable introduction, engaging in meaningful conversation, using humor and positivity, and leaving a lasting impression, you can become a skilled charmer and make a lasting impact on those around you.

From Small Talk to Big Ideas: Mastering the Art of Conversation

Have you ever been in a social situation where you found yourself struggling to keep the conversation going? Perhaps you're stuck in a never-ending loop of small talk about the weather or your job, and you're desperately trying to think of a way to steer the conversation towards something more meaningful. If so, you're not alone. Many people struggle with the art of conversation, but with a few tips and tricks, you can take your small talk to big ideas and engage in more meaningful and interesting conversations.

> **TECHNIQUE 20**
>
> *Ask open-ended questions*

One key to mastering the art of conversation is to ask open-ended questions. These are questions that can't be answered with a simple "yes" or "no," and they encourage the other person to share more about themselves and their experiences. For example, instead of asking "Do you like your job?" try asking "What inspired you to pursue that career?" This not only shows that you're interested in the other person, but it also opens up the conversation to more interesting and thought-provoking topics.

Another way to engage in more meaningful conversation is to actively listen to the other person.

This means giving them your full attention, asking follow-up questions, and showing that you understand and care about what they're saying. For example, if someone is telling you about a recent trip they took, you could ask follow-up questions like "What was your favorite part of the trip?" or "Did you have any unexpected experiences while you were there?"

TECHNIQUE 21

Share your personal experiences

Using personal anecdotes is also a great way to connect with others and engage in more interesting conversation. By sharing your own experiences, you're not only showing vulnerability but also allowing others to see your perspective on certain topics. For example, if you're discussing a recent news story, you could share a personal experience that relates to the topic, such as how you or someone you know was affected by it.

Another way to take your small talk to big ideas is to be knowledgeable about a wide range of topics. This doesn't mean you need to be an expert on everything, but having a basic understanding of current events, popular culture, and other relevant topics can help you engage in more interesting and informative conversations.

Real-life examples of using these conversation techniques are abundant. For instance, a colleague at work might mention that they are passionate about a certain topic or issue. By asking open-ended questions and actively listening, you can find out more about their perspective and what drives them. You might even discover a shared interest or passion that leads to a deeper conversation.

By asking open-ended questions, actively listening, sharing personal anecdotes, and being knowledgeable about a range of topics, you can engage in more meaningful and interesting conversations. So the next time you find yourself stuck in small talk, remember that with a little effort, you can take the conversation to bigger and better places.

Secrets of Storytelling: How to Leave Your Audience Begging for More

From the earliest days of human communication, storytelling has been a crucial way of sharing ideas, experiences, and emotions. But what separates a good story from a great one? How do you leave your audience begging for more? In this section, we'll explore the secrets of storytelling and how you can use them to captivate your audience.

One of the most important elements of a great story is a clear and compelling narrative structure.

> **TECHNIQUE 22**
>
> *Tell a clear compelling story using sensory details*

A well-told story has a clear beginning, middle, and end, with each part serving a specific purpose. The beginning should introduce the main characters and setting, while the middle builds tension and conflict, and the end provides resolution and closure. For example, consider the classic story of "The Three Little Pigs." The beginning introduces the three pigs and the wolf, the middle shows the pigs building their houses and the wolf trying to blow them down, and the end shows the wolf being defeated and the pigs living happily ever after.

Another key to great storytelling is the use of sensory details to bring the story to life. By describing sights, sounds, smells, and textures, you can create a vivid and immersive experience for your audience. For example, instead of saying "The sun was shining," you might say "The warm sun beat down on my skin, casting a golden glow over the landscape."

Emotional resonance is another important element of great storytelling. By tapping into universal emotions such as love, fear, joy, and sorrow, you can create a powerful and unforgettable story. For example, the story of "Romeo and Juliet" has endured for centuries because of its powerful depiction of love and tragedy.

TECHNIQUE 23

Acting surprised + humour = Mad combo

Using humor and surprise is also a great way to keep your audience engaged and begging for more. A well-placed joke or unexpected twist can break up tension and keep the story fresh and interesting. For example, in the story of "The Boy Who Cried Wolf," the unexpected twist at the end (the boy being eaten by the wolf) is what makes the story so memorable.

Finally, a great storyteller knows how to connect with their audience on a personal level. By using relatable characters and situations, and by showing vulnerability and authenticity, you can create a deep and meaningful connection with your audience. For example, the story of "The Ugly Duckling" resonates with so many people because it's about feeling like an outsider and finding your place in the world.

To better illustrate everything I've said here, I'll give you two stories right now, one is boring and the other is interesting, attention grabbing and will make the listeners yearn for moreeee…

Story: A Day at the Beach

Boring story:
It was a sunny day, so we decided to go to the beach. We drove for a while and finally found a spot to park. We set up our chairs and umbrella and sat there for a few hours. We went for a swim in the ocean and played some beach volleyball. We had some sandwiches for lunch and then sat

around for a while longer. We packed up and left in the late afternoon.

Interesting story:
As soon as we arrived at the beach, I felt the sand between my toes and the warm sun on my skin. The waves were crashing against the shore, and the salty sea air was refreshing. We set up our chairs and umbrella and started exploring. We found some cool shells and watched as a group of kids built an elaborate sandcastle. I dove into the ocean and felt the exhilarating rush of the waves pushing me back to shore. We played some beach volleyball and made some new friends. For lunch, we had fresh sandwiches from a nearby café, and I savored the tangy taste of the tomato and basil. As the day went on, we watched a beautiful sunset and toasted marshmallows over a bonfire. We left feeling refreshed and rejuvenated, already planning our next trip to the beach.

In the interesting story, the narrator/teller uses sensory details, emotions, and personal experiences to create a vivid and engaging narrative, while the boring story lacks these elements and simply lists the activities of the day without much depth or excitement.

In conclusion, great storytelling is a skill that can be learned and mastered. By using a clear narrative structure, sensory details, emotional resonance, humor and surprise, and personal connection, you can leave your audience begging for more. So the next time you have a story to tell, remember these secrets of storytelling and watch as your audience becomes captivated and enthralled.

DISCLAIMER!!!

Now I have to say this!
As much as we've been discussing how you can become a magnetic person, how to create connections, and how to captivate any audience,

It's important to note that I'm not saying that you should do everything in your power to impress people. No! There's a difference between building your social skills and pleasing people; there's a difference between entertaining an audience and seeking validation from an audience.

Sometimes, people fail to understand this fact and mistake the real aim for something that can cause serious damage in their lives.

In order to avoid such confusion, I recommend you get one of my books titled "How to Not Give a F*ck Guide." The book will show you practical strategies to stop stressing yourself out, feeling overwhelmed by what others think of you, or worrying about little things.

HOW TO NOT GIVE A F*CK GUIDE

JAMES RUGGER

You can get it on Amazon by clicking [HERE](https://a.co/d/6ptNUdG). *(Soft-copy)*

or typing this URL into your browser.
https://a.co/d/6ptNUdG
If you've been enjoying this book so far then you definitely will enjoy the book I just recommended.

Chapter Two

Hacking Your Brain for Maximum Fascination

Are you ready to unlock the secrets of your own mind and become even more fascinating than you already are? In this chapter, we will explore the fascinating world of brain hacking, and how you can use this knowledge to captivate any audience.

Our brains are incredible machines, capable of processing vast amounts of information and generating creative ideas, but what if we could tap into our brain's full potential? In this chapter, we will explore how to optimize our brain's function, including memory, creativity, and critical thinking. With these hacks, you'll be able to hold your audience's attention like never before, leaving them mesmerized and begging for more. So let's dive in and discover the secrets of hacking your brain for maximum fascination!

How to Develop a Magnetic Personality That Draws People In

Having a magnetic personality is an incredibly valuable trait in today's world. Whether you're trying to make new friends, network in your career, or simply charm your way through social situations, a magnetic personality can help you achieve your goals. But what exactly does it mean to have a magnetic personality? Simply put, it's the ability to draw people in and make them feel comfortable and at ease around you.

So, how can you develop a magnetic personality that draws people in? The first step is to focus on developing your interpersonal skills. This includes things like active listening, empathizing with others, and using positive body language. When you show genuine interest in other people, they are more likely to be drawn to you.

Another key factor is your attitude. A positive, optimistic outlook just like we discussed in the last chapter can be infectious, and people are naturally drawn to those who radiate positivity. Conversely, negativity and cynicism can be off-putting and make people want to steer clear.

Lastly, it's important to be authentic and true to yourself. Trying to be someone you're not will only lead to feelings of discomfort and inauthenticity. Instead, embrace your unique qualities and quirks, and let your true self shine through.

Here's an example: Let's say you're attending a networking event. Instead of focusing solely on promoting yourself and your business, take the time to genuinely connect with others. Ask them about their own interests and goals, and show a genuine interest in what they have to say. Use positive body language like smiling, maintaining eye contact, and leaning in slightly to show that you're engaged and present in the conversation. By focusing on building genuine connections, you'll naturally develop a magnetic personality that draws people in.

Mind Hacking 101: Unlocking Your Inner Genius

The human brain is an incredibly complex and powerful organ, capable of incredible feats of creativity, innovation, and problem-solving. Yet, despite its immense potential, many people find themselves struggling to tap into their inner genius and unlock their full potential. That's where the concept of "mind hacking" comes in - the idea that by understanding how the brain works and taking a strategic approach to cognitive optimization, we can unlock our inner genius and achieve our goals.

One of the first steps in mind hacking is understanding the power of the subconscious mind.

This is the part of the brain that operates below our conscious awareness, but is responsible for many of our thoughts, behaviors, and habits. By learning to tap into the subconscious mind and reprogram our thought patterns, we can unlock new levels of creativity and innovation.

One technique for doing this is called visualization.

> **TECHNIQUE 24**
>
> *Visualize yourself achieving your goals*

By visualizing our goals and imagining ourselves achieving them, we can train our subconscious mind to work towards those goals in a more efficient and effective way. For example, let's say you're an athlete training for a big race. By visualizing yourself crossing the finish line first, feeling strong and confident, you can program your subconscious mind to work towards that outcome.

Another important aspect of mind hacking is understanding the power of focus and concentration. In today's fast-paced world, distractions are everywhere, and it can be difficult to stay focused on our goals. But by learning to harness the power of concentration, we can accomplish more in less time and with less effort.

One technique for improving focus is called "single-tasking."

TECHNIQUE 25

Practice single-tasking

This involves focusing all of your attention on one task at a time, rather than trying to multitask or switch between tasks. By eliminating distractions and focusing your full attention on one task, you can achieve a state of "flow" where you're fully immersed in the task at hand and performing at your highest level.

TECHNIQUE 25

Take care of your body

Finally, it's important to understand the role that our physical health plays in our mental performance. By taking care of our bodies through regular exercise, healthy eating, and adequate sleep, we can boost our cognitive function and unlock our inner genius.

One example of this is the "exercise effect." Studies have shown that regular exercise can boost brain function and improve cognitive performance, including memory, attention, and problem-solving. By incorporating regular exercise into your routine, you can enhance your mind and unlock your full potential.

In summary, mind hacking is all about understanding how the brain works and taking a strategic approach to cognitive optimization. By tapping into the power of the subconscious mind, improving focus and concentration, and taking care of our physical health, we can unlock our inner genius and achieve our goals. With a little practice and persistence, anyone can become a master at mind hacking and unlock their full potential.

Secrets of the World's Most Fascinating People

The world is full of fascinating people who seem to have an almost magical ability to captivate those around them.

They effortlessly command attention and leave a lasting impression on everyone they meet. What is their secret?

It turns out that there are certain traits and habits that the world's most fascinating people have in common. By studying these individuals and learning from their example, we too can become more captivating and intriguing to others.

One of the secrets of fascinating people is that they are genuinely interested in others.

> **TECHNIQUE 26**
>
> *Pick genuine interest in people*

They take the time to listen and engage with those around them, showing a sincere curiosity and respect for other people's experiences and perspectives. This not only makes them more likable, but it also allows them to gain valuable insights and knowledge from a wide range of sources.

> **TECHNIQUE 27**
>
> *Tell compelling stories*

Another key trait of fascinating people is their ability to tell compelling stories. Whether it's sharing a personal anecdote or recounting a fascinating historical event, they know how to craft a narrative that captures their audience's attention and keeps them hooked until the end. You can always go back to the first chapter of this book where we discussed it in details.

> **TECHNIQUE 28**
>
> *Have a strong sense of purpose*

Fascinating people also tend to have a strong sense of purpose and passion. They are driven by a deep desire to achieve their goals and make a meaningful impact on the world. This sense of purpose gives them a natural confidence and charisma that draws others to them.

> **TECHNIQUE 29**
>
> *Get highly skilled in a particular field*

Finally, fascinating people are often highly skilled in a particular area or field. Whether it's art, music, science, or business, they have developed a deep knowledge and expertise that sets them apart from others. This mastery not only gives them a sense of accomplishment and fulfillment, but it also makes them incredibly interesting and valuable to others.

By incorporating these traits and habits into our own lives, we too can become more fascinating and captivating to those around us. It takes time and effort to develop these skills, but the good news is the rewards are well worth it. So why not start today and unlock your own inner fascination?

Chapter Three

Unlock Your Inner Genius: Mastering Knowledge and Skills

Have you ever looked at someone you met and thought, "Wow, they are just so interesting and knowledgeable about so many things"?

Well, the good news is that you too can become that person! By unlocking your inner genius and mastering knowledge and skills, you can become a fascinating and dynamic individual who always has something new and exciting to share. So, let's dive in and explore some tips and techniques for unlocking your full potential and becoming the most interesting person in the room! And don't worry, we'll throw in some jokes and humor along the way to keep things light and fun.

Ignite Your Passion: Unleashing the Power of Curiosity

Passion is what drives us to achieve great things and to push beyond our limits. It's what makes life exciting and fulfilling, and it's something that we all have the potential to ignite within ourselves.

One of the key ways to unleash the power of passion is through curiosity. When we are curious, we become open to new experiences and ideas, and we begin to explore the world with a sense of wonder and awe. This curiosity fuels our passion and inspires us to take action towards our goals and dreams.

TECHNIQUE 30

Get curious about things

To ignite your passion, start by cultivating a curious mindset. Ask questions, seek out new information, and be open to different perspectives. When you approach the world with curiosity, you'll find that there's always something new to learn and discover.

Another important factor in unleashing the power of passion is to follow your interests and pursue your passions.

Technique 31

Follow things that interest you, things you have passion for

Whether it's art, music, science, or something else entirely, find what you're passionate about and dive deep into it. Immerse yourself in the topic, attend events and conferences, and connect with others who share your interests.

It's also crucial to stay open to new opportunities and to be willing to take risks. Sometimes, the things that ignite our passion the most are the things that scare us the most. So don't be scared to step outside of your comfort zone and try new things.

Finally, surround yourself with people who support and encourage your passions. Whether it's friends, family, or mentors, having a strong support system can make all the difference in achieving your goals and staying motivated.

When we ignite our passion and unleash the power of curiosity, we tap into a wellspring of energy and inspiration that can propel us to great heights. So don't wait - start exploring your interests, asking questions, and pursuing your passions today, and see where your curiosity takes you.

Skill Up Your Game: Building a Diverse Skillset

In this part of this chapter, we're going to talk about how building a diverse skillset can help make you the most interesting person in the room.

First and foremost, having a wide range of skills makes you a more versatile and adaptable person.

> **TECHNIQUE 32**
>
> *Be versatile, possess a wide range of skills and knowledge*

You're able to take on different tasks and roles with ease, and you're not limited by a narrow set of skills or experiences. This makes you an interesting person to work with and be around, as you're able to bring a unique perspective and approach to any situation.

But how do you go about building a diverse skillset? The answer is simple: try new things! Take up a new hobby, sign up for a class, or volunteer for a project that's outside of your comfort zone. You never know what you could discover about yourself and your interests.

One of the best ways to build a diverse skillset is to learn from others. Surround yourself with people who have different backgrounds, experiences, and skillsets than your own. This will expose you to new ideas and perspectives, and you'll be able to learn from their expertise.

And don't forget to have fun with it! Learning new skills should be an enjoyable and rewarding experience. Don't be afraid to make mistakes or take risks - that's all part of the learning process.

Now, let's talk about how building a diverse skillset can make you the most interesting person in the room. When you have a wide range of skills and experiences, you become a more dynamic and multifaceted person. You're able to bring a unique perspective to any situation, and you're not limited by your past experiences.

Additionally, having a diverse skillset can open up new doors and opportunities for you. You may discover a new passion or interest that you never knew existed, or you may find that your diverse skillset makes you a valuable asset in the workplace.

So what are you waiting for? Get out there and start building your diverse skillset! Whether you're learning a new language, taking up woodworking, or volunteering at a local nonprofit, every new skill you acquire will make you a more interesting and well-rounded person. And who knows, you may just discover a hidden talent that you never knew you had!

Learn Like a Pro: Strategies to Rapidly Absorb New Information & Become Fascinating

Are you ready to learn like a pro? Great, because that's exactly what we're going to cover in this topic.

TECHNIQUE 33

Learn quickly and efficiently

Learning new things is not only a great way to expand your knowledge, but it can also make you a more interesting and dynamic person. Whether it's a new language, a musical instrument, or a skill you've always wanted to learn, having the ability to absorb new information quickly and effectively can give you a real edge.

So, how can you become a pro at learning? Here are some strategies to get you started:

1. Find your learning style: Everyone learns differently, so it's important to find the method that works best for you. Do you learn better through visual aids, like diagrams and infographics? Or are you a more auditory learner, who absorbs information through lectures and podcasts? Maybe you're a kinesthetic learner, who needs to physically engage with the material to understand it. Figure out your learning style and tailor your approach accordingly.

2. Break it down: When faced with a large amount of information, it can be overwhelming to try and take it all in at once. Break it down into manageable chunks, and tackle each piece one at a time. This will make the process more manageable, and you'll be less likely to feel discouraged.

3. Practice, practice, practice: Learning something new takes time and effort, so it's important to practice consistently. Dedicate a set amount of time each day or week to working on your new skill, and stick to it. The more you practice, the faster you'll absorb the information and the more confident you'll become.

4. Engage with the material: Don't just passively read or listen to the information - engage with it actively. Take notes, create flashcards, or try to explain the concept to someone else. This will help you to process and internalize the information more effectively.

Learning like a pro doesn't mean you have to sit in a library for hours on end, with a pile of dusty books stacked up next to you. In fact, it's quite the opposite! Learning should be fun, engaging, and even a bit silly at times.

For example, if you're learning a new language, why not practice by ordering food in that language at a restaurant? You'll get to eat delicious food and practice your language skills at the same time - talk about a win-win!

Or, if you're learning a new musical instrument, why not start a band with some friends? You'll have a blast jamming out together, and you'll all get to improve your musical abilities in the process.

The bottom line is, learning doesn't have to be a chore. By finding ways to make it fun and engaging, you'll not only become a more interesting and dynamic person, but you'll also enjoy the process a whole lot more.

Chapter Four

Adventures of a Lifetime: Living Your Most Interesting Life

Life is full of adventures, and each one has the potential to change us in profound ways. Whether it's traveling to a far-off destination, taking up a new hobby, or simply exploring the world around us, the adventures we embark on have the power to transform us, inspire us, and help us grow.

In this chapter, we'll explore the concept of living your most interesting life and the role that adventure plays in making that possible.

Through inspiring stories and real-life examples, we'll see how people from all walks of life have embraced the spirit of adventure and used it to create a life that is rich, meaningful, and fulfilling.

We'll meet people like:

Alex Honnold, the free-solo climber who scaled El Capitan in Yosemite National Park without a rope. His story of dedication, passion, and fearlessness is a testament to the power of adventure to push us to our limits and help us achieve our greatest potential.

Dan Buettner, the journalist and explorer who studied the world's "Blue Zones" - areas where people live the longest, healthiest lives. His research shows that one of the key factors in a happy and fulfilling life is a sense of purpose and a willingness to take risks and try new things.

Elizabeth Gilbert, the author of "Eat, Pray, Love" who embarked on a year-long journey of self-discovery after a difficult divorce. Her story is a reminder that sometimes the greatest adventures are the ones we take within ourselves - the ones that challenge us to grow, evolve, and become our best selves.

Through these stories and many more, we'll explore the idea that life is an adventure and that every moment is an opportunity to explore, learn, and grow. Whether you're embarking on a grand adventure or simply trying something new, the key is to embrace the journey with enthusiasm, curiosity, and an open heart.

So join me as we delve into the Adventures of a Lifetime and discover the joy, wonder, and magic that come with living your most interesting life.

Technique 34

Make every day a new adventure

How to Make Every Day a New Adventure

Dear friend,

Do you ever feel like your days are all starting to blur together? Like you're stuck in a rut and nothing exciting ever happens? It's a common feeling, but the good news is that you have the power to change it. You can make every day a new adventure if you're willing to put in a little effort and embrace a mindset of exploration.

Here are some tips to get you started:

1. Try something new every day. It doesn't have to be a big thing - it could be as simple as trying a new food or taking a different route to work. The point is to break out of your routine and open yourself up to new experiences. You never know what you might discover!

2. Look for opportunities to be spontaneous: When an unexpected opportunity arises, seize it! Say yes to that invitation to go hiking, even if you hadn't planned on it.

Say yes to trying that new restaurant your friend recommended. The best adventures often come from taking a chance and stepping outside your comfort zone.

3. Cultivate a sense of curiosity: Approach every day of your life with an open mind and a willingness to learn. Ask questions, try new things, and seek out information about the world around you. The more you learn, the more you'll be able to appreciate the beauty and complexity of the world we live in.

4. Make time for adventure: It's easy to get caught up in the demands of daily life, but it's important to set aside time for the things that bring you joy. Whether it's a weekend camping trip or an afternoon exploring a new part of town, prioritize adventure and make it a regular part of your life.

5. Surround yourself with positive, adventurous people: The people you spend time with can have a big impact on your outlook and your willingness to try new things. Seek out friends who share your sense of adventure and who will encourage and support you as you explore the world.

Here are some examples of people I know who make every day a new adventure:

My friend Sarah, who recently started a blog where she documents her daily adventures. She's always trying new foods, visiting new places, and meeting new people, and her blog has become a source of inspiration for others who want to live more adventurously.

My neighbor Tom, who retired a few years ago and has been using his newfound free time to travel the world. He's been to dozens of countries and is always planning his next trip, even if it's just a weekend getaway to a nearby town.

My coworker Emily, who makes a point of trying something new every week. She's taken up salsa dancing, learned how to play the guitar, and even tried her hand at skydiving. She's always up for a new adventure and her enthusiasm is infectious.

Remember, the key to making every day a new adventure is to approach life with a sense of curiosity, openness, and willingness to try new things. With a little effort and a lot of enthusiasm, you can turn even the most ordinary day into an exciting new experience.

Best of luck on your adventure-filled journey!

The Science of Adventure: Why Taking Risks is the Key to Happiness

What do skydiving, bungee jumping, and rock climbing all

risks, and they're all associated with feelings of excitement, joy, and happiness. But why is it that we feel so alive when we take risks and embrace the unknown?

TECHNIQUE 35

Take risks, calculated risks though

The answer lies in the science of adventure - the study of how taking risks can lead to greater happiness, creativity, and fulfillment. By stepping outside our comfort zones and exposing ourselves to new experiences, we activate neural pathways that stimulate the brain and release chemicals like dopamine and adrenaline - the same chemicals that are associated with feelings of pleasure and happiness.

Real-life examples of people who have embraced the science of adventure include:

Felix Baumgartner, the skydiver who became the first person to break the sound barrier in free fall. His willingness to take risks and push the limits of what was thought to be possible is a testament to the power of adventure to inspire us and drive us to greatness.

Diana Nyad, the swimmer who at the age of 64 became the first person to swim from Cuba to Florida without a shark cage. Her story is a testament to the resilience and determination that can come from embracing the unknown and taking risks.

Elon Musk, the entrepreneur and inventor who has built a career on taking risks and pursuing seemingly impossible dreams. His willingness to challenge the status quo and push boundaries has led to groundbreaking advances in technology and science.

The science of adventure teaches us that taking risks isn't just about having fun - it's also about tapping into our full potential and achieving greater levels of happiness and fulfillment. By embracing new experiences, challenging ourselves, and pushing the boundaries of what we thought was possible, we open ourselves up to a world of possibilities and discover the true joy of living life to the fullest.

So whether it's trying a new activity, taking a chance on a new job, or pursuing a lifelong dream, don't be afraid to take risks and embrace the unknown. The science of adventure is on your side, and the rewards of stepping outside your comfort zone are waiting to be discovered.

Chapter Five

Making the Most of Your Unique Talents and Abilities

We all have unique talents and abilities that make us who we are. Whether it's a natural gift for music, a talent for writing, or a knack for problem-solving, these abilities are what make us stand out and set us apart from others.

In this chapter, we'll explore the concept of making the most of your unique talents and abilities and how doing so can lead to greater fulfillment, success, and happiness. We'll delve into the idea that everyone has something special to offer the world, and that by tapping into our unique strengths and abilities, we can create a life that is both meaningful and rewarding.

We'll explore inspiring stories of people who have embraced their unique talents and abilities, such as:

J.K. Rowling, the author of the Harry Potter series, who turned her love of writing into a worldwide phenomenon that has captivated millions of readers.

Michael Jordan, the basketball legend whose natural talent and hard work made him one of the greatest athletes of all time.

Temple Grandin, the animal behavior expert and advocate for people with autism, who used her unique perspective and talents to revolutionize the way we think about animal welfare.

Through these stories and many more, we'll see how embracing our unique talents and abilities can help us achieve our dreams, overcome obstacles, and create a life that is interesting, rich, fulfilling, and uniquely our own.

Let's go!

Steps to Making the Most of Your Unique Talents and Abilities

TECHNIQUE 36

Find your unique talents and use it to your advantage

Discovering and utilizing your unique talents and abilities is one of the most rewarding things you can do in life. It not only helps you to achieve success and happiness, but it also makes you the most interesting person in the room. In this chapter, we'll explore the steps you can take to make the most of your unique talents and abilities and stand out from the crowd.

1. Identify your strengths: Start by identifying your natural talents and abilities. What are you naturally good at? What do people often compliment you on? What comes easily to you?

2. Develop your skills: Once you've identified your strengths, work on developing your skills in those areas. Take classes, read books, and practice regularly to hone your skills and become an expert.

3. Find your niche: Figure out how you can apply your unique talents and abilities to a specific area or industry.

Maybe you're a great writer who can specialize in a certain topic or genre, or maybe you have a talent for graphic design that you can use to create stunning visuals for a particular audience.

4. Take risks: Don't be afraid of taking risks and trying new things. Embrace the unknown and challenge yourself to step outside your comfort zone. This will not only help you grow as a person but will also open up new opportunities for you.

5. Network: Connect with other people who share your interests and passions. Attend conferences, join online communities, and network with professionals in your field. This will not only help you to learn from others but will also provide you with new opportunities and connections.

By following these steps, you can make the most of your unique talents and abilities and become the most interesting person in the room. You'll have a sense of purpose and direction, and people will be drawn to your passion and expertise. Embracing your unique talents and abilities will help you to achieve success, happiness, and fulfillment in your personal or professional life,

So, embrace your uniqueness, you don't need to be like another person. Take risks, and show the world what you're capable of. Your talents and abilities are what make you unique, and they have the power to change the world.

Standing Out in a World Full of Copycats

In today's world, it's easy to get lost in the crowd. With so many people trying to be like everyone else, it can be hard to stand out and be noticed. But if you want to be a truly interesting person, you need to learn how to stand out in a world full of copycats.

Technique 37

Stand out in a world full of copycats

The first step to standing out is to embrace your uniqueness. You are a one-of-a-kind person with a unique set of skills, experiences, and perspectives. Don't try to be like everyone else; instead, focus on what makes you different and use that to your advantage.

Another important aspect of standing out is to take risks. Don't be afraid to try new things or to take a different approach. Taking risks can be scary, but it's often the only way to achieve great things and to make a real impact.

It's also important to be authentic. Don't try to pretend to be something you're not or to put on a false persona to impress others. People can see through that, and it's not a sustainable way to live your life. Instead, stay true to yourself and allow your unique personality shine through.

Find your niche. Whether it's in your personal or professional life, find an area where you can make a real difference and become an expert. By focusing on a specific area or industry, you can become a go-to person and someone who is highly respected for their knowledge and expertise.

Finally, don't forget to have fun with it! Developing your own style should be an enjoyable and creative process. Don't take yourself too seriously and don't be afraid of making mistakes. The most important thing is to stay true to yourself.

By embracing your uniqueness, taking risks, being authentic, and finding your niche, you can stand out in a world full of copycats and develop a personal style that is truly one-of-a-kind and commands attention wherever you go. You would become the kind of person that people are drawn to because of your unique qualities and perspectives. You can make a real impact on the world and leave a lasting legacy.

So don't be afraid to be different. Embrace what makes you unique, take risks, and find your niche. By doing so, you can become a truly interesting person and make a real difference in the world.

What I'd advice you to do now is to brainstorm. Think about the things that make you unique, think about how to apply the techniques discussed here. That my friend is what will make the difference. You may read a thousand books but if you don't actually practice what you find in those books, it's no use.

People who embraced their unique abilities

Here are five inspiring stories of people who embraced their unique talents and abilities:

J.K. Rowling: Before she became a household name with the Harry Potter series, Rowling was a struggling single mother living on welfare. However, she never gave up on her love of writing, and her determination paid off when she finally got a publishing deal for her first book. Today, Rowling is one of the most successful authors in history, with her books selling over 500 million copies worldwide.

Michael Jordan: Known as one of the greatest basketball players of all time, Jordan's talents were apparent from a young age. He worked hard to hone his skills and became known for his incredible athleticism and competitive spirit. However, Jordan's success wasn't just due to his natural talent - he also had an unwavering work ethic and a fierce determination to succeed.

Temple Grandin: Grandin is a renowned animal behavior expert and advocate for people with autism. As someone on the autism spectrum, she has a unique perspective on animal behavior, which she used to revolutionize the way we think about animal welfare. Today, she is a professor of animal science and has written numerous books on the subject.

Another example is Elon Musk, who has used his talents and abilities in engineering and entrepreneurship to revolutionize industries such as space travel, electric cars, and renewable energy. By focusing on his strengths and working tirelessly to develop his ideas, he has become one of the most influential and successful entrepreneurs of our time.

Frida Kahlo: Kahlo was a Mexican painter who is known for her unique style and powerful self-portraits. She suffered from chronic pain throughout her life and used her art as a way to cope with her physical and emotional struggles. Today, she is considered one of the most influential artists of the 20th century and an icon for women and the LGBTQ+ community.

These five individuals all embraced their unique talents and abilities, and as a result, they made a significant impact on the world around them. They serve as a reminder that when we embrace our differences and let our true selves shine through, we can achieve great things and make a real difference.

So now I challenge you. Can you, make a difference? Can you uniquely be interesting?

Chapter Six

Overcoming Obstacles to Fascination

Have you ever been in a social situation where you just couldn't seem to engage with anyone?

Or maybe you feel like your interests and passions aren't resonating with those around you? It's easy to feel frustrated or discouraged when it seems like you just can't break through and connect with others. But fear not, because in this chapter, we'll be exploring the common obstacles that can impede your ability to fascinate others, and more importantly, we'll be sharing practical strategies to help you overcome them.

Whether it's mastering your nerves, dealing with difficult people, or finding common ground with those who seem vastly different from you, we'll provide actionable tips to help you become a master of engagement and captivation. So buckle up and get ready to power through any obstacle that stands in the way of your ability to fascinate!

How to Overcome Shyness and Social Anxiety

Do you ever feel like you're missing out on all the fun because you're too shy or anxious to put yourself out there? You're not alone. Many people struggle with shyness and social anxiety, but there are ways to overcome it and become the life of the party.

First of all, it's important to understand that shyness and social anxiety are not the same thing. Shyness is like being a wallflower at a party - you're not necessarily uncomfortable in social situations, but you prefer to hang back and observe rather than jump into the fray. Social anxiety, on the other hand, is like being a cat at the vet - you're on high alert and ready to bolt at any moment.

While shyness and social anxiety are different, they can both make it difficult to connect with others and feel comfortable in social situations. The good news is that many of the techniques for overcoming shyness can also be helpful for managing social anxiety.

For example, **practicing small talk** with strangers can be a great way to build your confidence and social skills.

TECHNIQUE 38

Practice small talk before you move into social gatherings

If you're feeling shy, you might start by complimenting someone on their outfit or asking for a restaurant recommendation. If you're dealing with social anxiety, you might try rehearsing some conversation starters or practicing deep breathing exercises to help you stay calm.

Another technique that can be helpful for both shyness and social anxiety is exposure therapy. This involves gradually exposing yourself to social situations that make you uncomfortable, and gradually building up your tolerance over time.

> **TECHNIQUE 39**
>
> *Go out there! Expose yourself to social situations*

For example, if you're shy about public speaking, you might start by giving a short presentation to a small group of friends, and then gradually work your way up to bigger audiences.

Now, I know what you're thinking - this all sounds great in theory, but how do I actually put it into practice? Well, the key is to take it one step at a time and not to put too much pressure on yourself. It's okay to feel nervous or awkward in social situations - everyone does at some point! The important thing is to keep putting yourself out there and practicing your social skills.

And hey, if all else fails, you can always rely on humor to break the ice. Just be sure to use it appropriately - you don't want to be the person telling dad jokes at a funeral.

So, whether you're dealing with shyness or social anxiety, remember that you're not alone and there are ways to overcome it. With a little practice, patience, and maybe a few good jokes, you can become the confident, interesting person you were always meant to be.

One of the best ways to overcome shyness is to practice. Start small by striking up a conversation with a stranger or attending a social event with a friend. Gradually, you can work your way up to bigger challenges like public speaking or networking events.

Another helpful technique is to focus on the other person.

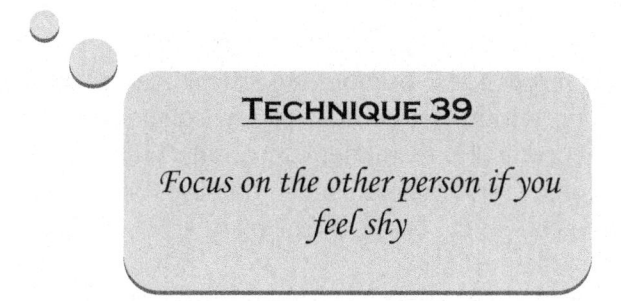

TECHNIQUE 39

Focus on the other person if you feel shy

When you're feeling shy or anxious, it's easy to get caught up in your own thoughts and worries. Instead, try to shift your focus to the other person and ask them questions about themselves. People love to talk about themselves, and showing a genuine interest in others is a great way to make a connection.

Absolutely! Shifting your focus to the other person is a great technique for overcoming shyness and social anxiety. It takes the pressure off of you and allows you to build rapport with the other person. Plus, you might learn something new and interesting!

To make it more fun, think of it like playing a game of 20 questions. You can ask about their hobbies, interests, or even their favorite type of cheese (because who doesn't love cheese?). Just be sure to listen actively and show genuine interest in their responses.

For example, let's say you're at a party and you're feeling shy. You could approach someone and ask them how they know the host, or what their favorite song is right now. Or, if you're dealing with social anxiety, you might try rehearsing some conversation starters ahead of time so you feel more prepared.

And don't forget to use humor to break the ice! If the other person is open to it, you could even turn the conversation into a silly game. For example, you could challenge each other to come up with the most creative use for a paperclip, or see who can do the best impression of a famous actor.

Overall, focusing on the other person is a great way to build your social skills and make connections with others. And who knows, you might just make a new friend or learn something new and interesting along the way. So go ahead, give it a try - and don't forget to bring your A-game cheese questions!

Humor is also a great tool for overcoming shyness.

> **TECHNIQUE 40**
>
> *Use humour if you run out of ideas in social situations*

Yes, using humor is a fantastic way to overcome shyness and make social situations more comfortable. It's like a magic wand that can instantly transform awkwardness into laughter!

But, as you mentioned, it's important to use humor appropriately. You don't want to offend anyone or come across as insensitive. So, let's take a look at some examples of appropriate and inappropriate humor.

First, let's start with a bad example. Let's say you're at a dinner party with new people, and the host serves a dish that you don't particularly like. Making a joke like "Wow, this tastes like something my dog wouldn't even eat" is not a good idea. It's offensive and could make others uncomfortable.

On the other hand, a good example of appropriate humor could be making a witty comment that relates to the conversation. For example, if someone is talking about their favorite TV show, you could say something like "Ah, yes, that show. The one that everyone has seen except for me." This can break the ice and show that you're interested in the conversation.

Another way to use humor is to make fun of yourself. Self-deprecating humor can be a great way to show others that you're approachable and not taking yourself too seriously. For example, if you spill your drink, you could say "I always knew I was a bit clumsy, but I didn't think I'd be this bad at holding a glass!"

Making a joke or a witty comment can help break the ice and make others feel more at ease around you.

Overall, using humor is a great way to overcome shyness and make social situations more comfortable. Just be sure to use it appropriately and remember that not everyone has the same sense of humor. So, don't be afraid to test the waters a bit before diving in with your funniest joke.

But in all seriousness, overcoming shyness and social anxiety can be a challenging process. It's important to be kind to yourself and celebrate your progress, no matter how small. Remember that everyone has their own unique journey, and there's no right or wrong way to be social.

By taking small steps, focusing on others, and incorporating humor into your interactions, you can overcome shyness and social anxiety and become the interesting and engaging person you were meant to be. So go out there and show the world what you've got!

The Art of Handling Criticism and Rejection with Grace

Criticism and rejection are inevitable parts of life. Whether it's in your personal or professional life, you're bound to face situations where someone doesn't agree with you or doesn't want to work with you. While it's natural to feel hurt or discouraged, it's important to learn how to handle criticism and rejection with grace. In fact, mastering this skill can help you become more confident, resilient, and ultimately more interesting to others.

One of the first steps in handling criticism and rejection with grace is to develop a healthy mindset.

TECHNIQUE 41

See criticism & rejection as opportunities for growth

It's important to understand that criticism and rejection aren't personal attacks on your character or abilities. Instead, they are simply someone else's opinion or preference. This mindset shift can help you approach criticism and rejection with a more level head and prevent you from taking things too personally.

Another helpful technique is to practice active listening.

TECHNIQUE 42

If someone criticizes you, just listen to what others have to say

When you receive criticism or rejection, take the time to really listen to the other person's perspective. Try to understand their own point of view and ask clarifying questions if it's necessary. This not only shows that you're receptive to feedback, but it can also help you improve your skills and knowledge in the long run.

It's also important to respond to criticism and rejection with grace and tact. Avoid getting defensive or argumentative, as this can escalate the situation and damage relationships. Instead, thank the person for their feedback and express your willingness to work on any areas for improvement. Similarly, if you're facing rejection, respond with grace and professionalism. Thank the person for considering you and express your continued interest in working together in the future.

Here's an example of how to handle criticism with grace:

Imagine you're presenting a project proposal to your boss, and they provide you with critical feedback. Instead of becoming defensive, you listen carefully to their feedback and take notes. You ask clarifying questions and show that you understand their concerns. Then, you thank them for their feedback and express your commitment to revising the proposal to better align with their expectations. This shows that you're receptive to feedback, willing to improve, and ultimately a valuable team player.

Similarly, here's another example

Imagine you're applying for a job and you receive an email notifying you that you were not selected for the position. Instead of becoming discouraged, you respond with grace and professionalism. You thank the employer for considering you and express your continued interest in future opportunities. This shows that you're a mature and respectful professional, and it can leave a positive impression on the employer in case they have future openings.

In conclusion, handling criticism and rejection with grace is a crucial skill that can make you a more interesting and well-respected person. By developing a healthy mindset, practicing active listening, and responding with grace and tact, you can turn these difficult situations into opportunities for growth and improvement. Remember, it's not about avoiding criticism and rejection altogether, but rather about learning how to handle them in a way that promotes your personal and professional development.

The Science of Confidence: How to Project it, Own it, and Love it

Confidence is a trait that is highly sought after in our society. Whether it's in the workplace, in social situations, or just in our day-to-day lives, having confidence can make all the difference. But what exactly is confidence, and how can we develop it? In this section, we will explore the science of confidence and how to project it, own it, and love it.

Confidence is often described as a feeling of self-assurance arising from one's appreciation of one's own abilities or qualities. However, it is important to understand that confidence is not something that we are born with, but rather something that we develop over time. While some people may naturally have more confidence than others, everyone has the ability to develop and improve their level of confidence.

So how can we project confidence to others? One of the key components of projecting confidence is body language.

> **TECHNIQUE 43**
>
> *Project confidence with body language!*

Our body language can convey a lot about our level of confidence, such as standing up straight, making eye contact, and using open body language. For example, if you walk into a room with your shoulders hunched and your eyes downcast, people are likely to perceive you as lacking in confidence. On the other hand, if you walk in with your shoulders back, head held high, and a smile on your face, people are likely to perceive you as confident and self-assured.

Another way to project confidence is through our tone of voice.

Technique 44

Project confidence with the way you speak!

Speaking clearly and confidently, with good volume and pace, can convey a sense of authority and command attention. Additionally, using positive and assertive language can also convey confidence. For example, instead of saying "I'm not sure if I can do this," say "I'll do my best to make it happen."

But projecting confidence is only part of the equation. It is also important to own our confidence and believe in ourselves. One way to do this is by focusing on our strengths and accomplishments. Take time to reflect on what you do well and what you have achieved, and remind yourself of these things when you start to doubt yourself. It is also important to practice self-care and self-compassion. Taking care of our physical and emotional well-being can help us feel more confident and capable.

Now, let's talk about loving our confidence. This means embracing our unique qualities and accepting ourselves for who we are. We all have flaws and imperfections, but these are what make us human and interesting. Embracing our quirks and imperfections can actually make us more relatable and likable to others. When we love our confidence, we are able to accept both our strengths and weaknesses and use them to our advantage.

Of course, it's not always easy to feel confident all the time. We all face challenges and setbacks that can knock our confidence down. However, it is important to remember that confidence is not a fixed trait, but rather something that we can work on and develop over time. By practicing the techniques mentioned above and persevering through challenges, we can become more confident and ultimately more successful in all areas of our lives.

As an example, let's consider a salesperson who is struggling to close deals. They may start to doubt their abilities and feel less confident in their sales skills. However, by focusing on their strengths and successes, such as a high customer satisfaction rating or a successful pitch, they can remind themselves of their capabilities. By projecting confidence through body language and assertive language, they can convey to potential customers that they are competent and trustworthy. By owning their confidence and practicing self-care, they can feel more comfortable and at ease in high-pressure situations. And by loving their confidence and embracing their unique qualities, they can connect with customers on a more personal level and ultimately close more deals.

The science of confidence is rooted in the understanding that confidence is not a fixed trait that some people are just born with, but rather a skill that can be learned and developed through intentional practice and mindset shifts.

Finally, when you overcome shyness and social anxiety, you become more comfortable and confident in social situations. You're no longer held back by self-doubt and can approach new people and experiences with ease. This makes you more approachable and interesting to others, as people are naturally drawn to those who are comfortable in their own skin.

When you receive criticism, whether it's constructive or not, and you remain calm and composed. It shows that you're open to feedback and willing to learn and grow, which is an attractive quality in anyone. By showing that you can take criticism and learn from it, you demonstrate that you have emotional intelligence and resilience, which are valuable traits in both personal and professional settings.

Lastly, confidence is contagious, and when you exude it, others are naturally drawn to you. When you're confident, you're more likely to take risks, try new things, and speak up for yourself and your ideas. This makes you a dynamic and interesting person to be around, as you're constantly pushing yourself to grow and evolve.

In short, by overcoming shyness and anxiety, handling criticism with grace, and projecting confidence, you become a more well-rounded and interesting person. You're able to connect with others more easily, learn from feedback, and take risks that lead to personal growth and fulfillment. All of these qualities make you stand out in a crowd and leave a lasting impression on those around you.

Conclusion

As we come to the end of this book, I hope that you have gained valuable insights on how to become a more fascinating and confident person. We have explored a wide range of topics, from mastering the art of conversation to developing your own personal style, from overcoming shyness and social anxiety to handling criticism and rejection with grace.

But what I hope you take away from this book is not just a list of tips and tricks, but a deep understanding of the science of fascination and confidence. We are all unique individuals with our own set of strengths and weaknesses, but by harnessing the power of our minds and personalities, we can create a life that is truly worth talking about.

Remember that becoming fascinating and interesting is a journey, not a destination. It takes practice, patience, and persistence to develop these traits. But with dedication and a willingness to step outside your comfort zone, you can unlock your full potential and become the most interesting person in the room.

So, don't be afraid to take risks, try new things, and embrace your own unique style. Don't let fear hold you back from pursuing your passions and achieving your goals.

And always remember that confidence is not something that you are born with, but rather something that you can develop and cultivate over time.

With that in mind, I encourage you to go out into the world and live a life that is full of adventure, passion, and purpose. Embrace your own unique journey, and always remember that you have the power to create a life that is truly worth talking about.

Strategies for Continuing to Grow and Evolve
Congratulations, you've made it to the end of this book! You've learned how to captivate an audience, project confidence, overcome obstacles, and live a more fulfilling life. But the journey doesn't end here. To continue growing and evolving as a fascinating person, you need to keep challenging yourself and pushing beyond your limits.

Here are some strategies for continuing to grow and evolve:

Keep Learning: Never stop learning. Whether it's through formal education, online courses, or reading books, constantly seeking out new information and ideas will keep your mind sharp and your curiosity alive.

Try New Things: It's easy to get stuck in a routine, but trying new things is essential to personal growth. Whether it's a new hobby, travel destination, or social activity, embrace the unknown and step outside your comfort zone.

Embrace Failure: Failure is an inevitable part of life, but it can also be a powerful teacher. Rather than letting failure discourage you, embrace it as an opportunity to learn and grow.

Surround Yourself with Positive Influences: The people you surround yourself with have a significant impact on your mindset and outlook on life. Surround yourself with positive influences, people who inspire you and encourage you to be your best self.

Take Care of Your Mind and Body: A healthy mind and body are essential to personal growth and well-being. Take care of yourself by eating well, exercising regularly, and taking time to rest and recharge.

By continuing to challenge yourself and embrace new experiences, you will continue to evolve and grow into the best version of yourself. So go out there, take on the world, and become the most interesting man in the room!

[PS: If you have any questions, you can reach me via email.

My email address is jamesrugger001@gmail.com.

If you enjoyed this book, kindly leave a 5 star review on the Amazon store. It really makes me happy and inspires me to create even better books.

It's time for the 7 day challenge!]

Bonus

7-Day Challenge to Become the Most Interesting Man

Congratulations on taking the first step towards unlocking your inner genius and becoming the most interesting person in the room! As a special bonus for purchasing this book, we're offering you a 7-day challenge to help you jumpstart your journey towards personal growth and development. We will focus on developing a diverse skillset, improving communication and social skills, and building confidence.

Each day, you'll be presented with a new challenge that will push you out of your comfort zone and help you build the skills and knowledge you need to become a dynamic and engaging individual. By the end of the week, you'll feel more confident, capable, and interesting than ever before. So, are you ready to accept the challenge?

VERY IMPORTANT: Get your writing materials ready. And if you purchased the soft copy of this book, get a fresh exercise book, write down the questions, and write down your answers for each of them. It's not about reading a hundred books; you achieve massive success when you apply and practice all that the books teach.

And don't skip any day's challenge or try to do days 1 and 2 on the same day; you won't be doing yourself any good. Give yourself enough time and space to brainstorm and reveal your true self.

Let's get started!

DAY 1 CHALLENGE

Embrace Your Unique Qualities

Welcome to the 7-day challenge on how to become the most interesting man in the room! Before we dive into the techniques and strategies that will help you achieve this goal, it's important to start by embracing your unique qualities.

Think about what sets you apart from others. Maybe you have a quirky sense of humor, a passion for a particular hobby, or a unique talent that you've been hiding. Whatever it is, embrace it and own it.

For today's challenge, your task is to identify one unique quality about yourself and find a way to showcase it. Maybe it's telling a joke that only you could come up with, wearing a shirt with your favorite band or sports team, or showing off a piece of artwork that you created.

The point is to highlight what makes you different and embrace it with confidence. Don't worry about what others might think - the most interesting people are the ones who are true to themselves.

So go ahead and take on this challenge - let your uniqueness shine! And stay tuned for tomorrow's challenge, where we'll focus on building your knowledge and skills to become even more interesting.

What qualities or skills set you apart from others?

Of all these qualities, pick at least one and describe how you plan to showcase it. (You can showcase as many as you want.)

_____
_____
_____
_____
_____
_____
_____
_____
_____
_____
_____
_____
_____
_____
_____
_____
_____
_____

DAY 2 CHALLENGE

Step Out of Your Comfort Zone and Try Something New

Welcome to day 2 of the "How to Become the Most Interesting Man in the Room" 7 day challenge. Today's challenge is all about stepping out of your comfort zone and trying something new.

It's easy to get comfortable in our daily routines and stick to what we know, but trying new things can broaden our perspectives and add depth to our character.

Here's your challenge for today: pick something you've always wanted to try but have been too afraid or hesitant to attempt. It could be something as simple as trying a new type of food or as adventurous as signing up for a skydiving lesson.

Whatever it is, take the plunge and give it a try. Embrace the excitement and uncertainty that comes with trying something new. Challenge yourself to try something new that scares you, such as bungee jumping, skydiving, or public speaking. You might surprise yourself and discover a new passion or talent along the way.

Remember, the key to becoming the most interesting man in the room is to constantly challenge yourself and embrace new experiences. Good luck!

What are those things you've always wanted to try?

_____
_____
_____
_____
_____
_____
_____
_____
_____
_____
_____
_____
_____
_____
_____
_____
_____
_____
_____
_____
_____

How do you plan to try them?

What are the things that scare you? How do you plan to give them a try?

DAY 3 CHALLENGE

Expand Your Knowledge Base

Today's challenge is all about expanding your knowledge base. To become an interesting person, it's important to have a wide range of knowledge on various topics. This not only makes you more knowledgeable but also gives you the ability to contribute to conversations and discussions on a variety of subjects.

Here are some actionable tips for today:

1. Read articles and books on different topics: Start by picking a topic that you don't know much about and read up on it. This could be anything from politics to science to cooking. The more you read, the more you'll learn and the more interesting you'll become.

2. Attend lectures and workshops: Look for lectures and workshops in your area on different topics that interest you. Attending these events will not only expose you to new information but also give you the opportunity to meet new people who share your interests.

3. Watch documentaries: Documentaries are a great way to learn about a wide range of topics. They're also entertaining and engaging, making it easier to absorb new information.

4. Learn a different skills: Learning a new skill is not only beneficial but also gives you something interesting to talk about. Whether it's a new language, a musical instrument,

or a sport, expanding your skillset will make you more interesting and dynamic.

Remember, the key is to keep learning and expanding your knowledge base. This will not only make you more interesting but also give you a better understanding of the world around you.

What new things will you start learning?

_____

_____

_____

_____

_____

_____

_____

_____

_____

_____

_____

_____

_____

How do you plan to expand your knowledge?

DAY 4 CHALLENGE

Connect with Someone New

Today's challenge is all about expanding your social circle and meeting someone new. This may seem daunting at first, especially if you're naturally shy or introverted, but remember that everyone has something interesting to offer.

Here are the steps for today's challenge:

- Identify a social event or gathering that you can attend, such as a networking event, party, or even a coffee shop.

- Approach someone who seems interesting and strike up a conversation. Start with a simple greeting, such as "Hi, I'm [your name], what's your name?"

- Ask them a question about themselves, such as "What brings you here today?" or "What do you do for work?"

- Listen actively and engage in the conversation. Show genuine interest and ask follow-up questions to keep the conversation flowing.

- Exchange contact information, such as phone numbers or social media handles, and make plans to connect again in the future.

Remember, the key to making a meaningful connection is to be genuine, show interest, and listen actively. Don't worry about being perfect or impressing the other person - just be yourself and let the conversation flow naturally.

Which social event or gathering will you attend?

_____
_____
_____
_____
_____
_____
_____
_____
_____
_____
_____
_____
_____
_____
_____

When you meet someone new there, write down seven (7) questions you will ask the person to talk about himself or herself.

Here are some additional tips for the day 4 challenge:

1. Practice active listening: When someone is speaking to you, try to give them your undivided attention. Show that you are engaged in the conversation by maintaining eye contact, nodding, and asking follow-up questions.

2. Expand your knowledge: Read up on current events, watch educational videos, or listen to podcasts on a variety of topics. This will give you a wider range of knowledge to draw from in conversations and make you more interesting to talk to.

3. Attend events: Attend events related to your interests or try something new. This will give you more experiences to draw from in conversations and help you connect with others who share similar interests.

4. Take up a new hobby: Trying something new can be a great conversation starter and can also help you develop new skills and knowledge.

5. Be open-minded: Avoid judging others based on their interests or beliefs. Be open to learning from others and having your own beliefs challenged.

Remember, the goal is to continue expanding your knowledge and experiences so that you have more to contribute to conversations and are seen as an interesting and dynamic person.

DAY 5 CHALLENGE

Master a New Skill

Today's challenge is all about stepping out of your comfort zone and learning something new. Whether it's a new language, a musical instrument, or a craft, challenging yourself to master a new skill can help you become more interesting and well-rounded.

Here's your task for today:

- Choose a skill that you've always wanted to learn but haven't had the time or motivation to pursue.

- Set aside at least an hour today to start learning and practicing that skill. You can use online resources, instructional books, or even take a class if possible.

- Make a plan to continue practicing and learning the skill over the next few weeks or months. Set achievable goals for yourself and track your progress.

Remember, the goal of this challenge is not to become an expert overnight, but to start the journey towards mastery. Learning a new skill can be a rewarding and fulfilling experience, and it will also give you something interesting to talk about with others.

Good luck and have fun with it!

Which new skill do you plan to learn and master?

How do you plan to start learning and mastering it?

Some additional tips for Day 5 of the challenge:

1. Take notes: Whenever you're learning something new, whether it's from a book, a lecture, or a conversation, make sure to take notes. Writing down key points and ideas will help you retain the information better and make it easier to recall later.

2. Use visual aids: If you're learning a new concept or skill, try to find visual aids to help you understand it better. This could be diagrams, flowcharts, or even videos. Visual aids can help you process complex information more easily and remember it better.

3. Practice, practice, practice: To truly master a new skill or concept, you need to practice it regularly. Set aside time each day to work on your new skill, whether it's practicing a new language or working on your public speaking. Consistent practice will help you improve faster and build your confidence.

4. Teach someone else: One of the best ways to reinforce your own knowledge is to teach someone else. Find a friend or family member who is interested in learning the same skill or concept as you, and teach them what you've learned. This will not only help you solidify your own understanding, but also give you a sense of accomplishment and fulfillment.

5. Take breaks: It's important to take breaks while learning new information or practicing a new skill. Your brain needs time to rest and recharge, so make sure to take short breaks

every 30-60 minutes. Use this time to stretch, take a walk, or do something else that helps you relax and clear your mind.

DAY 6 CHALLENGE

Mastering Presentation Skills

Improving your public speaking skills is a key component of becoming the most interesting person in the room. Today, your challenge is to practice a short speech or presentation that you can use to impress others in social and professional settings.

First, choose a topic that you're passionate about and that others might find interesting. It could be anything from a hobby or travel experience to a new business idea or industry trend.

Next, focus on using engaging body language and tone of voice to capture your audience's attention. Stand up straight, make eye contact, and use hand gestures to emphasize your points. Vary your tone of voice to add interest and emotion to your delivery.

Finally, practice your speech in front of a mirror or record yourself to review later. Take note of areas where you can improve, such as pacing or enunciation, and work on refining your delivery.

By improving your public speaking skills, you'll be able to share your knowledge and insights with others in a more engaging and impactful way. This will help you stand out and become the most interesting person in any room.

What topic will you be presenting on?

How do you plan to capture your audience's attention during the presentation?

DAY 7 CHALLENGE

Celebrate Your Achievements and Set New Goals

Congratulations! You've made it to the final day of the challenge. Take a moment to reflect on all the progress you've made throughout the week. Think about how much more confident and interesting you feel, and how much closer you are to becoming the most interesting person in the room.

Now, it's time to celebrate your achievements. Treat yourself to something you've been wanting to do or buy for a while, or simply take a moment to bask in your own awesomeness. You deserve it!

But don't stop there. Use this moment of celebration to set new goals for the future. Think about the skills you want to develop even further, or new areas of interest you want to explore. Write them down and commit to taking action towards achieving them.

Remember, becoming the most interesting person in the room is a journey, not a destination. Keep building on the skills and confidence you've gained, and continue to challenge yourself to learn and grow. Who knows, maybe one day you'll be the one writing a book on how to become the most interesting person in the room!

How do you plan to celebrate your achievements so far?

What new goals have you set for the future?

[PS: If you have any questions, you can reach me via email.

My email address is jamesrugger001@gmail.com.

If you enjoyed this book, kindly leave a 5 star review on the Amazon store. It really makes me happy and inspires me to create even better books.

Adios Friend!]

About The Author

James Rugger is a self-help specialist with a passion for empowering individuals to become the best versions of themselves.

Born and currently living in California, his journey to becoming a self-help author began when he realized that he had spent most of his life trying to please others and seeking their approval.

As a speaker and coach, within 5 months, James Rugger has helped over 700 individuals from all walks of life overcome their fears, doubts, and insecurities, guiding them towards a life of purpose, meaning, and joy.

His approach to self-help is grounded in his experience, along with science-based strategies and techniques that have been proven to work.

His philosophy is simple: you only have one life to live, so you might as well live it on your terms.

Attributes

All images used in this book were downloaded from *pexels.com* & *pixabay.com*

LOST IN SPAIN

A Collection Of Humorous Essays

SCOTT OGLESBY

Disclaimer

This book is true-ish to the best of my (very limited) knowledge and to
the best of my (terrible...pathetic, really) memory.

If you happen to think that you recognize one of the characters as
yourself or someone you know, you are wrong.

Stop being so delusional. I'm talking about that other guy.

The one over there.

Points

That guy, see him?

runs away faster than you'd think possible

The names have been changed to protect the not-even-close-to-innocent
and if real have been used fictitiously.

Also, and this is important, do not buy this book if you are easily
offended.

Copyright © 2014 Scott Oglesby.

All rights reserved. No part of this publication may be reproduced,
distributed, or transmitted in any form or by any means, or stored in a
database or retrieval system, without the prior written permission of the
author/publisher.

ISBN: 1495334767
ISBN-13: 978-1495334764

DEDICATION

This book is dedicated to all of the outcasts, misfits, loners, junkies, losers and those of you who can't quite figure out how to arrange your faces at parties. You are my people!

CONTENTS

1	Imagination Meets Reality	Page 1
2	Kappi And The Gypsies	Page 32
3	See This Vain	Page 50
4	Awkwardity	Page 61
5	One, Two, Three, Four	Page 78
6	Kasper And Nothing More	Page 102
7	Killing Time	Page 132
8	Broken Bad	Page 137
9	Political Discourse	Page 157
10	Market Day	Page 183
11	Awkward Insecurity	Page 191
	About The Author	Page 203

ACKNOWLEDGMENTS

I would like to thank all of the people who made this book possible, especially the inhabitants of Javaron who were unfortunate enough to exist in proximity to me and had the heartbreaking naiveté to tell me things.

To King George for allowing me to squat in his Spanish house for three years.

To Al Gore for inventing the internet.

To Kyle Wygle for being outlandishly stupid enough to change my life.

To Amy Severson for editing me, challenging me and not stabbing me in the face with a broken wine bottle. She is more than a friend; she is, quite possibly, a Time Lord.

To Megan McMeans who found more typos than I'd have thought possible. Without her help this book would have looked a lot like what happens when a cat walks across a keyboard.

Lastly thank you to my beautiful and talented wife Karen. She did all the real work to get this book out there.
You are my light.

I love you all!

1

IMAGINATION MEETS REALITY

I moved to Spain with the idea that I'd party hard but play it cool, knowing that if I stuck to my principles I'd fall in with the right group of glamorous, globetrotting socialites who would, upon the first impression, fall into a deep and needy love with me. They'd fly me first class on the best airlines where we would guzzle Cristal and lick the gelatinous goop of the world's finest Fentanyl patches before sneaking off to the toilet for inductions into the mile high club with mysterious and extraordinary strangers. After I'd been properly vetted, wealthy individuals or shady corporations would hire me to travel the world doing their nefarious bidding. This vocation would leave me filthy rich, with an ample amount of free time. I'd enjoy VIP status at the most exclusive clubs in Western Europe, where hordes of beautiful but average people would stare, trying to meet my eyes and hope to gain favor with the Special One. In Monaco I'd be met by a limousine and an emissary of the royals to whisk me away to the tables where I'd intimidate and bluff the world's rich and powerful elite. Afterward, against my own wishes, I'd be seduced by their undersexed trophy wives. After they'd heard

that I'd taken Prince Rainier's private helicopter to meet Brad and Angie in Paris, these gorgeous creatures would attempt stoicism by putting on a brave front only to break down and weep into silk scarves while their husbands hushed them with irritation. These heart-broken waifs would hold onto the private and dim hope that they might be rescued by my loving and generous embrace again one day. They are only human after all.

I'd soon move on to the arts, where someone like me belongs. I'd be persuaded into acting one cocaine filled night by the Coen Brothers and the good looking Olson twin. The role, something about a devastatingly handsome ne'er do well street kid made good would win me my first in a long line of successive Oscars. I'd quit acting at the very peak of my success and my public would gnash their teeth and tear their garments in mourning, much to the consternation and dysphoria of the other proletarian actors who would think, "Well, what about us then?"

One night, high on lust, avarice and peyote I'd create a brand new art form by combining sculpture, painting, music, and against all common sense, dance, into a work that would bring one New York Times critic to his knees in rapturous ecstasy. He'd had no choice after sampling my hors d'oeuvres, which contained actual ecstasy. That my parties tend to feature food infused with cosmetic hallucinogens would be one of my beloved eccentricities. They'd call me a virtuoso of Right Now and legions of art students and professors would drop their books, pick up their White Crosses and follow me. I'd take us all to my private island in the Bahamas where I'd explain that the whole thing was a silly accident and I had no memory of what I'd done. They'd be torn between their belief in the inerrancy of my words and the physical proof of my obvious genius before agreeing to worship me as a demigod anyway.

My fantasies never came to fruition. I assume that this was due to the total absence of glamorous, globetrotting socialites

LOST IN SPAIN

in the rural mountains of Southern Spain.

Where did I come up with such lofty and impossible aspirations in the first place?

People have always said I have a ridiculous imagination. Other people accuse me of psychosis with delusions of grandeur but I always have those people publicly flogged and thrown in my ostracization pit. This only happens in my mind though because I don't want anyone to know I'm a megalomaniacal overlord. In large part though, I blame Karen's brother George, the benevolent benefactor of our three year Spanish sabbatical.

It all started when George and Audrey visited from London. We were living in a large two bedroom beach house on the water in Florida. Karen was working as an accountant and I was running a painting company. By running a painting company I mean I was painting houses, working for myself. I had no employees or insurance or expensive equipment but I did have homemade business cards and managed to rake in a few dollars during the Champagne years of the housing bubble. We had a dock and a boat lift, although no actual boat. Very white trash chic. We had an amazing house, nice furniture and Fuck You sized big-screen TV. That's what the box it came in said. There were 38 inch, 45 inch, 54 inch, and Fuck You. So I went with the Fuck You because that's how I rolled at the time. I felt in control of my destiny for the first time in a chaotic and tumultuous decade.

I smelled a change in the air however. It smelled like the outerwear section at a thrift store. It smelled like an old mattress left out in the rain. It smelled like despair and it portended bad things. The economy was just starting to slip and the jobs first slowed then stopped. Karen was starting to feel the pinch as there were fewer beans to count. We were blowing a large chunk on rent every month and no longer owned any property. When we found out that George had a few houses sitting unoccupied in Spain I thought, *I'm going to squat the fuck out of one of those!* I'd always fancied myself possessing just the right kind of pretentious Americanism to

3

tell people I'd taken leave in Europe indefinitely. Perhaps I'd see to that Masters of Fine Arts, Barcelona I'd had my eye on. This was all nothing more than speculation, mental masturbation for the drifter's soul. Until it wasn't.

Karen's brother, King George, is attractive in a non-classical, disheveled kind of way. Yet, he is the most attractive man I've ever met. He's attractive like a superconducting solenoidal magnet. With his communicable optimism, infectious enthusiasm, and contagious joy of life, King George is a force unto himself. He's got a whole Steve Jobs/TV preacher/self-help guru vibe about him. He's imbued with the charisma that, in the wrong hands, can make opening fire on the FBI seem like a good idea. The day after you've spent time with King George anything seems possible; you feel like you should study theoretical physics in your spare time and create an interpretative dance based on the collected works of David Foster Wallace and narrated by Morgan Freeman. "There, There, Gately's Last Tango" you'd call it.

Two days after he's left you struggle to remember the urgency and have a George shaped hole in your motivation.

George's fiancée Audrey is an exquisitely beautiful woman who carries an air of High Art to which I've always aspired but never pulled off. She's the perfect match for George. She worked in fashion, theater, and video production. If so inclined she could both choreograph and film your "Infinite Dance." In the time I knew her she'd become the youngest Reiki Master in Europe, became a licensed hypnotherapist, birthed an angelic child who may or may not turn out to be the Messiah, and beaten Kate Middleton at Winning Life. She is the kind of person who can make a midnight excursion to a 7-Eleven glamorous and titillating.

Audrey is forever elegant, graceful, and always, always positive. She never has a negative word to say about anyone, a quality I find infuriating. How else can I pull myself up from middle class obscurity than by clawing and tearing down

my betters? I can charm beautiful faces in my own inept, clumsy way. I'm capable of feigning academic sophistication to impress brilliant minds on a short-term basis. When you put them both in the same person however, and add in that je ne sais quoi of High Art that combines tragic beauty with cultural sophistication with killer fashion and top it off with an accent that American stage actors have been trying to mimic without success for centuries, I become an awkward disaster. She once asked me the courses I took in college and I, literally, could not name one. It's as if my desire to be accepted as a member of the elite becomes a palpable force, a physical entity that drowns my brain in white noise and fills my throat with congealed glue. Glue made from all the awkward tears and dried napkin semen of every teenager who'd ever snapped a bra strap to show affection or wrote a love poem out of Tupac songs only to have the teacher find it, read it in class, and inform the student (who is not, nor ever was, me) that he should cite his sources.

"You're welcome to stay in our Spanish house," George said during the turkey dinner that Audrey had whipped together. "I love the thought. I just don't want you to get the wrong idea."

I had the wrong idea.

"No, no, I'm a realist." I said, because I was lying.

"It's in a remote village in the mountains." He said.

It's a country estate, I thought.

"I mean, it's pretty isolated. Until you guys get a car, you're going to have a hard time getting what you need."

I'll become Henry David Thoreau, I thought.

"But is it livable?" Karen asked.

"We had a friend who stayed there for six months," Audrey said. "Gordon, lovely man, you'll meet him at the wedding. He managed to do massive renovations; redid the plumbing, wired for electricity, but we're not sure how far he managed to get."

Nail gun! I thought.

"It sounds amazing, just what we need right now," Karen

5

said, as I aggressively concurred.

George said, "It is amazing, and you'll love it. As long as you understand what you're getting into. The floors are still bare cement."

Bare under the layer of priceless, oriental rugs, Italian marble and Moroccan tile, maybe, I thought.

"I don't think there's much furniture."

More room to rollerblade!

"Not sure if there's a fridge or if the oven works."

Fine dining every night then!

"There may not even be mattresses in there for all I know."

Really? Shit. "I'll buy one, we need a mattress." I said out loud.

"I'm telling you Scott, this is not what you're expecting. It's going to be very, very different from your life right now."

I'll become the Champion of Spain!

"There's no Champion of Spain." He said.

"How can you hear my thoughts?" I asked, alarmed.

"You were moving your lips. Every time I said something you moved your lips. You learn to lip-read when you've spent too much time in clubs." George explained.

I will develop my own superpowers, I thought, fighting to keep my poker face. I looked at him and he just lifted an eyebrow. I was already winning.

Once King George knew that we were serious about it and had some idea of what we were getting into, his irrepressible optimism flourished like an invasive species of fish in a small pond.

"You're going to love it." He said.

"It's going to change your life." Audrey agreed.

"I was a bookie back in Pittsburgh," I said because I was feeling insecure. George and Audrey were just telling us about how George had been a producer for MTV Europe, and putting out a weekly show for Underground TV in Ibiza when they'd met. Before that he'd been executive producer for the morning show on BBC Radio after starting out as a

DJ. This was after a dozen other ridiculous accomplishments accumulated like so many notches in a New Jersey beach house bedpost. His life spiraled upwards, a magic elixir of success, to swirl around him like animated bluebirds in his very own Wonderful Life.

George had turned into Don Draper during his time in Spain, a country that everybody else visits to smoke pot and get off the grid. Using nothing but a phone booth and lots of loose change, he'd managed to start up an advertising company. Remembering he was there for only three months—as infuriating as that is—it's also remarkable that he'd written a book in that short time, his third. Now he was creative director for a multinational advertising company in the UK.

"After the bookie thing," I said, not wanting to be outdone, "I worked for the turnpike. Then I moved to Florida and painted houses. Now, maybe I'll write a book."

"That house is the perfect place." Audrey said.

"It is," George added. "I was able to complete the outline of another book while I was there as well."

"In three months. You wrote one book. Then you started another. In three. Fucking. Months?"

But before he could answer I stabbed him in the face with a roasted potato, which turned out to be a more lethal garnish than you'd think. I then deleted his LinkedIn profile and created my own using his resume. Karen and Audrey both took to calling me Sexy Beast, a moniker I accepted out of pure honesty. I wrote his outlined book, and then wrote three best sellers all while directing and starring in an ironic movie about identity theft that broke Hollywood. Finally, I wrote another outline, to be completed when I could find a spare week. All of this only happened in my brain, but it didn't make it any less real.

"Holy wows, amazing." I said because my vocabulary is terrible while my imagination is in overdrive.

"Thank you but no," George replied.

"No what?" I asked.

"Each person on this planet is amazing. Each person has the potential to be amazing, to do amazing things. Just by being alive you've already hit the cosmic lottery, beating infinitely long odds. Everything you do after that is just icing on the cake."

"That is so true," said Audrey, beaming. "What a lovely thought!"

"My problem is I think of amazing things all the time." I said, explaining my deepest psychological issue, "but then all I can see are the roadblocks and hurdles and I become paralyzed with inaction. So I sit on the couch and drink adult beverages."

"Don't do that," he said because he's clearly not a trained psychologist. "You want to write a book, lock yourself in a windowless room…"

"Or I could close the blinds." I said, trying to be helpful.

"Yyeeaa, or that. First write chapter headings on separate notebook pages. Then make a rough outline. Tape the notes all over the walls and lock yourself in for four hours a day. Every time you look around, trying to escape, you're getting ideas, even subconsciously."

"That's just crazy enough to work," I said and winked at him.

"It's how I did it," he said. "And you like to gamble right?"

"I used to be a bookie in Pittsburgh." I said because I was stuck on stupid.

"You can open a casino in Java. The Spanish love their cards and they love to gamble. This is what you do…" He spread his fingers and placed them on the table but it had the effect of a fist slamming down, such was his presence. "Start a small card game and see how it goes. Make it a weekend thing. House takes ten percent right? Put aside the money and rent one of the old, massive buildings in the town square. Make some money and buy slot machines. They love those slot machines."

"What about the laws," I asked, pretending to not be a

LOST IN SPAIN

criminal.

"Just make friends with the mayor, he's a great guy."

"He's a remarkable man." Audrey said. "His wife is a fabulous cook as well."

"We got him to let us use the town's old radio equipment. Every day we'd walk up the mountain and broadcast a weather report."

"How did you know the forecast?" I said.

"We just looked across the mountains. You can see a storm coming four, five hours before it gets there. A four-hour-cast."

"Artists, painters, photographers, anyone looking for inspiration and natural beauty would go up there all the time." Audrey said. "The views are spectacular. You can see from the Sierra Nevada all the way down to the Mediterranean."

"It really is unbelievable," George agreed. "So we'd see a storm coming in somewhere, I don't know, off the coast of Africa, and we'd tell them that rain was expected.

Karen and I sat there and looked stunned and wholly impressed and felt overwhelmed with a nervous excitement neither of us knew quite what to do with. There were so many possibilities. Maybe I would become an anchorman for an all gambling channel? Or perhaps I'd start a commune for non-hippies that just really like drugs and sex… and gambling?

"I mean, it's not like Telemundo or BBC has a Javaron affiliate is it?" George said, laughing. "They loved us because we paid attention to Javaron. Not enough people do that."

"We would broadcast the week's upcoming events as well," Audrey said.

"Are there many, events?" Karen asked because Karen is an aficionado of Things To Do and See. I like the idea in the abstract more than the actual reality of doing and seeing things.

"There is always something going on." Audrey said, tucking a strand of gently flowing hair behind one perfect ear.

9

"There are dozens of fiestas a year, the children put on plays, there is Flamenco dancing, horse races and soccer games. There is constantly something. If you immerse yourself wholly within the culture you will experience a rich and vibrant community."

"It really does sound lovely," Karen said, and I agreed even though, in my experience, immersion is hard and painful.

"And you don't have to open a casino," George said. "Once you're there you'll get plenty of ideas of what you want to do."

Olive-monger! I thought, because my mind had finally snapped.

"You'd have stiff competition." George said.

I really had to stop moving my lips.

We solidified our plans during the remainder of their stay. We were really going to do it. I'd been afflicted with a cross contamination of George's inveterate passion and exuberance and Audrey's poetic energy and obdurate equanimity. I felt ready to become the Champion of Spain, and if not that, a friendly recluse. Either would do.

It turned out that they weren't lying after all. The house did not feature Italian marble or Moroccan tile. I did not alchemize into Henry George Thoreau. The rooms were too small for rollerblading and there was nowhere to buy rollerblades. There wasn't even a nail gun lying around. There was a working oven though, and enough mattresses that I was able to cover the entire bedroom so that it resembled a harem tent. I enjoyed the fact that every night I could tell Karen that we had to 'go to the mattresses' like a mafia family in hiding. I was overwhelmed and culture shocked but felt we could make it work, despite the fact that it was not casino ready. I loved the house, they even had what I called a Moroccan room, which gave me the perfect excuse to light candles and smoke pot. Javaron was antique but new to us,

strange, with onion-like layers that would take years to uncover and appreciate.

Karen and I had barely settled—certainly hadn't yet developed any real sense of Javaron—before it was time to hit Ibiza for George and Audrey's wedding. It was this trip that tipped the scales of my imagination to reality balance. As soon as I stepped off the plane I could smell magic in the air, taste possibility. It was as if ecstasy was pumped into the atmosphere and the simple act of breathing became an initiation into a previously inconceivable state. Happiness, unity, passion, and purity of love were all suffused with a sense of peace and satiation to create a state that could only be enlightenment. Then we hit traffic. Karen checked us into the hotel while I took our suitcases to the room. The walk was close to a mile uphill within the sprawling, oversized compound. *This is the problem with corporate greed,* I thought, and knew I'd lost my trip.

My natural high rebounded with ease the next morning. I knew I could drink that night and that made all the difference. First we walked past George's beach house, down to the beach itself. I was awestruck by the natural, and in some cases, manmade, beauty that surrounded me. Light brown mounds topped with exquisite points, dark, oily hills rolling gently down, perfect orbs of white and black and brown, and that golden color that only Polynesians can attain. There were bare breasts everywhere, spread out before me in the rapturous sovereignty of what was surely Valhalla. The island was nice as well. There were olive trees ensconced in ancient white stone, fine white sand and water that was almost day-glow in its fervor to reach blue green perfection. It was an amalgamation of colors which perfectly showcased the perfect blue of my eyes. I was stunned by the breasts though. I've traveled to a lot of countries where ladies felt free enough to shed the confining mass of their bikini top but this was the first time where what I saw belonged to people I'd actually want to see naked. It was glorious. That's when I knew beyond shadow or doubt that Ibiza was the molten ore

from which rum soaked fantasies and afterlife revelations are forged.

Karen dragged me away and we went back to the beach mansion. Did I call it a house before? If I had overlooked its size and splendor it was only because I had been rendered senseless by the siren song of breasts calling out to me from the waters below. We were buzzed in through the solid, very large, intricately carved, wooden security gate. It was a classic Spanish style villa made by and done for those with the hard cash to go full-on House of Bonaparte. Real Italian marble with under floor heating. Granite countertops. Mahogany paneling and trim. Real Madrid—a few key players anyway, had stayed there for two weeks the previous summer.

The day before the wedding George took me to run some last minute errands: pick up the extra booze, borrow a serious DJ deck, buy seven ounces of blow and rent the topless models who would parade it around on silver serving trays. The last two things only happened in my head because George and Audrey are obviously terrible wedding planners.

On the way he pointed out a villa on top of a hill that would have told my Fuck You TV to piss off. Or maybe it would have politely reminded my Fuck You TV that it was not to presume to fraternize above its station and to get back to the servant quarters at once. I'm not sure why a Spanish villa would speak like a character on Downton Abbey but that's how I heard it.

"That's the flat we lived in while I was here." He said.

"Jesus, must have been expensive."

"It was. They gave us cars and motorcycles as well."

I looked out the window at the hodgepodge collection of vehicles and the erratic drivers. There was an old Spanish man in overalls with goats in the bed of his truck, a carload of bikini clad girls in an open jeep, and anything and everything in between. They were all braking and swerving and beeping and preening as greenery gave way to desert vistas and back again.

"I'd be dead in a week. I've totaled a car and crashed two others and none of this was going on." I said gesturing as a group of drunken Brits raced alongside the bikini jeep to exchange numbers and evening itineraries at seventy miles per hour.

"Wreck?" No I never wrecked, not accidentally. Well..." he haltered considering, "maybe the bike. I used to race dirt bikes right? Well I was thinking about it one day and decided to give it a run down that hill on the side of the villa."

"Mountain." I said. "That was a mountain."

"We all went outside, and I have my two camera guys filming it, one up beside me and one at the bottom. I ease the bike to the edge and titter at the top, rev the engine for dramatic effect. My mate counts down three, two one... and it all went terribly, terribly wrong."

"Did you die?"

"No. But this wasn't a dirt bike was it?"

"I don't know," I said, hoping it wasn't a trick question.

"No it was a new motorcycle, one of the fast ones. It was meant to look posh but it was really just plastic glued on top of plastic with a tiny little rocket engine buried under more plastic."

"So what happened?"

"I went off that mountain like a goddamned rocket is what happened. Only down, not up. The brakes might as well been decoration. I'm careening off of trees, scraping rocks, lifting off who knows what involuntarily, flying through the air and slamming into more organic detritus."

"Sounds kind of fun."

"Oh, it was. You look at the tapes after we edited them and it looked like one of those fast forward deconstruction videos, taking apart a motorcycle. Only with more violence."

"Lucky you didn't get deconstructed."

"Yes. One good thing came out of it though."

"A morphine drip?"

"No."

"Insurance money?"

"No."

"You found a genie"

"Scott, man, no. Now the bike had a cup holder."

"You're high." I said because I wanted some.

"You're the one talking about genies and morphine. I was happy I finally had a cup holder."

"You had a cup holder."

"Yes. Yes, I did and it was brilliant! Where the speedometer used to sit there was now a perfect cup sized hole. This is Spain, it gets hot. I like to drink orange juice in the morning. Now, I had a cup holder for my juice and it was awesome. I loved that cup holder."

"Eventually though I had to trade it in, it was too dangerous."

"Too dangerous to sip orange juice on a crotch rocket speeding down Spanish highways?"

"No, there were spiky chunks of bent metal sticking out all over the place. It was very Road Warrior."

"This is the perfect place for that." I said as I pointed to a Volkswagen camper van that lost something soft looking from its roof that splattered on the road.

"The cars didn't get wrecked but they got lost."

"Lost like misplaced or lost like Jack, Sawyer, Freckles and Hurley?

"What?"

"I used to be a bookie. In Pittsburgh. I was kind of a big deal."

"Yeah, you might have mentioned that once. Just lost. I parked a car somewhere and when we came out of the club in the morning it was lost."

"You never found it?

"It was lost." He said with finality.

"I'll bet it's on some island in the middle of the Pacific pushing buttons right now, probably unstuck in time." I said, mixing my references.

We took an exit and after three dizzying round-a-bouts we were in a trendy, colorful neighborhood. George parked and

LOST IN SPAIN

before he was out of the car a man rushed from a café, aggressive with friendliness towards George. They talked in Spanish and the small Middle-Eastern looking man kept slightly bowing, smiling as if to show off his wisdom teeth. Just as George had managed to pull himself away, a petite blond of Nordic descent and a large, beautiful Spanish man came rushing out of a storefront carrying DJ equipment. Both wore an unmistakable look of abject adoration.

"You're a fucking legend man." The pretty girl said.

"Uhh, George, nice to meet you." He said, popping the trunk. We all loaded up the car, the first responder and the Spanish guy kept chattering away in Spanish, patting his back and beaming at him while the blond muttered happily the way stoners do when they're living in the moment. All three barraged him with non-specific praise. When we drove off, all three were standing where we'd left them in the street, staring us off like love starved mistresses in a closing scene of a strange soap opera.

"What exactly did you do here?" I asked because I was starting to get a distinct Bruce Wayne/Tony Stark-like vibe.

"Started off I was sent to do weekly shows for Underground TV on the dance music, the club scene here. The top clubs were all keen to be featured on the show. We got the VIP treatment everywhere we went. Front of the line. Free drinks. Stuff I can't mention without having to kill you twice then burn your corpse. Unspeakable offers which had to be politely declined of course."

"Of course," I said because I was lying. I'd never turn down an unspeakable offer.

"I'd always loved to DJ so I convinced the manager of Pasha to let me spin one night. Ended up with a regular spot. A couple weeks later Space asked me to play their busiest spot.

"Wait, they're really out there? And they love dance music?"

"No you imbecile, Space as in the world's biggest club."

"Right, yes of course."

15

"On top of that I started my own night that quickly went out of control. We got ahold of this dilapidated old building that was the island's infamous brothel for centuries. It sat unused—full of squatters and junkies—for ten years. One night I threw a party, started spinning, and everyone wanted to do it again. The basement was pitch black except where we strung strobe lights and neon. The floors were bare dirt, turned to two inches of mud when things got going... everyone was just covered in filth and it got them off harder. The building went up for seven floors, every wall covered in psychedelic graffiti and Day-Glo tags. It got so big that queues were going around the block, clubbers dressed to the nines to get in this ancient, filthy whorehouse."

He noticed that I was slamming my head into his dashboard.

"Why are you doing that?" He asked, clearly not used to Americans.

"This was the late '90s right?" I said, "I was a bookie in Pittsburgh and working for the turnpike."

"We ended up being voted best night in Ibiza," he continued. "One night, Grandma Funk showed up and performed. Head Candy played once, as a supporting act."

My life is going to be exactly like this, only I won't have to do things, I thought. "You were really, really busy," I said, feeling bad for him now.

"After all that we'd wake up Monday morning hung over, sunburnt, just smashed, and it would be like, shit, we still have to do a TV show."

"I think I'd be locked in a rehab for 'exhaustion' after a week of that."

"I was so jacked up with adrenaline Scott, the pure thrill of it all. I knew that all of this would never happen again. Not even on this island."

"But it would be a very Pete Doherty-y kind of exhaustion."

"I don't doubt that Scott."

LOST IN SPAIN

The next day was the wedding. Audrey was staggeringly beautiful, resplendent. She embodied a transcendental elegance that took your breath away and made you want to order a highball and talk about jazz. Even if you didn't understand jazz. George lost his disheveled trademark, thanks to an extra attentive hair stylist and looked dapper and handsome.

My wife performed the ceremony. Karen was gorgeous. She stepped outside herself and personified an ageless, eternal priestess of love. We all knew she'd be perfect for the part given her history of high school drama and walking around the house talking to the pets in flawless Dalek. She can also do Italians, her boss, George Bush, and a wicked Winston Churchill.

The reception was held in the mansion-y villa. One of Audrey's friends—an opera singer out of London—sang Fields of Gold while rose petals fell from a hidden rose petal depository in the sky. She made my face leak which normal people have told me means crying. The guests were millionaire club owners, famous DJ's, artists, musicians, TV producers, radio people; sophisticates of every stripe, all sipping drinks and dancing and being nice to me.

The smokers congregated in a semi-secluded corner, so as not to contaminate the purity of the party with images of death, disease or floating ash. Also because that's where the ashtrays were. It was in that comparatively seedy atmosphere that I met Gordon the Godless. Gordon is a tall, broad, good looking man. The kind of man's man that Earnest Hemingway would have taken one look at and called brother. Or, Hemingway would have tried to decapitate Gordon with a sword, depending on the Old Man's BAC and whether or not Gordon had yet bedded The Old Man's wife. The sort of man who simultaneously makes me want to try a five-o'clock shadow and makes me realize I don't have the testosterone. I got the idea that he held onto his boyish good looks only because it helped him get laid. Lovable, cute and tough, Gordon reminded me of a panda. A panda that has massive

amounts of drunken sex on a global scale.

Gordon's love of rum, women and food was legendary up and down the Mediterranean. Yet he carried a cultured sophistication easily and well. The way a Kardashian might carry a rhesus monkey in her purse, say. He'd chartered boats all over the world, designed and built sets for TV spots and movies, and was presently building a farmhouse in the woods of Northern England. He's the one who did the initial work on the house in Javaron, to make it habitable.

I took to calling him Gordon the Godless not because he was an atheist—he might've been a Mormon for all I knew—but because he reminded me of a Viking warrior, someone who should carry a moniker. He looked like a man answerable to no one. This man, this great, hulking, swarthy panda of a man, was also in awe of King George.

"Did he ever tell you about the time he stopped a war?" Gordon asked with the coolest sounding posh accent I've ever heard.

"I used to be a bookie," I said.

"What…"

"Oh," I said. "I said, what a rookie. For stopping a war. What a rookie move. Joking. I was just being stupid. So wait, what? He stopped a fucking war?"

Gordon chuckled. "Who would stop a fucking war? Fucking wars are fabulous. I've had my share with exes, and it's not something any man should stop. But no, he stopped a killing war. Guns and bombs, senseless slaughter and such. He didn't actually stop it, but he did slow it down for a few weeks."

"Please elaborate," I said, hoping I'd finally found a crazy person—someone on my level—in that sea of perfection.

"The U.N. or NATO, one of the world bodies, funded a study at the time and one result surprised the experts more than any other; the right music retards aggression. So somebody gets the idea to start pumping tunes through some central communications network in the Balkan war. And guess what they used? Yep, George's London radio shows.

And it worked. The fighting slowed, even stopped in some small pockets."

"Jesus Christ!"

"Not him. George."

"So what happened?"

"Don't know. Maybe Milosevic turned it off."

"He was a complete dick. He probably put on Slayer or something. To make up for lost time." I said.

"Imagine if that experiment had stopped the whole thing. He would've won a Nobel Peace Prize."

"That would have been just like King George."

At some point we were interrupted by a series of toasts and speeches. When it came time for Audrey's thank you speech, a hush descended over the frivolity. From the moment she took hold of the microphone the breeze stilled but Audrey's silken hair did not notice and kept going about the business of gently flowing. The birds stopped chirping, and time, humbled by its clumsy existence, stopped. It was like watching Michael Jordan with 15 seconds left in a game seven, being there as Louis Armstrong blew his heart and soul onto the stage at the Apollo, holding the door while Lance Armstrong shot steroids into his thigh; it was watching someone do what they were born to do. It was watching poetry. All I kept thinking was that someone had snuck a barstool onto the Oscar stage. Despite being surrounded by matrimonial ornamentation, and despite the stool, she looked for all the world to be accepting an Academy Award for Best Person on an Island. Her dress had something to do with it, sure, as well as the perfect makeup and hair but it was more than that. Something in the tilt of her head, charm of her voice, passion in her eyes, love radiating from her soul, the poise, grace, humility, mixed with a fierce determination, had red carpet mythology written all over it.

When Audrey finished time started up again because it didn't want distance and speed to overtake it. The birds started singing again and the crowd let out a long held breath

in unison. Afterwards the drinks started flowing in earnest and it wasn't long before a bridesmaid jumped into the pool and we partied in a manner that would please the ancient and nascent Gods alike. I didn't throw up in public or spill a drink on anyone. I was ready for the gilded life.

When we arrived back on mainland Spain I was abuzz with possibility, fortified by borrowed confidence and airport espresso. My future spun out before me like an optimistic top, my fate gilded with glamour and something that looked like naked windsurfers. The only thing interfering with my prescience was a lingering and persistent hangover.

"Not long now and I'll have a personal assistant/doctor to shoot me up with B12 and just a hint of morphine for these days." I said.

"What?" Karen asked.

"Oh, just thinking about the near future," I answered cryptically.

It was all going to start from here. The world was mine, all I needed now was four hours a week of hard work for a month or two and my success would be the meta unstoppable force. I could see it all so clearly. As we drove up into the mountains though the air grew thick with fog and an acrid smoke. Not knowing any better the rural farmers used plastic bottles to light and spread their fires. It was a smell that burnt your eyes and stuck to the inside of your nose.

We kept hitting potholes filled with litter and passing elderly pedestrians as they walked up the steep mountain road, their backs laden with long pointy sticks that I imagined they used to kill small, helpless animals. We drove by abandoned houses tagged with terrible graffiti. Names like Flippo and Chica Peaz with hearts over the I's and underlined as if significant. They were monochromatic: white, and done with no artistic expression whatsoever. If there is a more depressing sight than a dusty, litter strewn, lonely mountain road it's an abandoned cement block shed with shitty graffiti on a lonely mountain road. The scene was out of Nine Inch

Nails video that was directed by Sylvia Plath. The video would end with Flippo and Chica Peaz lying down in front of a lame mule in an act of self-obliteration.

We got home just as the downpour began. As we pulled suitcases from the car I felt my skin prickle, even more than usual, and found an old lady standing in the rain, drenched, staring at us with an open, toothless mouth and angry, vacant eyes. She looked as if she was daydreaming of intense violence. I thought, *So, this is how you want to play it, Javaron. You're messing with the wrong man.*

I said to Karen, "This town really needs a denture and umbrella emporium."

"Boy you've got a regular en-tre-pre-neur-ial spirit. You should send a telegram to that Henry Ford fella. You're fixin' to be a land-holder someday aren't cha?" Karen said. But she said it in an old fashioned accent and I think she was being sarcastic because Henry Ford was dead and we had the internet for messages.

The sky stayed low for weeks as if it were depressive and strung out on barbiturates, the streets were gray like a late stage alcoholic. Clouds had blown in on winds of despair, hung frozen in place out of stubborn menace and were patient enough to wait out my fever dream of optimism. Javaron looked old and dusty, the people smelled ancient with a less than subtle vinegary aftertaste. I knew that most of the Spanish had lived here all their lives; working, supporting their families, remaining steadfast and loyal to their faith, their heritage, their country. I was mortified. The principle made me heartsick. The old men continued to shuffle around in their blue pants which would have given me some hope for capitalism but there was already a blue pant and flannel shirt market a few stretched pork hides down the road, which is how I thought they measured distance at the time. As we'd walk to the stores the old women seemed to multiply and stare even harder. They were beginning to test their prey, growing impatient and aggressive. I thought I saw them spitting at us and flashing gang signs. I realize that perception

changes how we see reality and I was in a dark place, so it is possible they were simply trying to welcome us. The meat cleavers and butcher knives they were holding suggested otherwise.

I've always been struck by the perfect pitch blackness when I first turn out the bedroom light to go to sleep. It's disappointing when, ever so slowly, gray outlines begin to appear as my eyes adjust. For me that pure obsidian represents limitless possibility and the nascent appearance of the murky shadows of lamps, bookshelves and hobgoblins represents roadblocks, restrictions and, sometimes, actual hobgoblins. Depending on what my day's been like. Leaving Ibiza and coming to Javaron was like this for me. Spending so much time with King George and the fabulousness of Audrey on that fairytale island had me seeing stars, blinded to reality. As more and more time passed in Javaron, reality asserted itself more and more forcefully, and it was this sad, tenebrous, shit-smeared-on-my-shoe version of reality that made me reach for blackout glasses.

Karen took the transition from the glitz and glamour of Ibiza to the donkeys and drunken elderly men of Javaron with inspiring alacrity. While I spent the first months battling a losing fight to stay positive, daydreaming of movie theaters, casinos and improbable, instant stardom, Karen did what she's always done. Karen lived.

Every Saturday Karen scours the weekend edition line by line, a Day-Glo yellow highlighter like a bit between her teeth. Her feet will tap in anticipation, her eyes wild with excitement. Sometimes, a small whinny escapes containment from her mouth as the steam fans out from her head. I watch her from the corner of my eye, wary. I rush off to other rooms, feigning a purpose other than mere escape. She's onto me though, always onto me. She follows at my heels, obdurate and irrepressible. There are Things To Do and See you see and Karen will not be denied these pleasures.

"The Museum of Agriculture is having a lawn party at

noon," Karen might say. "Something about regional grasses. They'll be serving tea and it's only an hour's drive."

Or,

"Diabetes Research Foundation; sugar free jelly tasting at four. Be there or lose a foot due to peripheral neuropathy."

I'm terrible at going places and doing things. I like the idea in the abstract—something to be able to post on Facebook or brag about—but the actual doing and seeing is so much like work. I manage to avoid all but the inescapable. "This [Thing To Do and See] is really important to me Scott," she'll say, and I know we're going.

Karen is fascinated by people, interested in activities people are interested in even when she's not interested in the actual activity. "Come look at this tattoo that Lynda Sue is having done." She'll say with real zeal, gesturing wildly at the television.

"Why are you watching Miami Ink?" I ask. "You hate tattoos."

"I do not hate tattoos. I just don't think people should put them on their body."

"You hate my tattoo."

"Well, it's on your body. But look. Lynda Sue is getting a back tattoo of her dead mother. Get this, the mother died of tetanus."

"Is that still a thing?"

"Well the mother is dead, I guess it is. But the tattoo… she has flames where her hair should be and look at the eyes… what would that even mean?"

"It looks like she's in pain."

"Another reason not to put tattoos on your body."

"You don't like tattoos, you like art."

"I like body art. It just shouldn't be on your body." She'll explain with finality.

"You should see the 1973 Electra Glide Paul Sr. just finished." She'll say during dinner.

"What?"

"Retooled the whole thing from tits to toes. It's beautiful.

He took it for a ride and the chrome was shining like the evil boy in the Stephen King, novel about the hotel...."

"The shining?"

"That's it, yeah. The demon spawn boy. "

"The boy wasn't evil, he could see evil. You're confusing "The Shining" with "The Omen" I said.

"Whatever."

"Are you talking about a motorcycle?"

"Not a motorcycle, you nerd," she said pointing at me with her fork, "a chopper. He rebuilt the engine while his kid was being all insolent. That kid's evil."

"What do motorcycles...?"

"Choppers."

"What do Choppers have to do with your life?"

"I am large, I contain multitudes," She'll say, quoting Whitman.

Karen will watch The Ultimate Fighter with me just because she gets to see how they interact in the house. I'll yell at the screen, "Kick him in the face" before she reminds me that Shane has three children to support and there's not much work in Missoula Montana and he really needs this. I'm pretty sure I could make her a die-hard Steeler fan if only they gave longer pre-game interviews. As it is she can pick a Cowboy cheerleader out of the dizzying sea of silver, glitter and silicone because she happened across a reality show one night.

She was able to handle the transition much easier because she's totally at peace wherever she is. She's a Dali Lama or a Gandhi, or more accurately, a female Yoda. It's why I married her. She balances the negative energy of my own bitter black soul. She has always truly loved people where I love characters. I can get down with TV, movie, and book characters, people in the abstract, all day but interaction with flesh and blood humans exhausts me.

Karen's affability and genuine love of people served her well when we got back to Javaron, as I'm sure it would in any far-

flung corner of the globe. She's the type who would assimilate well in Afghanistan, North Korea, even Texas. While I walked up mountains alone, or sat in the house cold and moping, Karen went out and did actual things with actual people. We lived in the same village but her Javaron was communal, while mine was becoming increasingly monastic.

She had coffee or tea with British compatriots. She took a Spanish class in a house full of cats. It started off with a gaggle of foreigners clumsily trying to conjugate verbs and after three weeks it was just Karen, the teacher, and approximately five hundred and thirty two cats and exactly four dogs. She'd come home proud, repeating phrases like, *"Cuanto para los zapatos,"* and *"Creo que el gato ha muerto."* She'd be coughing and sneezing and had horrific looking scratches on her arms but she was beaming with newfound knowledge and the acquisition of another friend.

She took a creative writing course a few months later, put on by—in my opinion—Javaron's strangest couple. They were a lily white, well-heeled couple from the English countryside. What made them unique among the eclectic eccentrics of our village was that they were hard core evangelical Christians that believed in end time/rapture theology. They were ecstatic about it. In other words they were crazy, like the other ninety-five percent of non-native inhabitants of our village, but not from drug use, unlike the other ninety-five percent.

They believed in an angry, vengeful God and a criminally violent Jesus. Father, Son and the Holy Arsenal were going to come down to Earth and slaughter all the New Agers, Catholics, Muslims, Atheists, Pagans and Rick Warren in an orgy of blood and death. They shared this 'good news' with ear to ear grins and a genuine glee. They were lovely people once you got past them wanting to see humanity obliterated, and they made delicious pastries. They wore bright Christmas colors all year round and stood as if Norman Rockwell was watching with a paintbrush at the ready.

Creative Writing for a Fallen World met every Thursday

morning at the coffee shop/bar/casino. Karen's work was surprisingly powerful given that she wrote about anything. One of her poems was, literally, called Anything and was about everything in Javaron. When I'd ask her to describe the couple's writing, a dark and curious expression would come over her as she described glittery staircases, white horses, human entrails, famine, plague, pestilence and blood raining from the sky like money in a strip club on rap video shoot day.

"How did it go today?" I asked.

"Great thanks. They wanted me to meet their closest friend."

"And personal savior?" I guessed.

"How did you know?"

"I'm a prophet. You'll hear all about me soon."

"The only thing you prophesize is proselytizing. Hey, I like that," she realized, "I'm going to use that phrase in my next stream of consciousness essay."

"So how was he?"

"Who?"

"The friend. The Christ?"

"Oh. He was a lot more like the Terminator than you'd think."

"I'll be back?"

"That part too, I guess. Yeah."

The only invitation Karen ever turned down was when the apocalypse couple asked her to go caroling on Christmas Eve. Caroling isn't a thing in Spain to begin with, and singing is the one Thing To Do that Karen will not Do. So they went it alone, knocking on the doors of the Spanish and English alike, persistently, like debt collectors or Jehovah's Witnesses. They clutched candles between woolen gloves, wholesome, winning smiles showing white capped teeth. They sang merrily about the coming war between Gog and Magog, about death and destruction and the wicked writhing in agony, about the thousand year reign of the antichrist. They sang about the Glorious Reappearing and Jesus, smiling,

LOST IN SPAIN

causing blood to boil and heads to explode. They sang fa la la la, la la la la.

She soon found another Thursday evening replacement: an exercise class with a burned out dominatrix as instructor. The crazy couple, unfazed; began posting flyers about a new 'book club meeting' they were going to host. Karen was content and happy and learning to live another life in another land. She wrote a children's book about our dachshund being afraid to move but finally fitting in. The irony was not lost on me. She watched video tutorials and learned how to write and sell ebooks, learned how to build websites and optimize search engines. When I asked her what that even meant, she replied, "I'm making Google my bitch."

Meanwhile, I did what I've always done. I took long walks and lifted weights. I read books and watched movies. I drank way too much and slowly lost my mind. I waited for fame or fortune—I'd have taken notoriety at that point—to knock on my door and whisk me into another reality. "Where is Satan with my contract?" I thought, as I tapped a pen against my leg and listened for the door.

"Nobody has emailed me from Ibiza yet." I said one morning.

"Why would they?" Karen asked.

"I don't know. Maybe somebody wants me to manage their club, or star in a movie, or partner in a business venture and is willing to put up my half."

"Try refreshing your browser." she said as she slowly took over the internet.

I wallowed in self-pity and possibly a little ass sweat—we didn't have air conditioning—frozen with indecision, stuck in stasis. I'd write the beginning of an outline for a genre changing zombie novel and scrap it when I couldn't find the character arc for Supporting Zombie #2. I wondered why some people have the ability to follow through on ideas while I, after a short burst of excitement or revelation, found myself stuck in a lackadaisical malaise.

After I made the most profound decision of my life and

27

quit drinking I felt sure that my dreams and fantasies would simply fall into place. Had not the entire universe been created by an explosion? My life up to that point had been nothing if not catastrophic. Now, I just had to sit on my couch and wait, I thought, failing to notice that I was doing what I've always done.

Weeks stretched into months and still I waited. There were no emails from Ibiza. Inspiration did not slap me in the face. Nothing happened. I read self-help books that claimed all I had to do was imagine what I wanted really hard... which, looking back, may not have been the best advice for me. Still, I was sober and beginning to learn myself. I settled into happiness, contentment. I learned some of what Karen was doing but could never sit still for long enough. I couldn't gather the motivation to fully grasp it all. I was still bouncing around between interests, like I've done the whole of my life, when the miracle happened. Across the great expanse of the Atlantic Ocean a man named Kyle Wygle got himself a DUI on a motorized bar stool. I happened across the story and wrote about it. In doing so I was reminded that the source of golden material was all around me in the ingenious, hilarious, obnoxious, audaciously stupid, willfully ignorant, violently insane, wretchedly beautiful humanity that populates this earth.

I didn't need to invent characters that may or may not be undead if I didn't have the heart or the chops for it. I could draw from the bizarre, exceptionally amazing people I met every day. Karen suggested that I start a blog and I'd asked her if blogging wasn't a way for socially inept, nerdy sociopaths to passive aggressively blame society for their own miserable failings.

"Yeah, pretty much. And penis jokes."

"Show me where to sign." I said, still holding my red pen.

"This," she said pointing to the computer, "is where the in-ter-net lives. You don't need a pen anymore sweetie."

My first post was up an hour later and I knew I'd found a

home. I opened up about things I never dreamed I would. The experience proved more cathartic than talk therapy with a Xanax IV. I found that I could entertain (a few) people just by being myself. By observing the world around me and listening to my internal dialogue I somehow became more me. A me more fully realized. All the great novels are ultimately about people and I could never know how to write people until I knew myself.

I wrote about stupid criminals, about right wing websites and feminist communes, about celebrity meltdowns and personal catastrophes. I wrote about the unbelievably interesting denizens of our village. I ventured out amongst them armed with only a camera and bought endless coffee, took infinite pictures. I watched them and listened to them and got to know them. I occasionally bought them wine as a bribe to get them to tell stories, open up. I once regretted buying them wine after an irate Gypsy chased me from his compound with a rusted shovel.

Most importantly, I found my calling. It didn't matter if I wasn't good at it—I wasn't at first, maybe I'm still not—I was going to write for the rest of my life. I found the one thing that I loved to do without any of the usual qualifiers: how much can I get paid?, how much will I get laid?, will people love me enough to name children after me? It didn't matter. I found the first thing calling me that did not say, "Drink me, smoke me, snort me, shoot me… hey, ever try a suppository?" I found I was finally living life on its own terms and as long as those terms allowed me to drink lots of coffee, eat four meals a day and start watching my shows at exactly 7:30 pm, I was free as a bird.

Old friends would message me on Facebook and ask about my living in Spain. They would tell me I was a "fucking rock star" and I'd think, "This is exactly what I've always wanted out of life." Then I'd ask them if they remembered when I was a bookie. Wasn't I kind of a big deal back then? They would laugh and laugh. Not physically, perhaps, but they'd certainly LOL and even ROTFLMFAO which is the

five star version to my way of thinking. Without the drinking, drugs, depression and self-pity I was finally able escape the dark, confining hellhole of my head and appreciate what I had. Despite everything, I still had a lot. I was happy.

I stopped looking down on Javaron as a place where mules go to die and began to first appreciate it for its uniqueness then to love it. It's counterintuitive to most people's thinking but blogging got me into the world, doing things I would have never done otherwise. I wanted to write about Things To Do and See so I went with Karen, even made suggestions. We went to all the fiestas, religious festivals, even some funerals. I brought coffee and a notebook and a well thought out excuse to leave early. At some point I stopped seeing the people as small minded worker bees and learned just how cohesive and efficient their way of life was. Not unlike worker bees, actually. Here, right in front of me was exactly the sort of communal utopia I'd always wanted to try. Every citizen had a place, whether it was farmer or mayor or the guy who has to chase the idiot American away with a rusted shovel. They were all worthy, sacred. Here was a place where everybody knew your name. They knew everything about you and because of that, you belonged. It may not be the life for me, but it was a life well lived.

I got to know Hollywood Jose, Hippy Tom; the Aging Drug Lord, American Anne, Kaspar; my own, pet Timberlake and dozens more. Once I let go of my preconceived notions I fell in love with the village and its people. I found serious intellectuals to argue with, hilarious people to laugh with, interesting people to write about and crazy people to run from.

I had disliked them because of their imperfections. They reminded me too much of my own limitations and weakness. After I allowed myself to get to know them, I loved them for those same qualities. More importantly I realized that King George, Audrey the Fabulous, Gordon the Godless and all the amazing souls I'd met in Ibiza were only human as well.

LOST IN SPAIN

They struggled and cried, became frustrated and failed. Sometimes they got constipated. Occasionally they got a mustard stain on their shirt. They were human too. The only thing separating us was my frame of mind and an opera singer or two.

I'd already realized I didn't need fame; if I spent my life in a proletarian pool of obscurity, so be it. The most freeing revelation came when I realized that didn't even need a lot of money to be happy. Just enough to live in a warm climate with quality lawn chair and all the notebooks and pens I'd need. I'd be content as long as I could find a place I could sit in the sun. As long as I could write and had people to write about. If, every few months somebody called me a fucking rock star that would be great. If someday I could make a modest income doing what I loved then I really will be a rock star. As close to rock star as I'm ever going to get, anyway.

When King George would visit us he'd re-walk his Spanish house, touching the walls as he roamed from room to room. During these meanderings, while we showed him Karen's latest artwork or the rocks I found in the river and arranged in The Moroccan Room he'd invariably say something like, "You know, you could open a petting zoo in here, keep some exotic animals in the fields….charge a fortune."

Strolling in the kitchen he might suggest, "Fried peanut butter and jelly sandwiches, you could sell 'em like hotcakes!"

Now though, instead of rushing head first towards a brick wall, I'd just cock one eyebrow up as if to ask, "How soon can we get the permits?"

31

2

KAPPI AND THE GYPSIES

After the long, arduous journey, we had finally arrived in the quaint mountain village we were to call home for the next three years. I was still in my Bukowski Years, so as soon as the suitcases hit the floor I declared, "We're officially Spanish now! *Vamos a trabajar mañana.* Tonight. We. Fiesta!" I was feeling the Latin vibe, mostly because I was culturally confused and was impressed with my barely functional Spanish.

We left the house and stopped in the first open establishment we saw. The bar glistened as if sprinkled with pixie dust, the tiles sparkled, and the slot machines rang out with vigor. The bartender polished glasses and a sultry senorita came to take our order. We ordered wine and a fried "something" and cheese platter. I'm not a big fan of cheese, but *the fried something will be good*, I thought. Besides, I didn't want to ruin my appetite for booze by trivialities such as food.

I went off to waste my first of many euro notes on the slots and returned thirty seconds later to our plate of odorous cheese and grease laden, fried octopus. I spent a half hour

32

sucking vegetable oil while discreetly spitting chunks of rubbery cephalopod into tiny napkins and stuffing them into my pockets. I didn't want to offend the locals, not yet, or allow Karen to know that I hadn't actually consumed anything.

There were only three other patrons, all elderly farmer types, who sipped their drinks in the stoic silence of the alcohol- dependent. *Boring*, I thought. We decided to pay our bill and find somewhere more fiesta-like. So we went to the British pub.

The Blues Brothers was set back, its entrance at the end of a short alley. I saw a group of people passing a joint, sitting on a picnic table just outside the bar. They spoke German and had large backpacks at their feet.

"Damn tourists," I mumbled to Karen as I parted the translucent plastic bead curtain and walked through the threshold.

BB's was nothing like the bar we'd just left. If the Spanish place looked like it had been shit on by a unicorn, this place looked like it had been shit on by something not as magical or rainbow-y as a unicorn. A rhinoceros, say, or maybe an ill dinosaur. The bar was brown Formica and the tiles were muddy Moroccan and looked like they had been slapped down by someone who didn't have a wet saw or the ability to pass a breathalyzer. It took my eyes a minute to adjust to the smoke-filled gloom and I could hear a lone acoustic guitar softly strumming the sounds of the sixties.

This was when I first saw Tommy Wales, who was at least thirty years old in the sixties, but seemed to be still living them. He had a bandana wrapped around his head, a joint stuck between his lips, and his eyes closed tight against the reality of the second millennium. I noticed four people playing pool and a half dozen others sitting around the bar, rolling cigarettes laced with hash and drinking with aplomb.

Well this is alright then, I thought, pleased with myself for thinking with a British accent.

"A shot and beer and she'll have a shandy," I called.

"A shhoott aand a beeerr." I heard to my right.

This was to be the first of many, many, over enunciated attempts to mimic my American accent. I immediately felt bad for all the times I had teased my wife with such lame mimicry. This wasn't humor, this was outrageous.

The man seated next to me was at least six foot two and two hundred forty pounds of pure muscle. The many scars on his hands and the fewer scars on his face told me he liked to fight and fought well. As I unclenched my shoulders and tucked my chest back in, I turned my frown upside down and shook his hand with all the superlative charm I could muster.

"Scott." I said. "This is my wife, Karen"

"Weell alllriiight theenn, I'm Dean, nice to meeett yaaa."

Dean was my age, but like most of my peers, he seemed more grown up, more like a real man, while I felt like an aging boy. This may have been due to my smallish stature—five-eight, one-sixty—but, more likely, it was due to the fact that when anything serious happens that requires responsible action—a burning orphanage, a flat tire, having to renew my car insurance—I tend to call in a real adult to handle it. I'd call the fire department for the orphanage, Triple A for the tire, and Karen is more than capable of handling the bureaucratic thing; she practically lives for that sort of stuff.

"Tell me something then mate," Dean started in. "Why are American footballers such pussies with all those pads and helmets? Why do they wear the bright, shiny spandex... are they worried their vaginas will fall out?"

"You better get used to this," Karen said with no small amount of glee.

I mumbled back something about size, speed, and head trauma prevention, and then added the excuse of steroids as a sort of apology while Dean exhorted the virtues and manliness of rugby. He was only "taking the piss," of course.

It took me a long time to understand and accept the practice of torturing people for sport and even longer to appreciate the exquisite art form that it is. I'm sure I would

have acclimated myself much sooner if I had a few more inches and pounds. Or played rugby as a youth. Two years later and Dean would leave his own bar open, just so I could watch the Super Bowl. As my beloved Steelers lost to the Green Bay Packers, I was able to allow the barrage of insults to bounce right off my tiny, birdlike chest.

Dean then introduced me to his wife, Dani, a forty-something that dressed like a twenty-something and usually pulled it off. The bartender came over with our drinks and offered me his joint. I hadn't smoked weed in years, but I didn't want to look like an NFL player, a pansy, so I took a hit, making a big show of it while not really dragging too much. Karen simply waved it away because she's smarter than I am.

The bartender introduced himself as Frank Black, the proprietor of this fine establishment. Frank was a well-connected guy in London, a Face they'd call him, and he ran a number of shady operations. He had three sons, all chemically dependent in one way or another, but all genuinely nice guys like their father. Frank also ranked as a local celebrity due to his casting in a dozen or so westerns that were filmed in Spain during the seventies. I don't remember seeing British gangsters in any John Wayne films, so I'm assuming he played an American outlaw. He fit the part: six-two with a ruggedly handsome face and cleft chin, framed by long brown hair that looked good even in a ponytail. He also walked with natural swagger. *Now this is a guy*, I thought, *who played some rugby growing up.*

The small amount of pot I'd ingested wrapped itself around all the booze I'd drunk, which was a lot by then, and added a healthy dose of paranoia to the awkwardity I'd felt since realizing I wasn't going to fit in as seamlessly as I'd daydreamed.

In that vulnerable moment, trying to figure out what condition my condition was in, I heard a voice full of gravel speak with a thick, guttural accent. "Sexy, sexy, beautiful

womans." He motioned towards my wife. "Marry wanna."

Although he was a foot shorter, he had Dean's build and disposition. "No, she's MY sexy wife." I held my masculine ground, thanks to the blessings of alcohol-induced lowered brain function.

"Hi," Karen said. "Sorry mate, I'm with the American footballer."

"That's not the right phrasing.," I said trying to recover.

"Hahahaha!" The man's voice boomed across the room. "No no no no. Marry wanna?" he repeated this time sucking at his fingers.

"No gracias. I'm more of a drinker," I said.

"You. You. Have. Marry. Wanna?" he asked with a series of points and gestures. "Me gusto marry wanna."

"You just put it out," Frank said as he walked away into the kitchen.

"More. Marry wanna." He said ten minutes later.

"No. Maybe ask Frank."

"He gave to me. Me gusto more marry wanna."

"I don't have any more. I don't have any."

"Sexy, sexy womans." He pointed to Karen and performed a little gyration, his mouth curled in a wolfish grin. "Hahahaha."

"No. My. Wife," I said with steely resolve.

"He's very charming," Karen said coquettishly. "You're very charming."

"Hahahaha." Then he slumped over and stared into his quadruple espresso like his power had gone out.

"Don't mind Kappi," Frank explained, coming back with supplies. "He's a little loco. He's a local gypsy. He's totally harmless unless he drinks or goes off his meds."

"What happens then?" I asked.

"I guess he killed two guys when he was younger. Spent a decade in a prison-type mental hospital. They probably did the shock treatment on him. Savage bastards."

I narrowed my eyes at Kappi and decided I'd always be nice to this man. I was an enlightened being, after all.

36

LOST IN SPAIN

"What, did he shoot them or pull an O.J.?" I asked while making the pirate throat slashing gesture.

"No. These were two separate deals, yeah? Both were gypsies, which is why he isn't still locked up with a car battery stuck to his testicles. One was his uncle or cousin or some shit. He choked the guy out, then waited a few hours and threw the little guy over his shoulders and carried him to the hospital. He walked in, put the relative on a chair like a rag doll, and tells the nurse, 'Man sick.'"

"Man beyond sick." I said. "And there was another one?"

"A few years later he was down in Adra, at the gypsy camp there. A couple thugs tried to rob him. Kappi took a knife to the stomach, but managed to grab one of them. Beat the bastard to death while the other guy ran off. Broke his face all up, I guess."

"Ugh," Karen said.

"So he didn't go to jail for choking his relative, but he did for fighting back against two armed robbers?" I took a furtive glance over at Kappi, but he was still studying his coffee. A crazy cool robot switched to "off".

"It's a funny country. Police don't like to get too involved in gypsy affairs. It's like in your country, with the blacks, or Mexicans now, I guess."

"No, it's not," was all I could manage.

"Ha." Karen laughed.

"Anyway, he had the guy pinned under him and he was still bashing his head into spaghetti when they showed up. By then the bloke's head's practically gone. He was drunk, see? So all that's behind him. Almost no one lets him drink now. They won't even sell it to him in the stores. Sometimes the idiot kids will buy him a fifth, just to see what'll happen, but usually, no."

"So he's on medication, too?" I asked.

"Oh yeah. Some heavy shit, I guess. Lithium. A couple anti-psychotics. A few psychotropics, you name it. His medicine cabinet's like a salad bar, only instead of lettuce and vegetables and shit, it's all drool-inducing drugs, man. He gets

a nice little check from the government every month. We keep him swimming in weed. It evens him out."

"So nothing's happened recently," Karen wondered.

"No, he's been mellow as a tree frog, man. Oh, except for during winter. Kappi doesn't appreciate the chill factor, man. Does some shit to make them lock his ass back up."

"Does some shit like what?" I glanced over and saw that Kappi was reanimated and staring at us, his eyes darting between Frank, Karen, and me.

"Hahahaha," Kappi said.

"Oh nothing too mad," Frank answered. "Just small mischief. One year he put his head through a window. One time he finds a sledgehammer and knocks out a wall."

"Of a house?"

"Of the supermercado. Said he wanted some cigarettes and everything was closed up, I guess. One time he set some old car on fire."

"Shit," I said.

"Yeah." Frank walked away to serve some drinks.

"That's not very nice, Kappi." Karen said.

"Marry wanna?" Kappi replied, his smile almost charming.

"I'm all out." I shrugged my shoulders, palms face up. "Lo siento amigo."

"Hahahaha."

A few minutes later, Kappi noticed the Germans outside and sat smoking pot with them the rest of the night.

Over the months, we grew fond of Kappi and began to regard him as a cute, but potentially dangerous, pet. Like a howler monkey, or a Great Dane that comes down with intermittent bouts of rabies. We'd feed him and make sure he drank enough water in the summer. We'd occasionally buy him cigarettes and sometimes even marijuana. But we didn't allow him in the house and refused to clean up his messes.

I couldn't help but feel a certain empathy for him, a kinship, for here was a fellow outcast. I always said the wrong thing at parties and was kind of clumsy. He'd killed two men. We were brothers in spirit. Even the large, revolving-door

gypsy population shunned him. And if there was one demographic I could identify with, it was the misunderstood social pariah.

Kappi had a big heart. He'd offer what little resources he had. A bite of his mauled sandwich or a drink of his coffee was always up for grabs, no matter how many times he was politely declined. Anything but his dope was as good as yours. He was also a curious and insatiable connoisseur of tobacco. He'd always have cigarettes, but was forever wanting to trade and sample. I'd give him one of my Pall Mall Menthols and his eyes would light up like a kid who realized he'd found the peanut butter cup house on Halloween. He'd always say the same thing with a wide grin after his exhale: "Mucho frio, me encanta!" (Very cold, I love.)

All of my previous cultural knowledge of gypsies had come from books and movies. I knew they were revenge-minded carnival nomads with a terrible weight loss plan, fortune tellers, and hard-drinking, ridiculously good-looking Irishmen with a killer right and an incomprehensible accent. While the hard-drinking part was right on, the rest was, well, off. None resembled Brad Pitt in the least and, certainly, none could enact horrific curses. I'd asked.

The gypsies of Javaron seemed to be divided into two separate factions or camps: those who came to Spain from Romania and those who came to Spain from Romania earlier. Their incomes and class rankings varied considerably. Some owned businesses, owned and rented properties, even horse stables, while others lived in shanty town-like houses without water, electric, or plumbing. It wasn't that this last group couldn't afford things like utilities; they preferred to spend their money on other necessities like booze, drugs, and weapons. They also had an affinity for beater cars, which they could use to buy drugs or, when necessary, as a weapon. Our house was set just above a compound-like house belonging to this last class, although they were just out of view.

During our first Saturday in Spain, I sat outside on the

terrace, trying to figure out who our elderly, drunken, Spanish neighbor was talking to (himself) and what he was saying, ("fuck you, fuck them, fuck it" over and over again) when I heard another strange sound. It was as if three chickens and four spider monkeys had learned to speak gibberish and were arguing over amphetamines. As it went on, the strange sounds increased in pitch and aggression. The noise both grated the nerves and inspired a train wreck voyeur curiosity.

I had to see. *This will be just like watching Cops,* I thought. *Only live and without any cops.* I felt a mild disgust with myself, but because I've lived with that feeling for most of my life, didn't allow it to deter me. I leashed the dog, my prop in this little endeavor, and carried him out the door. We walked down a litter-strewn stream that ran directly in front of the gypsies' house. The stream was handy for them as they used it as a personal garbage shoot, toilet, sink, dishwasher, and laundromat. Before I could get around the corner to the front, I heard a revving engine, a high pitched screech (the spider monkey, I assumed) and, finally, the unmistakable sound of metal changing shape. Once I crept within viewing distance, I set Luca Brasi down, careful to keep him away from the broken glass and used adult diapers scattered over the ground.

From what I could gather, after polishing off a few half gallons of homemade hooch, the gypsy cousins began fighting over a love interest, another cousin. The first cousin, who I named Clubby Gypsy, grabbed a two foot length of thick rebar and tried to assault the offending cousin, NASCAR Gypsy, who jumped in his Peugeot and tried to run him down like a cartoon roadrunner in an Acme tank.

By the time I arrived at the scene, NASCAR Gypsy was standing on the roof of his car throwing river rocks at Clubby Gypsy, who retaliated by smashing at his own terrace with the rebar. Shrapnel rained down like a cement chip and broken electronics waterfall. They were both shrieking an indecipherable mixture of Spanish and Romanian. The only word I could make out, mainly due to its repetition, was

LOST IN SPAIN

"puta". I wasn't sure if they were insulting each other or still arguing over the female. They were joined by a chorus of screams and admonitions from the four ladies present who were taking half-hearted swings at each other as well. Or perhaps, they were consoling one another. It was hard to tell. By the time the dust cleared, NASCAR Gypsy drove away in his wrecked vehicle, Clubby Gypsy passed out, or knocked himself out, and their property looked like it had been sodomized by a tornado.

The matriarch of the clan was wheelchair bound, forced to wear diapers under a tattered moo-moo. Despite this, she carried, or rather sat, herself with a subtle grace and quiet elegance that was lost to the latter generations. I didn't know half of their names and couldn't pronounce the rest, so I followed my earlier examples of naming them after their most identifiable characteristics. Just like The Smurfs, only white trashier.

Grandma Gypsy was, at one time, a prominent member of village society. She and her husband bred and sold horses and owned land and a successful produce market. Unfortunately for Grandma Gypsy, Grandpa Gypsy ran off with Gold-Digger Gypsy and left the clan to fend for itself. As the children grew, the four sons began mating with a harem of five women, producing thirteen children who, in turn, hooked up with gypsies from other clans as well as their uncles and cousins. All this breeding produced an untold number of offspring with multigenerational parentage. Maury Povich couldn't have sorted through this mess if you gave him a year and his own DNA lab.

Most of the clan moved on. It's kind of their thing. Only Clubby Gypsy, Stabby Gypsy, Junkie Gypsy, Huffy Gypsy, and Whorey Gypsy stayed behind to live with, and take advantage of, Grandma Gypsy. The Javaron Clan also served as hosts to the myriad of relatives—and they're all relatives—of roving gypsies passing through. These visits often ended in violence and bloodshed like the incident I'd witnessed with

NASCAR Gypsy and his two brides, The Polygamy Twins.

There's an ancient legend that a gypsy woman stole the fourth nail that was to be used to crucify Christ. This was why one nail was used on both feet. I'd always assumed Jesus had a wonky left foot and was just trying to hide it, knowing the image would be immortalized in gold on every Italian's neck for the next two millennia. I must have been wrong. Legend has it God saw this act of mercy and blessed the bloodline with the ability to be the most talented thieves in the world.

Our gypsies did not possess this gift. They were terrible thieves. Every day they'd get caught trying to steal everything from liquor to licorice at the local stores. The shop workers would shoo them out, but concede a loaf of crusty bread as a consolation prize. They didn't really need the booty; like Kappi, they received a monthly stipend from the government. Every month they each got a check, Spain's version of food stamps, and a voucher for free medicine from the *pharmacia*. Although most of them sold what they could for drugs and weapon money, there was more than enough left over for them all to live well. That wasn't the Javaron Clan's inclination, however. They were hunter-gatherers by nature and simply stuck to their instincts, saving most of what was left of the food stamps for posterity. They always impressed me as the consummate survivors. In the event of a zombie apocalypse, they'd live the exact same life, not even having to adjust to the unpredictable violence and danger that would cripple most of society.

Every morning, Junkie Gypsy and Whorey Gypsy would sneak onto the local farmers' land and steal the produce they needed right from the source. Potatoes, carrots, zucchini, peppers, dozens of fruits and nuts; it was all grown in the area. Huffy would stay home with Grandma while Stabby and Clubby rummaged through all the village dumpsters. They would discover great treasures such as chairs only missing a few legs, broken china, and used disposable razors, in

42

addition to the protein for their nightly meal. They had iron stomachs and could eat anything.

The proof of this occurred when a local pig died of an unknown disease. When it got sick and started acting un-pig-like by lying around all day in its own feces and throwing up a lot, the farmer had to do the humane thing: put it down and bury it. Normally they'd eat the pig, but since nobody could determine what had stricken it, they didn't take the chance. Clubby and Stabby heard about this and, three days later, dug it up in the middle of the night. This happened in the spring, so it wasn't too hot, but it wasn't anywhere near refrigeration temperature, either. The next day they cooked it, outside, and the aroma that wafted through our street resembled that of a bag of colons left out in the sun. It smelled as if a three hundred pound bucket of blackhead pus were roasting over an open fire. Even the hearty Spanish were gagging as they walked by. To the best of my knowledge though, none of the gypsies ever took ill from the rancid meat.

Every morning, after their daily chores had been attended to, they began drinking. The production and consumption of alcohol were the two things they were obsessively responsible about. Their formula was simple: add fruit and sugar to water and yeast and wait. Within two months, they'd have something not even the Spanish would call wine. It wasn't wine but it was alcohol and it was strong and they loved it. So much so there were dozens, perhaps hundreds, of casks, gallon-sized glass bottles, and garbage cans lined with plastic marinating amongst their landfill of treasures. To me it looked like catastrophe in waiting.

At two or three p.m., the high-pitched screaming would commence, echoing through the quaint white-washed streets like an airborne toxin, infecting everything it touched. Cats mewled and fought, dogs howled, and even the elderly married couples would turn on each other with perplexing hostility and aggression. It was like all the serenity and good will had been sucked out of the atmosphere and replaced with

black rage. By four p.m., we'd hear the sounds of inorganic objects colliding with organic humans, which would precede an indignant howl of pain followed by the chirping of an ambulance.

I spoke often with an ambulance driver who was known among the village as Hollywood Jose, both for his dyed blond hair and for his well-known affinity for American entertainment. The paramedic had spent many hours attending to the clan over his career and was more than willing to gossip. Jose would often be found nursing a beer and poring over the *National Enquirer* or *People* magazine. "To improve my English speaking," he'd say. We became friends due to the fact he was one of the only Spanish I could easily communicate with and one of the only people willing to talk to me in any language.

I soon learned that Stabby Gypsy would have been better represented by the nickname Bleedy Gypsy, since he took a lot more punishment than he gave. He'd been bludgeoned, lacerated, or, ironically, stabbed, over a dozen times in the three years Jose worked in the village. Stabby Gypsy's face looked like raw material, an ore, which had yet to be melted down and cast into human form. Now I knew why.

"He's like your American Sly," explained Jose. "Whether Stallone is playing the Rocky or the Rambo, yes? He is having pain and the blood always. I tell you now."

If the clan's fighting was mostly amongst each other, the small and short Clubby Gypsy was a lot more agile and wiry than I'd given him credit for. He'd only been stitched up a handful of times. I thought again of Brad Pitt in *Snatch* and when I brought this up to Jose he was adamant.

"No, no, no! He is ugly of the face and *loco* like the Britney Spears and violent and stupid in the head. Brad Pitt is the beautiful man with the golden hair as mine. He is talent and strong and so very happy. This is why the California is for gay, yes?"

"Probably," I answered, but I was sure he didn't

understand the concepts of underground fighting or Americanized homosexuality.

Junkie Gypsy was on methadone, but would mix whatever she could get with an entire week's supply. This resulted in overdose, shots of adrenaline and Narcan, and in-home follow up visits from a state social worker. Why they didn't remove Grandma Gypsy from that environment I'll never understand.

The Spanish authorities thought of the Gypsies as another entity, existing entirely outside their purview. They'd do what they could to help, after the fact, but refused to intervene or take preventative measures. It was like Alaskan fishermen throwing cod to a stranded polar bear floating adrift on a stray iceberg or casting dwarfs in bad comedies; people trying to help an ugly situation, but not doing enough.

Huffy Gypsy was diabetic and clinically obese. She also suffered from sleep apnea, but since they chose to live without electricity, a CPAP machine wouldn't help. Huffy also drank and smoked and every time Jose saw her, he was surprised she was still alive.

"Huffy is like the Tom Cruise when he had the big hair with fancy suits and was making the sexy looks with beautiful Brad Pitt," he said.

"What?" I asked.

"The Vampire Interviews... when they were the sexy evils." I noticed as he answered, he crossed himself with a visible shudder.

"So you think our Gypsies are like vampires?"

"Yes, yes, like that. But with the ugly and fat. Not with beautiful. I tell you now. Never die, never. Like that."

If they were vampires, Grandma Gypsy was The Queen of the Damned. At night—once the rest of the clan were passed out or in the emergency room—Karen and I would bring her some food and wheel her up into the kitchen. I'd place her before the fireplace and Karen put the food on her lap. She'd stare into the fire, eyes glowing crimson, and as she took the first dainty little bite, nod in an almost imperceptible gesture

of gratitude.

The clan had an endless stream of relatives that came to enjoy their unique brand of hospitality. The thieves, addicts, and thugs would never last long—a day or two max—before the bucket of shit they kept outside the door would hit the non-proverbial broken fans scattered on the terrace. Their innate nature would overwhelm their desire for familial companionship and one of the visitors would say or do something that made Stabby become stabby or Clubby reach for his trusty rebar. There were only two sets of relatives who beat the odds and stayed for a longer haul.

The first were two sisters and a brother: Baby Mama I, Baby Mama II, and Baby Daddy. They were fifteen, seventeen, and twenty, respectively, and arrived in Javaron with five children between them. I never found out which babies belonged to whom because I'm not one to pry into affairs which don't concern me. The Baby Mamas cared for them all while Baby Daddy kept busy by bedding anything that wasn't nailed down. Gypsy, Spanish, English, tourist, young, old, male or female, Baby Daddy was the horniest person I'd ever met. Someone straight out of a Chuck Palahniuk novel. He was only five-six with a slight build, but he had a pleasant face and a winning, rakish smile. If the rumors were to be believed, he also had a horse-like penis which helped even more than his obvious charm.

The Baby Mamas were quiet, didn't even drink. Every time they saw me they'd smile and sometimes even wink. I like to imagine they found me uniquely irresistible or ridiculously good-looking, but it was more likely my American passport they fancied.

There were no major incidents for months until one day Clubby Gypsy went after Baby Daddy with a table leg after Junkie Gypsy admitted to an affair with the boy. Luckily, Baby Daddy was fast and agile, kept in shape by his endless libido. Three days later, there were rumors of an underage pregnant Spanish girl and before the pitchforks could be

LOST IN SPAIN

sharpened and the torches lit the three baby makers pulled up stakes, leaving behind angry gypsies, furious Spanish, and lots of diapers.

The second family to stay was a young couple with kids and they were all good people, genuine. Phillip was a goat herder by trade. While he didn't look like Brad Pitt he bore an uncanny resemblance to Antonio Banderas. He had a dark, rugged handsomeness and light brown, gentle eyes. Every day, Phillip brought his two horses to the water fountain/horse trough and let them drink while he dipped a brush in the water and wet their silky coats, horse and man muscles rippling and shining in the Spanish sun. One day as Karen gazed down at the scene with a look I'd describe as hungry, I remarked that the image would make a great Harlequin romance novel cover.

"Mmmm hmm," she replied, biting her lip.

Phillip's wife, Maria, was a plump, pretty woman who went nowhere without their two adorable children. One day Phillip rode by on his horse calling out "Jojo" in a desperate voice. I assumed one of his charges had escaped and he was simply doing his job to find the goat. For the next few hours he rode up and down, back and forth, growing more and more agitated. At dusk we heard Maria and the kids, from blocks away, calling out balefully for Jojo. The cries grew nearer and I went out onto the street to see if I could help. All three faces were wet with tears and wholly miserable. Using my clumsy trio of English, Spanish and pantomime to communicate, I found that Jojo was their pet goat and, yes please, they wanted me to find him "en este mismo instante" (this minute).

"Here Jojo, Jojo Jojo!" I joined in the chorus.

An hour later, we rendezvoused back at the fountain in front of my house. It was then I heard how Jojo had escaped. The mischievous goat had run away just as Phillip had tried to cut its throat. Maria already had the stew cooking and everything. The kids were heartbroken because they knew it

was their grandmother's favorite meal and she was arriving the following day.

This sort of thing might be old hat to people living in rural areas or working for fast food conglomerates, but it caused me to consider, for the first time, where my food came from. Had a little girl named the chicken that was even now lying in my refrigerator? What if she'd tied a pretty pink bow around its neck and took it for long walks around the pen? Did she stroke its soon-to-be lemon-pepper marinated breast while cooing terms of endearment? Had I been eating that same chicken's eggs every morning? The eggs may not be fertilized—I don't know how eggs work—but I imagined a husky, patrician rooster clucking home from a hard day of pecking up the social ladder, fighting for alpha status, whoring himself out for the greater good, only to find his future babies vanished. It must have happened every single day. Was this a cause of conflict in their lives? I imagined him blaming his wife while she grew ever more perplexed, despondent, and resentful, her only joy now gleaned from the affectionate fingers of the human girl. I saw the rooster avow to be a better husband, to support her, and to lay the matter of the missing eggs to rest. He'd arrive home bearing daisies and bits of the day's finest grains and find her gone, along with the fucking eggs again, only a pretty pink ribbon lying torn in the sad brown dirt.

As tears welled in my eyes, I knew I had destroyed a family and vowed to go vegan. That evening, however, I grew hungry. Desiree—that was her name in my fantasy—was already in the fridge and I couldn't allow her sacrifice to have been for naught. I did eat that bird, a little slower though, truly savoring it in appreciation of a good chicken, wife, mother, pet.

The family never did find their goat. Perhaps the other Gypsies got to it first, or maybe—and this is my hope—it escaped over the border into a small hippy commune in Southern France, where they'd enjoyed Jojo not for his protein rich flesh, but for his offbeat personality and

LOST IN SPAIN

anecdotes of Spanish life.

In addition to the permanent, seasonal, and overnight Gypsies, there were the carnies. Instead of setting up and operating rides—as they do in America—they sold cheap, Americanized goods made in Taiwan and the Philippines. The arrived in the morning in raper vans and trucks and were gone by nightfall so they never had a significant impact on our Gypsies, other than to increase their dysfunction. I suspected that they operated as a narcotic super highway. Three days after Market Day, Junkie, Stabby and Clubby could be found nodding off anywhere and everywhere around town.

I ran into Hollywood Jose the week before we left and he got me caught up on the Gypsies' emergency health care.

"The one you are calling Clubby? He gets shot by an old hunter rifle from the brother. He only hurt his leg, very minor. The Stabby wanted to kill him like Michael is killing Fredo in Godfathers. Too bad he doesn't have the fishing boat huh? That's how you do that!"

"How's my girl?" I asked.

"The old *madre*? She is perfection. Never see her for anything. No sickness or hurt, ever. She is really vampire. We are right. I tell you now."

I still often think of the Queen of the Damned, Grandma Gypsy. Gone is the dirty moo-moo and diaper bump. In my mind's eye she is sitting on a marble throne, ancient and proud, while people, customs, and cultures change around her like so many stage props being cleared away and replaced between acts. I know she'll outlast this current crop of relatives just as she outlasted the Egyptians and Greeks in centuries past. She has alabaster skin and wears an elegant black silk dress. And her hair... is perfect. To me she is as beautiful as Tom Cruise, Brad Pitt, even.

3

SEE THIS VAIN

"See this vein, how it looks boiled?" A bald, twitchy man walked up and asked me by way of introduction.

"Yeah, wow." I said because I didn't want to admit to not knowing how a boiled vein would look.

"That happened when I tried to inject straight MDMA. Hurt like holy hell! It burned and itched and shot flaming lasers of acid up into my brain. It was like shooting fiberglass into your eyeball, yeah? It was like I had blasted boiled tar heroin right straight into my fuckin' hand. But while it was still boiling, yeah? I didn't know what to expect shooting ecstasy but I didn't expect a boiling tar bubble. And look; that's just what it looks like! Can you believe it?"

"Huh uh." I said, because I couldn't believe it.

I'd been standing off to the side, minding the business of smoking a cigarette, while my wife Karen sampled homemade jelly in one of the tents. A brand new fiesta had sprung up around the country. Companies and schools had come and set up an interlocking maze of tents where one could sample and buy wine and cheese, get a reading from the good folks at scientology, or remortgage their house for centavos on the

50

Euro. This fiesta was based on an American inspired idea of consumerism and did not do well in the rural mountains of Southern Spain.

We'd just moved to Javaron and I was pleased that an English speaker had sought me out. He didn't seem as judgmental as the first few residents I'd met and I took that as a good sign.

He stood sweating and twitching, cursing and spitting while the Spanish sun beat down upon him like a punishment. He was wearing a cherry red jumpsuit with a matching Kongol hat and looked like he came straight from a Beastie Boys video in which they were being ironic. Or retro. Ironically retro maybe. He had an angry, painful looking skin condition. I think it was psoriasis but it could have been an allergic reaction to veterinary pharmaceuticals. He introduced himself as Lugs.

It was close to one hundred degrees that day and the sweat was exploding from his pores like midgets escaping a medieval carnival. The surrealism was punctuated by his dog, a white Alaskan Huskie, who whimpered with displeasure and lunged at the groins of pedestrians all while his master juked and jived and itched and scratched, but mostly sweated, never missing a beat, making it look even more like a satirical play on "No Sleep Till Brooklyn."

"….. Smoking crack in Ibiza. Sparkly high and drunk, right? We went back to this DJ's camper van and just orgied it up right there. Everybody was sexing everything…. a 300 pound Black Princess from Somalia pulled out a 13 inch dildo from I don't know where and shouted, 'I'm fucking somebody right here and now, don't care who. I'll fuck every one of you bad if I can't fuck somebody good.' So after the seven of us untangled ourselves I went off with her to the beach to get well and truly fucked…. Good times, fast times!" he said while worrying at a scab beneath his eyebrow, which broke open and produced a sickly flow of purple, muddy blood.

"Aww now look 'atcha done ya fuckin' twat." The woman

materialized from nowhere, rocking on her heels and sucking the oxygen right out of the atmosphere. She was between the ages of 40 and meth addict. Taking in her countenance I was re-motivated to give clean living an honest shot.

"Motherfucking Lugsy aren't cha?" she said, staggering but somehow maintaining an upright posture. This Hensonesque character stood at my height, 5'8" but seemed to possess another foot of stature which was pure personality. It looked as if she were punishing her hair for misbehaving in an earlier decade. If it was bottle blond then the bottle said 'rubbing alcohol.' Her skin was the shade of yellow that usually signifies an overworked and underpaid liver.

"All right Boo?" Lugs asked his life partner.

"Aye. Good as you, ain't I? Ya fuckin' Lugsy." She answered.

Both the couples' eyes were the same shade of pale brown—pretty brown—but made considerably less attractive by their erratic and unpredictable movements. Her haggard, doughy, scarred face sat atop a body which was alarmingly perfect. She wore cut off, '80s style jean shorts and a halter top made out of something resembling pasta. Thin, athletic, with a runners' muscle tone, she looked like a beach volleyball player from the neck down. Above the neck she looked like she'd played volleyball with a broken bottle and lost.

"Now I mixed me sausage in wit' plenty o' dark meat. Hit plenty o' winged birds… if you get me meaning, but this was something else altogether. Plus, the crack was right. My willy was hiding like a fuckin' sea turtle in a shark tank and it only made Big Princess angrier and violent seeming." His gestures were wild in imitation of the amour.

"She was that big?" Boo asked in response to his waddle.

"Aye. She slapped me in the face with the dildo, hard. Now I'm having to fend off blows from an errant dildo while trying to chub up myself, still hitting the pipe every three or four minutes … you know how it is… eh?"

"Mmmm" I answered, non-committal.

"Don't ya have any stories where your cock works Lugs?

LOST IN SPAIN

Don't mind im', he gets lost in his high all the time." She said to me. "I'm Boo hun. Good to meet ya."

Boo was a thirty-something hustler from Manchester. She'd spent a dozen years in Amsterdam working as a dominatrix and small time ecstasy dealer. She'd met Lugs, or Lugsy—depending on the use of the word 'fucking'—at a sex club in Holland where he was a paid submissive. For the uninitiated that means he got paid to be the victim in S&M games where there are no winners, only varying degree of loser. They got on like a house on fire. The house was filled with drug addicted sex freaks that love heat and pain. Like many immigrants to our tiny village they had fled to Javaron after finding themselves pursued by both sides of the law.

"After a half hour of abuse, my face is swelling up now… me mate comes by and we're able to hold her down and tie her up. This was lucky. Big Princess meant to kill me, I think. After that I was able to get myself right, and so was me mate, so we asked her if she still wanted sexed. She did. So, we did. But we wasn't untying Ebony Mountain until we was done. By then she was halfway normal so we all just kept smoking all night. Drugs are better in Ibiza."

When Boo went off to hustle up a beer Lugs seemed to fizzle out, like a crack pipe left out in the rain. He made attempts at another few short stories but they never went anywhere. I wasn't sure if Boo had stolen his mojo or he'd smoked it while I wasn't paying attention. I said my goodbyes and left him to his private thoughts.

Boo and Lugs were living in a cortijo: a Spanish farmhouse with surrounding land, up in the mountains above Javaron. They lived with the huskie, four to seven cats—depending— and an odd assortment of hangers on, random backpackers, and armed fugitives in a crumbling structure that was missing two walls and a third of the roof. Their living quarters would shrink by at least a foot after heavy rains, when more and more of the roof would collapse. This was one of many reasons for the erratic feline population.

53

The next time we ran into Boo and Lugs they were in Blues Brothers—the local British bar—ankle deep in drug induced nostalgia.

"This little blind fucker," Boo said, "he wandered into my club one night. The poor bastard just liked him a techno beat, right? He hears the music and wanders in off the street bobbing his head and snapping his fingers. He doesn't have any bloody idea that this is an S&M club with a live sex show poppin' off only a few feet away from where he's standin'. I'm surprised he couldn't smell it, the deaf are meant to have superhuman smells, yeah?"

There was a crowd gathered around Boo. This happened often, making her a natural for the adult entertainment industry. In the three years we knew her, she had only worked once in her chosen field. Boo took a position as manager of strip club/whore house for exactly three weeks. She brought Lugs along and got him hired as a faux big spender: someone the club hires to throw around big money in an effort to get the party started. Rumor has it that Boo had an affair with a stripper, they got half the club addicted to drugs and Lugs embezzled far too much food and booze to have any hope of not getting caught. All we know for sure was that on the twenty-second day Boo got fired, Lugs got beat up and they came home to Java.

"...So I'm feeling charitable, yeah? This bloke wasn't half bad looking. He wasn't gimpy in any other way but he's blind. So I pull 'im onstage and he's still thinkin' he's in an ordinary club and just got lucky. I start snoggin' 'im right there. Hard. Me mouth prolly wasn't tastin' too good. Not after the first act, but I'll give it to the blind bloke, he kissed me back. Little shy at first but good. Dude starts getting hard, can feel it firmin' up in me hand, so I take him out of his trousers."

She accentuated the story by showing us the heft and length in her cupped hands.

I looked around for Lugs and saw he was just behind her, like an old timey Japanese wife. He was staring at his mistress's back with something akin to rapture.

LOST IN SPAIN

Boo and Lugs survived in Spain by hustling. They'd drive into Orgiva or Malaga and pick up drugs for people. They'd find abandoned property to strip for copper and land to strip for firewood. They'd pick up scrap metal and sell glass bottles. They'd show up at bars and announce that they'd just gotten married to get free drinks and food out of suspicious but willing tourists.

"Hung like a Cuban, he was. So I wanked 'im off right there. I bent down and let 'im cum all over me face and tits. Not that he knew where it was going. Then the bloke got all shaky and surprised and shit but the crowd went bonkers. Four hundred plus in Euros that night. Great fuckin' night."

A few listeners in our present crowd offered a few hardy claps before thinking better of it and stopping mid-clap. They let their hands hang suspended before finding something better to do with them.

Boo also exercised a surprising prowess as a fitness instructor. She'd find an empty area, the local park, or the pool, and lead a loose gaggle of alabaster skinned, pear shaped women in an uncoordinated ensemble of disco moves, boot-camp style punches and kicks and traditional aerobic exercises. It was like watching an hour long, satirical YouTube clip with no punchline. After the class they'd all go to a British pub and congratulate themselves over bangers and beans while Boo smoked cigarette-con-hash and slammed beers.

She was a great motivator and, against odds, the classes would grow alongside her income until one of two things happened. Either Lugs took their saving to Orgiva for a well-earned crack binge, or Boo slipped off the alcoholic diving board and belly-flopped into the meth amphetamine and vodka deep end, which was always open and quite deep. After that they'd both slip under the radar—having spent everyone's money and goodwill—until they got hungry or bored enough to start the whole cycle over again.

Karen and I tried to help them out by buying wet firewood or surprisingly pure ecstasy—anything for charity—

but they never managed to stay above that dark, tumultuous water for long. They managed to hold a positive outlook on life and always had a master plan. Something just around the corner that they were sure would bring them prestige and fortune. One time it was a crude internet Ponzi scheme, another, a sadomasochistic sex tape. Despite no investors for the former and no interest in the latter they held out hope for a brighter future. You can imagine their exuberance when they heard that one of Lugs' mates had just inherited seventy thousand British pounds and was on his way over from Manchester.

"We ain't about to fuck this gift horse in the arse." Boo told me.

"Punch," I said "Don't punch it in the mouth."

"You're a sick fucker Scotty." She replied with a smirk, not understanding my correction.

Chalky was 5'10", barrel chested and dark skinned with piercing blue eyes. He was a fine looking man, one who would be perfect if cast as a Miami Vice style villain. He also sported the kind of symmetrical bald head that makes me think it won't be so bad when I go bald myself. Until I feel all the bumps and crevices on my own misshapen dome and realize that it's going to be horrific. Chalky was pleasant and amicable when he was sober but turned into an angry and violent brute when drunk. He inherited his money from his mother who had owned and operated an illegal brothel for over three decades in Northern England. This is where he'd learned his trade, which consisted primarily of fighting, whore management and counting money. Chalky loved his crack in the way a mother loves an ugly and stupid child: with a resentful but ruthless loyalty. Crack did not love him back, however. The drug made him paranoid, controlling and even punchier.

I met him the day he arrived in Javaron. He arrived flush with the promise of a new land and the hope that his demons could not traverse that small expanse of the Atlantic between

the UK and Spain. Karen and I were sitting outside the bar drinking strong Spanish coffee while Boo and Lugs hustled drinks out of tourists. Chalky pulled up in a newish Ford Explorer and got out carrying a state of the art MacBook and a bag of frozen English cod.

He wore a black Armani shirt open to the midriff, linen pants, and handmade Italian shoes. The Rolex was a powder blue Sea Dweller. His air of sophistication and class evaporated as soon as he opened his mouth.

"Boos, Lugsies!" He shouted, "Me mum's dead as dirt, I sent the birds back to Russia, and it's time we had us a party, hey?" Lugs wore an expression on his face of a man who's been told his bail has been paid, who's just been saved from some nameless fate. It was the look Daniel had walking out of the lions' den, the look OJ had when he found out that the prosecutions' case rested on the testimony of Kato Kaelin and that the gloves had shrunk in the laundry. Lugs and Boo both stood on shaky legs, squealed, and ran up to touch the hem of Chalky's garment.

"Let's do it proper then, hey!" Lugs cooed, his voice humbled by awe at his good fortune.

After a half dozen beers, shots, joints and suspicious trips to the bathroom each, the three jumped in the Explorer and took off, the sound of techno beats and laughter fading into the late afternoon sun.

I was walking up to the baker to buy my daily bread when I next saw Lugs and Boo. It occurs to me now that I'd never seen them apart, then or after, through the three years I knew them. They were sitting on the steps outside Blues Brothers' and I walked over to get the story.

"Three fuckin' weeks, Scotty. That mad fucker had us locked up tighter than a Catholic girl's arse in that stinkin' pit."

The 'pit' that Boo was referring to had been a luxurious Spanish villa that Chalky had rented at two thousand Euros a week. That first night, after a few hours of light partying, they

drove into Orgiva and bought an ounce of blow. After a few lines on the drive home Chalky stopped in the store and came out with an entire case of scotch, a box of baking soda and Spain's version of Chore Boy, which, for all I knew was Chore Boy. When they got home he put on his chef's hat and cooked the powder into rock.

They looked the worst I'd ever seen them, and that was a feat in itself. As if they'd been in a Bosnian death camp since the early '90s and escaped only to be bitten by a zombie on the way home. Both were a waxy greenish gray. It was like looking into a kaleidoscope of Ebola and AIDS and vomit. Lugs was covered head to toe in psoriasis, a condition that flares up when he's stressed or held hostage. His golden jumpsuit was torn, stained and covered in burn holes and what I guessed, hoped, was mud. Boo had two inch black roots beneath the sizzled and fried blond mane. Both of their lips and fingers were blistered and cracked. Lugs had a black eye and Boo was missing two teeth from her lower jaw.

"Once he hit that pipe, the depths of hell opened and the devil 'imself came into that fuckin' lunatic." Boo explained while Lugs stared at the ground with demoralized lassitude. He only moved to pick at a scab or stick a random finger in his mouth and suck.

"He started movin' furniture around right off and we thought, what the hell, we's jus' getting high? Before we knew what was what, he'd barricaded us in the kitchen, big ass, posh kitchen too. Had shit all up against the doors an everythin'. Then he starts waving a big ass butcher knife around like the one in that movie, yeah?

"What movie?" I asked.

"The one with the butcher knife. Anyway, he'd only move all that shit and open the door when the dealer guy was comin'. He'd put his cash in a box outside the door, then slam it shut again and look at us all mean an shit. The dealer boy would take the dosh and put the coke in the box and leave. Didn't even get to see the bloke, to ask for help or nothin'. Then Chalky, the bastard, would start cookin' and

wavin' that big ass knife around again. Four days in and he passes out, yeah? So me an Lugsy tries to make a break. Movin' shit from the door. The mad fucker wakes up an' punches me right in the mouth an' starts slappin' Lugsy like Lugsy was some kinda bitch."

"Like I was a bitch." Lugs mumbled with torpor.

"At least he didn't kill us. We thought he was going to. Here we is pissin' and shittin' in a pot, like we was home an' not in a big ass, posh kitchen. Why shit in a pot when you got a toilet in the other room, yeah? Crazy lunatic fucker."

"How did you manage to escape?" I asked. I never had to pretend to be interested in their stories.

"Cause Chalky might be dead for real. He jus' fell on the floor and started twitchin'. We moved all that shit from the door, took five or ten last hits from the pipe and hauled ass out. I hope he's alright an' shit but I ain't lookin' in on 'im. No, I ain't the one."

It was another ten days or so before we saw Chalky again. He looked a lot different than he did during our first encounter. The watch and all the toys were long gone, and he was living in his Explorer. He'd removed much of the interior, including seats and carpeting to make room for his sleeping bag and meth lab. This was his plan to get back on his feet. I loved his entrepreneurial spirit. I finally understood what those people meant when they said, "Just pick yourself up by your bootstraps." I thought of *Breaking Bad* and knew he could do it.

"Then the fuckin' thing blows up. Lucky we didn't get all burnt up like toast." Lugs told me a week later over beers I paid for. Lugs and Boo were holding court in Blues Brothers', again to the delight of a rapt audience.

"We did the first batch up an' it was shit. Made us all sick, yeah? So the next one we figures we needs more ephedrine and phosphine, but we ain't no bloody chemists. Boo's breakin' down the matches when a fuckin' fireball engulfs the truck. Nasty shit."

"I thought I was dead for a minute." She said. Boo looked a little singed, lacking eyebrows, eyelashes, and the front of her hair, but otherwise as healthy as a horse who's been on a month long drug binge.

"So we just let it burn man, jus' like that song says. When that shit went out and cooled down some we pushed it over the side of the mountain. Lucky we was parked on a mountain, eh?"

"Lucky indeed." I replied.

Chalky ended up moving in the couple's Casa De No Roof and two months later all three were arrested for attempting to grow forty-some pot plants behind the house. After spending a few months in a Spanish jail, Boo and Lugs came home. Chalky got somebody to wire him some money and abandoned Spain for the promise of a new, better life in Wales where, surely, his demons wouldn't follow.

It was a year later when we heard how much damage they caused to the rented villa. The rental agent was talking to Boo and Lugs while we listened in and took the occasional hit of whatever they were smoking. We were in the town's newest bar—another British pub that opened after Blues Brothers' shut down.

There were thirteen thousand in damages, mainly in the kitchen. For some inexplicable reason, Chalky had torn out five feet of tile along with two cabinets, and dug a four foot hole down into the earth. This psychotic excavation apparently ended when Chalky hit a water pipe and the place began to flood.

"He was a crazy fucker, mad fucker." Lugs said, and we all had to agree. The couple didn't feel the need to shoulder any of the blame and nobody else—not the owner or the real estate agent—made them carry any responsibility either. They were as hapless and innocent as baby sheep, following each other blindly off a mountain cliff.

Lugs choked and laughed, "Did I ever tell you about the time I was smoking crack in Ibiza?"

4

AWKWARDITY

When people think of only children they think of selfishness, of emotional immaturity, of delusions of grandeur. They can't imagine the down sides.

When you have no siblings there is no one else to blame for all the things that go wrong in a seven year old's life. When your parent comes home to find a broken lamp or the cat made up like a 1980s TV preacher with her expensive makeup, she doesn't ask "Who did this?" There is only you. GUILTY may as well be written in Maybelline Cherry Red across your forehead just as it's smeared across Snowball's lips, cheeks, and head. The mother will drop subtle hints that because the piece of shit father walked out and she has to work full time to avoid you both being sold into white slavery, maybe, just maybe, you could pick up the slack and just be fucking normal for five fucking minutes. But if you're anything like me, that's just not possible.

Soon you begin to internalize the feeling as the heavy finger of God pointing at you through the clouds, convicted by a jury of your peers, all inclusive, GUILT and carry it around with you like the broken Lady Timex hidden in your

pocket so your mother doesn't find it in the trash.

To this day I walk around with this inexplicable, constant sense of guilt. Not even guilt for the things I've actually done. I have done a lot of bad things in my life. I feel shame for some of them and I feel nothing for others. What I mean is a constant feeling of people thinking I'm worse than I actually am, that I've done things I haven't.

When I walk through a store I feel like I'm being watched as a potential shoplifter. When I was younger I'd steal things just to give the feeling validation. Then, a day or a week later, after the guilt got the better of me, I'd sneak back into the store and hide five or ten dollar bills in miscellaneous merchandise. Ironically I ended up getting caught at this last part. Instead of calling the cops the store clerk followed me out the door with crumbled up bills telling me I dropped my money in the pocket of a plus size faux fur coat *That's one hooker without cheeseburger money*, I thought and sighed, resigned. That's when I was young and stupid though. These days I make a big show of NOT being a shoplifter. I theatrically hold an item up at arm's length—a shirt, say, or a four pack of toilet paper—and if I don't want it I frown with concentrated consternation, shake my head in mock disgust and theatrically throw it back on the shelf.

When a serial killer is caught the neighbors are interviewed and inevitably say things like, "I never would have guessed it, he seemed so normal." If I was falsely imprisoned for the same crimes I just know my neighbors would say, "I just knew it." and "He always seemed 'off' to me." and "You'll find more bodies, look around back."

On the beach with Karen I often point out the creepy old men staring at bikini clad spring breakers, distancing myself from their ranks and thrilled at having patsies to pass blame onto. Karen will look from the men to me and back again as I stare hard into her eyes, searching to find my fault.

Another thing about being an only child is the isolation. Until I was school age, I never had anybody to play with, so I

learned to entertain myself. I learned to use my imagination as a sort of twenty-four hour movie channel. I had the usual boy stuff: bottom of the ninth, bases loaded, full count...home run!, G.I. Joe killing communists in the woods, California Highway Patrol Officer looking tan and saving hikers from mountain lions... drivel that is as pedestrian as it is dated. But I also concocted elaborate scenarios where I was the immortal king of the universe, adored by all of creation and acted them out amongst my G.I. Joe and CHIPS action figures. I loved the idea of being adored, and was always shocked when it so rarely happened. I loved the idea of people. I loved people, but only in the abstract. The reality never lived up to my expectations. Mostly because they so often failed to adore me. Instead of being good characters in my fantasies, real people had their own needs, desires, agendas. When my own mother would shut down my Curious George and I Save the World From Rabid Mountain Lions Remote Controlled by the Atlanta Braves story so she could take a shower and go to bed, it felt like an unforgivable betrayal. I could never comprehend why real people didn't do exactly what I wanted them to do the way my imaginary people did.

I got the sense that I was never really that good at being a child. I enjoyed having friends but I preferred spending time with only one at a time. I could handle two, even tolerate three, but any more than that was pure Nietzschean hell.

I could never shake that hyper-intense self-awareness that always prevented me from being at ease, being myself— whatever that meant. "This is my birthday party," I'd say to myself, watching the little demons and imps run and jump and puke and scream everywhere.

Why are they doing that? I thought but I couldn't understand it, not really. That never stopped me from trying to pump myself up and go for it.

Ok, you're going to scream at the top of your lungs and run as fast as you can across the room and dive headfirst into that ball pit! I thought. I was at Chuck E. Cheese during my 8th birthday

party and not enjoying myself at all and hating myself for it.

But what if there's a man with a knife in there?

What?

You know how many generations of germs are inbreeding in that cesspool?

Just do it.

Ok....AAAaaagggghh... this feels so fake... hhhhweeeeee!

I get stuck in an awkward inception; a self-conscious watcher watching a self-conscious watcher watching a self-conscious watcher. Only there's no end to the loop and I can never wake up.

Sports were one area where I actually felt comfortable. Not because I could lose myself in the competition but because I could lose myself in the role—or persona—of an athlete lost in the game. I knew how they ran and jumped, how they moved, how they celebrated. I knew because I watched them, I studied them. Those hours spent watching sports were class credits towards being human. When I stepped up to the plate I crossed myself just like I'd seen Clemente do, when I drove to the hoop I stuck out my tongue and usually bit it because I was not Michael Jordan.

I brought this same academic scholarship to high school and it served me well. Not with excellent grades mind you, because I wasn't studying for classes. I studied the cool kids the way an anthropologist studies an ancient culture. I felt like an alien trying to not get caught. So I watched the way they walked, talked, danced, how they ate, how they talked to girls.

It was exceedingly rare for me to make a move without asking myself, *What would a normal person do here?* When I failed to consult with myself or my mouth got ahead of my head and the real me slipped out, the results were unequivocally horrific. I would do or say that worst possible thing at the worst possible time.

As a junior I put a freshman to sleep with a sleeper hold. I wasn't trying to be a bully; I didn't even think it would work. One moment we were just messing around after football practice and the next I had a forearm tourniquet around his

LOST IN SPAIN

head and the next he was limp and the next he woke up and puked and the next I was suspended for a week.

Another time I launched into a stand-up routine about one of my teachers while she was just around the corner. My friends were trying to warn me but my brain-mouth connection was shut off and I'd just seen Eddie Murphy do Raw and wanted to try out some of those new cusses. I was in middle school.

As frequently as these incidences occurred however they were the exceptions. The rule was the polar opposite. If I didn't keep an iron, vise-like grip on my conscious action I stopped dead like a run-down robot. I'd sort of come to a few minutes later and find myself standing mannequin still, arms folded, hands clenched in the middle of a busy hallway or gyrating dance floor. People would look and point and I'd play it off by doing an Eddie Murphy routine.

When that happened I'd remind myself that THIS is NOT what a normal person should be doing and get back to walking or dancing again. The whole time, before, during, and after, knowing that this was all wrong, knowing that I looked off.

Those bursts of self-consciousness, although face-saving, could be brutal. They'd come sudden, unexpected, like bird flu in Asia or public transportation in Detroit. One second I'm talking to a girl at a party and everything is going well. The next second my internal point of view shifts with an almost audible click and instead of seeing from my own eyes I'm suddenly seeing—with crystal meth clarity—through her eyes. Through everyone's eyes within ten feet. That kind of blinding self-awareness is the most powerful form of torture. I can see myself and wonder why I keep looking down, I wonder why my tongue keeps moving like that—it looks obscene—and it's all just too much.

I also have a knack for clumsiness that comes out at the worst possible times. When I was fourteen, trying to emulate a fearful batter, I jumped back as if from a fastball and fell ass first through my friend's parent's glass coffee table. At fifteen

65

I drove a perfectly good golf cart into a lake near the 17th green. At twenty-two, full of testosterone, arrogance and Southern Comfort I walked through a closed screen door. It wouldn't have been so bad had the door only fallen on the charcoal grill, immediately burning through the screen and adding a taste of plastic to the flavor of the burgers. Unfortunately it also hit a girl on the way down. A pretty girl that I happened to like. It hit her in the face. Violently. I was lucky she didn't require stitches—a butterfly bandage was enough to slow the gush to a trickle—but the bruise was horrific.

I hoped that moving to Spain would instantly transform me into a suave, linen wearing aristocrat. I imagined my hair thickening, my skin glowing luxurious in the gentle Spanish clime. Women would see me smoking a thin cigar and buy me drinks. Single malt scotch, probably. It would arrive in a cut glass tumbler and cause my eyes to sparkle with the iridescence of wealth. Crowds would surround me wishing to hear tales of the wild and exotic lands from whence I came: Pittsburgh and Florida respectively. They'd want to know if Miami was really like Dexter and Miami Vice portrayed it and if Baltimore was really like The Wire. I assumed that Europeans would be terrible with American geography. I'd instantly be able to roll my R's and have sex twice in the same day. People would treat me with the reverence and admiration usually reserved for movie stars and men who can have sex twice in the same day.

Unfortunately, my awkwardity followed me across the ocean like the shark in Jaws followed that family to the Bahamas. Inexplicable but true.

Although reasonably intelligent and genial, I'm as likely to have an intelligent conversation as Charles Bukowski after climbing down a half-gallon of vodka, or Hunter S. Thompson after a few days in Vegas. I stammer and stutter and fumble words until I find one to hold like a security blanket. After I've found it I masticate the word continuously

throughout the whole conversation. This will continue with every conversation I have with that person until one of us dies. "Amazing" happens a lot. "Wow you look amazing." "This bottled water is amazing." "What an amazing funeral... I mean, amazing sendoff. Mr. Bernshaw looked amazing in that amazing casket. He would have been amazed at the turnout.....amazing." It's like a facial tic but with words. It's like Tourette's without the amazing vocabulary.

I know that part of my awkwardness stems from the fact that, by nature, I'm hopelessly introverted but in an effort to fit in from an early age have pretended to be an extrovert. Introverts have more filters between their brains and their mouths than extroverts and cable news personalities. So to be the fun loving and gregarious guy I wanted to be I had to bypass all my natural gatekeepers, never knowing what might sneak out. This was successful in elementary and high school—being the class clown and making people laugh—but proved to be disastrous as an adult. I've made an effort to be more true to myself but because I can't stand awkward silences I never make it. The pressure builds inside my brain until I have to say something, anything. "AIDS really is an amazing disease, when you think about what it does," I've actually said at a rehearsal dinner for my cousin's wedding.

At a loss for conversation I'll resort to the latest gossip, more often than not it'll be about someone's best friend or relative who happens to be trapped in my company. When I become nervous or anxious I tend to let loose a stream of expletives that would make Richard Pryor blush. This was especially troublesome at weddings and funerals. "Fucking amazing cake, it's good enough to make you not mind having AIDS!"

After a few weeks in Spain I noticed that instead of supernaturally transforming into the most interesting man in the world, my social skills only seemed to deteriorate further. Aside from my ability to say "hello", ask where the bathroom was, or order two breasts of penis, I couldn't even speak the language. I was unable to even spew profanity in any

meaningful way. I was reduced to pantomime and crude drawings I'd sketch on a tablet I kept in my back pocket. I had to walk into the pharmacy and rub my belly, pulling a frowny face in order to convey my upset stomach. The charades I acted out for diarrhea was unspeakable.

The grocery store was an adventure in awkward because they only displayed half of their foodstuffs and left the rest in the back room, bringing it out by request only. I would draw a large fish on my pad, puff out my lips, and pretend to pour a bottle of water over the drawing, to request my tuna in spring water. They kept it in the back for the finicky tourists who didn't want their seafood floating in unidentifiable grease.

We had three biblically old Spanish neighbors who would often come to the door bearing gifts. A burlap sack filled with just starting to rot potatoes or a five gallon blown glass jug of wine filled with wine and floating vegetables and smelling strongly of gasoline were both customary. After a valiant effort to say no I'd be forced to acquiesce and accept the gift. Then they'd come in and settle into the furniture that used to belong to them or their parents. I'd say thank you with a clumsy gracias and offer an Asian style bow with my hands pressed firmly together as if in prayer that they would soon leave. Not knowing the formalities of these situations I might offer them one of their own rotting potatoes or sometimes a can of tuna fish in spring water. They would smile and wave one finger in a reproachful manner and every one of them, every single time, day or night, would say one word, finger still wagging: vino. This was when I knew I was fucked. They'd sit for three or four hours, draining glass after glass of thirty proof V8, babbling away in increasingly incomprehensible Spanish while I nodded and said, "Si, si," "si claro," and "amazing," to everything. Eventually they'd begin lighting cigarettes, joints or cigars. "Please not in the house." I'd say while they laughed and laughed. I'd try the reproachful finger wag and it would send them into fits of hysterics.

One particular neighbor often stayed so long and got so drunk that he pissed himself sitting in our chair. His smile would turn into a frown of distaste and resentment as he blamed me for not dragging him home to piss in his own bed, sooner.

I didn't have any luck with the British population either. They seemed to all fall into easily identifiable stereotypes which annoyed me to no end. There were the posh, upper class types with nice cars and modern homes. They drove into Granada or Malaga when they wanted to shop or buy groceries and when they drank they drank well. They were nice enough to my face but I could sense their sense of superiority.

There were the lager louts who you could easily spot by their soccer jerseys, shaved heads and willingness to do violence. They talked with a cartoonish Cockney slang and only smiled when someone was being made fun of or getting hurt. They didn't care much for my American football and I could tell that they disliked me on sight.

Last, and by far the most common, were the dirty haired, drug addicted hippies who all looked like they'd just woken up from taking a long nap in a dirty litter box filled with hash. I got along with this last group the best. I'm not sure if they were the most accepting or if they were too high to care that I was so different. Most of them lived in cortijos and were forever complaining or bragging—sometimes both at the same time—about the lack of electricity and running water. They wore sandals and their clothes were always dirty and loose, like an aboveground pool cover in a shitty neighborhood. They usually had dreadlocks, not because they found it fashionable but because that's just what happens to hair when it's not washed for months. They bandied about with an air of disillusioned superiority and chilly contempt for the mainstream, but you could see a certain desperation in their eyes. They needed to be judged the way a bong needs water. Without that energy—if people didn't give a shit about

them not sending their kids to school—they'd simply burn out and float away like worthless ash. They fancied themselves outlaws, staying off the grid and under the radar, until they ran out of weed or food or money for weed and food. When that finally happened, every few months, they dropped all pretense, called their parents in Bristol or Glasgow and had some funds wired over posthaste.

Not long after we moved in Karen and I were stopped on the street by one of the posher British couples. It was what normal people called chatting but I still think of as time rape. The woman soon complained of having her bicycle stolen over the weekend. My guilt radar began to scream in alarm drowning out all rational thought and some motor skills.

I started an internal dialogue based around one common theme: How would a normal person act? I only have TV, movies and book characters to guide me. But because people in TV and movies are often guilty I'm led astray from how a normal person would act and end up looking guiltier than ever.

"Well. I. Never!" I said in outraged old lady speak. *That's not right, you're not an eighty year old woman*, I thought.

"I don't know what the world's coming to." I said. *Not believable*, I thought.

"Oh don't worry," she said. "It wasn't too expensive and we did file a claim with the police. These things happen."

"Where I grew up, we'd handle this ourselves." *Stop stop stop*, I thought. "Find whoever did it and make sure they didn't do anything like that again."

Karen and the couple just looked at me.

That was all wrong, I thought.

"I mean, now, I just call the cops. Probably. Sucks snitching though." *Wrong. Stop. Idiot!*

Then they were talking about the weather and I said, "I haven't had a bike since I was a little kid." And I thought; *now they think I had motive*.

They were talking about the grocery stores in Motril and I

said, "I wouldn't even want a bike, not here. Too many hills. Too many cobblestones and potholes and mule shits." *I sound defensive, shit.*

They had moved onto soccer and I said, "Thieves used to have honor. I think it's ok to steal from a corporation or the government but you'd have to be a scumbag to steal from just people." *I'm not looking good here. Shut up shut up shut up!*

Finally they were talking about an upcoming holiday in France and I said, "When do you leave?" *No No NO NO* "Do you want us to watch your house, we're very trustworthy." *This is like a Gypsy curse,* I thought.

It was more ignorance and awkwardity than curse though. I just, literally, don't know how to act. My biggest fear is that someone will go missing or turn up dead someplace that I live. Not because of the sadness or tragedy of it but because I just know I'd be suspected and charged and finally executed. I imagine they'd go old school with me as well: a public hanging or firing squad. It's what I'd deserve. I'd be smoking my final cigarette and wondering if this was how Johnny Depp would smoke if he were playing Benito Mussolini.

The well-defined groups I described could blend with each other reasonably well, considering their vast differences. Drugs have a way of bringing people together like that. But after the MDMA wore off the lager louts would stagger back to the bar, the posh would retreat to their villas for a week of rest and the hippies would continue the party until they spent all the money they made selling drugs to the other two sets. The one thing that all three had in common was their preconceived notion of what an American should be. The judgmental bastards tried to stereotype me. Me! It's like they expected me to don a Wal-Mart baseball hat and red, white and blue nylon track suit and loudly complain about my large penis while chewing a bacon cheeseburger and bragging about shooting homeless people. As if I couldn't get good beef over there even if I wanted to, and I let them know it.

For the first year none of them would miss an opportunity to make fun of my American accent; which was in fact a

Pittsburgh accent accentuated by my nasal voice and tendency to complain. It didn't help my cause that there was one other American in our village who went by the moniker American Anne. American Anne was a small, birdlike woman who had a disturbing habit of noticing me from a solid block or two away and, with a calm but supernaturally projected voice, say, "Hello Scott! What's for dinner today in the Casa Oglesby?"

Because I lack the larynx of a stage actor, I had to march the fifty or seventy five feet to where she was standing. I still would have felt uncomfortable but it wouldn't have bothered me as much if she'd just asked how I was, or mentioned the weather like a normal person. Then I could just mumble a, "good" or "true, windy" and turn the corner making my escape. But because she always asked a question that needed an articulated answer, and because I would have felt even more uncomfortable being rude, I had to shuffle to her, head down, like a scolded child. For three long years I did the same thing, never responding even a nod until I was face to face, and then with all of the passive-aggressive hostility I could muster, answer her god dammed question. "Oranges," I'd say, followed by an attempt to shame her into never doing it again.

"I was on my way home from the pool but since you yelled I came over here to answer you. I think I saw a few sleeping babies a few blocks back." She never took the hint, leading me to believe that Americans are incapable of understanding subtlety and nuance.

I've always looked at the many, many differences I had with people. We might both love sports but I'd focus on how the sports they loved sucked. We might both love drugs but I'd focus on the dirt under their fingernails. We both might love money but I'd focus on me not having any. All my life I've done this, and it's kept me from having to get too close to many people. I liked it that way. I really thought I did.

Then I developed an awkward but lasting friendship with an elderly burnout named Tommy Wales. Wales wasn't his

surname of course; it was where he was from. Like American Anne and Penitentiary Pete, it was just an identifier. Tommy was in his 60's or '90s when I met him, it was impossible to tell. He had the kind of craggy, wrinkled face and long, grey, thinning hair that makes you think of granola, free love and big, bushy pubic hair. In that order. Tommy looked like Abe Lincoln might have looked if he were a child of the '60s. He looked like Keith Richards would look if he couldn't afford all those blood transfusions and Asian pussy. If Tommy were capable of standing upright he would have been at least six foot. With his unfortunate posture however, he only made it to my height. It looked like he was perpetually fascinated with his groin; looking for signs of movement maybe, or just trying to hear it whisper. These were both possible since he chain smoked pot in a way that would make Snoop Dogg whimper. Tommy could roll a joint or even a cigarette laced with hash (much harder) while walking his dog on a leash. The dexterity this required was doubly amazing considering that he had a devil of a time getting his glasses back on when he took them off to polish them.

I tend to trust the character of older people, no matter what condition their condition is in. At least I can be sure that they are genuine, real. Not putting on an act for the cameras of the reality show that my generation believes is invariably filming. We seem so hungry for fame. Resentful and bitter when it doesn't come. We are so sure that wealth, notoriety and a book deal are around the next corner, we act as if it's already happened. And that makes us decidedly unreal.

I'd run into Tommy every night while walking my dog along a creek that ran the length of Javaron. It started near the top of the Sierra Nevada and stretched all the way down to the Mediterranean Sea in Adra. Tommy was an extremely gentle soul who spoke with a soft voice and loved animals. He pointed out a puppy hiding under a broken down Peugeot that we saved, brought back to the US and named, Puppy. That's only part of his legacy though. I talked to Tommy

more and more every day and we soon began to trust each other enough to open up. I learned that he had been in the game, from the way way back. In the '60s and '70s he ran a small crew of friends that ran weed and bricks of hash from central London up to Wales and into Scotland. They'd made a fortune and partied two away. Once blow hit the markets and things got violent, he got out. "We was just havin' fun, havin' a laugh, the time of our lives, really," he'd told me. "Then that other shite came along with all of its shite people and its shite troubles. Boys killin' people and all. So I quit muckin' around, found a wife and stayed to me self."

Tommy's wife Berta was a severe alcoholic and mentally unstable. The latter may have been due to a constant contact high. Some people don't have the constitution to withstand an immaculate stoning 28 hours a day, 9 days a week for 20 plus years. She was in her 50's, short and plump with the permanent sunburn of the heavy drinking Irish Protestant. To see the two of them together made me miss American sports because he looked like a long, curved hockey stick while she looked like a cheap, pleather basketball. If there was ever a drinker 'born two martinis below par' it was Berta. She'd manage to abstain from Tuesday through Thursday, wondering around in tattered clothing and mumbling incoherently. The few times she managed human interaction during these intervals, the most absurd and offensive things would spew from her lips while she wore an oddly detached smile and stared with glazed yet peaceful eyes.

"Americans and Spanish wear cunt ugly hands. You," she'd say, pointing at my feet, "wear the ugliest hands."

"Sorry."

"You should coat balls. I haven't been sucked on three months and the stereo's fucking hearing drove dildo hats."

All you could do was try to slink away before she got too worked up. If you happened to catch Berta on a Friday through Monday, however, when she'd had just enough alcohol to act as medication but not yet enough booze to be rendered paralytic, it was another story. You'd meet a

thoughtful, kind, fiercely intelligent, well-spoken woman.

"If we long to believe that the stars rise and set for us, that we are the very reason there is a universe, does science do us a disservice in deflating our conceits?" Berta might ask, quoting Carl Sagan.

During one of these slightly lubricated conversations I realized the futility of attempting to label or judge anyone, let alone write them off. She was discussing the socioeconomic impact that David Cameron's election as Prime Minister would have on the large Islamic population in Great Britain when I found a new appreciation for the value of America's pharmaceutical culture. Get this woman on 50 mgs of Zoloft or Seroquel and she's a professor of political science at Cambridge before the decade is over. Or, at minimum, she'd host a wildly popular daytime talk show.

I came to find that Berta had written three science fiction novels that were not only published but met with critical— although not financial—success. And this made me sad for humanity all over again. If a woman this intelligent and promising can fall this far, how low can I go? Then I realized that I'd probably have fun as a crazy person—I'm probably already having fun as a crazy person... and let it go.

Although Tommy was as incapable of debating Nietzsche as his wife Berta was of hosting a garden party on a Tuesday afternoon, he was always at an even keel: happy, affable, honest, slightly confused, and intensely likable. Together, they were a hot mess, ostracized by a town full of outcasts. Having been typecast and dismissed by polite society myself many times, I felt a strong sense of loyalty to these people. This surprised me. And changed the way I looked at the world. It was this couple, who I would have made fun of in my teens, ignored in my 20's and shunned even a year before, that caused me to step back and question my snap judgments and proclivity to pigeonhole everyone I encountered.

The human condition is one of frailty and courage, weakness and purity, hopelessness and faith, cowardice and honor, but most of all profound, unfathomable complexity. It

somehow causes us all to retreat to certain tents and huddle down against the harsh winds of suffering. In other words, I realized in my moment of clarity that I had been a walking colostomy bag for most of my life. I began pushing myself to interact and socialize—awkwardly of course—with all of the people I had previously swept into neat little tents and labeled too rich, poor, dirty, stupid, English etc., etc., for friendship.

It helped too that I quit drinking. My first year there I'd been a heavy drinker. And when I drank I turned from an introverted asshole into and extroverted, obnoxious asshole. I'd boast of my former accomplishments and talk openly, exaggeratedly of my shady (but in my drunken opinion) glamorous past. Once I sobered up, I'd shut myself up, preferring to stay home and watch movies or read than having to mingle and talk to the people I'd just embarrassed myself in front of.

We still went out. I just didn't pour barrels of asshole maker juice down my throat any longer. I soon learned that one lager lout was an ex-boxer who'd had a semi-successful career throughout Europe. Another owned two thriving car dealerships before cashing out and heading for the hills. One of the great unwashed burnout types was a computer programmer and another owned a stable of horses and offered scenic trail rides to tourists at a couple hundred an hour. One hippy couple were Israelis who had finally had enough after their home was destroyed in a bombing and another were highly educated, well-read, new-age enlightened types who built yurts and hosted guided meditation to gurus from the world over. They neither drank nor did drugs, which is probably why I hadn't known they existed before my own enlightenment. If only I'd realized sooner, I would have found profound friendships with so many more people.

So it was that I found myself just outside a local bar, at another party, my third since my new perspective took hold. I'd grown to tolerate even the worst of this ragtag menagerie, and to sincerely like the vast majority.

As I was sipping a Pellegrino water Tommy's wife Berta

LOST IN SPAIN

was taking healthy slugs from an 8 ounce glass of vodka. Tommy was beside her smoking a joint down to the quick.

"You have to understand that in the West, we subconsciously... haha... approach postmodern art with a Jungian, or egocentric, mindset." Berta said, gesturing to her brain. "Our interpretive process is all about ME. What the artist intended is not considered or relevant. The East, especially the predominantly Islamic Middle East sees absolutely everything through the lens of family/culture/race/class. If you look at...."

Tommy distracted her when his beard momentarily caught fire and when I looked up I noticed American Anne far off in the distance.

"Hi Scott," she said from a quarter mile away. "What are you up to?"

As her voice thundered like a conscience through my head, I waved at her to come and join the party. "Amazing," I said to Berta, "Interpreting interpretive art is just amazing."

5

ONE, TWO, THREE, FOUR

"One-Two-Three-Four." I count out loud. My fingers twist at the brass knob of the deadbolt, feeling, listening, for the satisfying little click at the end as metal slides across metal and into place. No, not this time. One-Two-Three-Four. I went too far again and the lock bounced back open so that it only looks locked. I know that the minute a roving band of rape-y tweakers try it, the door will open faster than a smuggled bottle of Nyquil in a rehab because IT IS NOT FUCKING LOCKED!

"One-Two-Three-Four." Yeah ok, I think that was good. Now I back away carefully and tear my eyes from the front door before they trick me into seeing it unlocked. As I look away I hear a weird sound from outside. Shit, shit, shit, now I have to do it again.

"One-Two-Three-Four," I count silently so as not to accidentally spit on anything which would ruin everything. I don't mean spit like a tobacco chewer or a lifetime smoker who carries his own spitting handkerchief; I mean the kind of spit a hungry man emits when ordering pizza at a hockey game. The little, tiny specks of spit that you can barely see but

78

could unlock a door or cause an electrical fire. Or spread the zombie plague. My fingers have to be bone dry as well, not an easy task when I am sweating profusely due to the enormous pressure that keeps building, reaching a screaming crescendo within my taxed brain. Sweat, spit, moisture of any kind is as dangerous as a crackhead with a winning lottery ticket. It can find a way into the locking mechanism and make it un-lockable. Besides, I just can't stand the thought of it. Now I want to take my sleeve and pull it down over my hand so I can make sure that the damn door is as dry as it is locked. So I do just that. How can I not?

"One-Two-Three-Four." Wait. How many times have I counted to four in this go-round? I count to four because four is lucky. Four is a happy number. I can't end anything anywhere near a six. When I was little someone terrified me by telling me of the devil and his magical three sixes. So now I'm afraid of six. Also anything that ends in six. Also twelve and especially eighteen since eighteen IS essentially three sixes; maybe even worse since it is three sixes trying to, almost literally, sneak in the back door. I'm ok with twenty-four though, maybe because of the four, unless I think too much about it, but thirty-six can go right to hell. Where it lives. Thirty-six will bring colon cancer and irritable bowel syndrome and Jehovah's Witnesses and death. These rules make reading a book a little like playing a game of Twister with a double-jointed octopus who cheats. There are no situations where I can put down a book with the page number on a six. Or a twelve. Or an eighteen. If the phone rings and I'm on page 316 I'm more likely to throw the phone out of a window than answer it. If I'm reading a book over six hundred pages I do not stop—under any circumstances—until I get past the six-y territories. I don't care if it is four a.m. or I'm late for work.

"One, two, three, four." I smell my own sweat and fear. I snap my head back violently, whiplash quick, but don't turn around. One cannot simply turn their head on a locked and checked door. I backpedal slowly, carefully. If I bump into

anything it would be disastrous. I make it back to the entrance of the kitchen which has already been checked. I've rubbed my palms against the window locks, rubbed my finger over the off button on the coffee pot as well as the end of its cord and it's definitely turned off and unplugged. I think. No, it is, I did it four times. Of course it is. I've moved all the appliances to the center of the counter and all debris to the center of the kitchen table. I've stared at the electrical outlets and blown on them ever so lightly. I've turned the faucet to the cold side just in case it starts dripping. If the faucet started dripping hot water it might cause the water heater to flare up and explode somehow.

"One, two, three, four." I taste frustration and a metallic flavor that must be rage. Or maybe it's blood. I might have been biting the inside of my cheek again. The stove has six knobs—most of them do—and I can't even begin to relate the horror of this. I've turned all those knobs totally, completely, 100% vertical. I've touched them, rubbed them and tilted my head every which way to make positively sure that they were all the way off.

"One, two, three, four." My vision keeps dimming and filling with stars. I know that breathing in hectic little fits and starts and holding my breath for two minutes at a time probably isn't good for me. I'd hate to give myself a stroke. Shit, now I have to think about perfect health and count. "One, two, three, four." Ok now just breathe. Ok, kitchen's safe. I start to turn… hesitate. Fuck. "One, two, three, four. One, two, three, four. One, two, three, four. One, two, three, four." Ok, all better, now stop this. Kitchen's good. Doors are good. I put my head down, hold my breath and softly walk backwards towards the bedroom. If I don't make it before I exhale I know I'll have to start over. But I make it. I always make it. Fuck yeah! I'd sooner pass out from oxygen deprivation than get raped by crazy tweakers while my stove catches on fire and my hot water tank explodes. I see stars but I make it.

It wasn't always this bad. It used to be a whole lot worse.

But before that it wasn't this bad.

As a little boy I remember touching things while I was walking. I'd see a wall and brush my knuckles against it. But after I touched it with my right hand, I'd have to touch it twice with my left hand and once more with my right to balance things out. I never believed anything as childish as stepping on a crack would break my mother's back. That kind of nonsense was for girls and little foreign boys who were prone to break into song at a moment's notice. My only issue was stepping on a crack would lead to having to step on two cracks with the other foot, then yet another crack with the original. I'd end up looking like one of those disabled kids who got free toys at school because people felt bad for them. So naturally I grew to loathe cracks and crack-like fissures in the ground. Better to just avoid them.

That was the extent of it though, just the one, one-two, one, (four!) back and forth while walking and occasionally feeling like I had to tell my mother I loved her and making her say it back until it sounded just right. None of the weird stuff, not yet.

My mom acted a little crazy sometimes. It occurred to me even as a child that if we had money people would call her eccentric. We were poor though, so people mainly ignored us. People don't really pay attention to poor people, despite what you hear. She went to bed early most nights, around nine or ten, but she allowed me to stay up. I cherished this time by myself at night. I'd pretend to be a gangster on the lam, having to hole up in this shithole of a house until the heat died down. I'd pace from room to room checking out the windows for the dirty Feds, making sure that my water gun was full and practice looking angry or villainous in front of a mirror.

I was always getting jolted out of my reverie by my mother's jarring voice. "Will you make sure I turned the coffee pot off?"

"I already did that ma," I yelled back. I could find no

suitable way to incorporate these interruptions into my mental movie, so I became increasingly frustrated and hostile.

"Did I turn off the stove?"

I'd mope back to the kitchen, throwing an evil glance into the mirror before standing in front of the stove and counting the dials.

"Off, off, off, off, off, off. Yes, the stove is ALL OFF!" Loudly enough so that my mom could hear my petulance.

"Thanks hun. The coffee pot's off, yeah?"

"Yes, I just told you that."

"Check again, yeah?"

"Ok. Yeah. Whatever," I'd yell. I just knew that Al Capone or Jesse James never had to put up with this.

Other than the occasional certainty that someone really was after me, none of my mother's oddities got to me at all. My mental health was rolling along as smoothly as a peyote trip in the desert. It wasn't until I was twenty-seven and had to move into "The Aunts" house that the trip started to go bad and I contracted The Fear. Whether it was Hunter S. Thompson's melting face or just having to relock a door forty-four times in a row, fear is fear.

I had three great aunts who had never married. Only one of them had ever even dated. They spent their entire lives in a house that was two decades older than them. And they were old. They'd been born in that house, watched three of their siblings die young and eventually their parents die old, in that house. They had married off four other siblings in that house, and they were intent on dying in that house.

They were the original Golden Girls, only more prone to moo-moos and violence. All three were lovely people—at least until senility set in—but they smelled strongly of BenGay and witch hazel. I'd grown close to them because I only lived three blocks away and hated my mom's side of the family. It also helped that they often cooked me pancakes and slipped me little wads of cash, trying to outdo one another. By the time I'd reached adulthood, I'd taken on a semi-

LOST IN SPAIN

caretaker role, doing their shopping, painting, paying their bills, and occasionally getting one unstuck from somewhere or other. I sensed my main role was simply making sure they didn't murder each other. When I was twenty, they were in their eighties. This was about the time they all started to go downhill. The oldest, Leona, hid her marbles all over the house before losing them for good. She had always had strange habits, like throwing the occasional foodstuff at one of the others or screaming at a babushka as she held it up to her face. As Leona got older though, the strange bent and stretched and finally snapped into full blown crazy.

She started crumpling up cash into little balls, wrapping them in tissues or napkins and flushing them down the toilet. I got called over one night to unclog their commode and found $143 in very wet money. She had always hid food. It used to be sensible hoarding—crackers, boxes of cereal, or cans hidden in her closet—but it evolved into lunchmeat, raw eggs and uncooked, loose pasta in her hamper or under her pillow.

Her favorite thing to hide was herself. The other aunts would frantically search the house, terrified Leona had wandered off only to eventually find her sleeping peacefully at the back of a walk-in closet. She often hid under her bed as well, but couldn't fit much more than her head and torso. Her butt was what seemed to hang her up from fitting all the way under. I'd walk into her bedroom and just see a butt and two chubby little old lady legs sticking out from under her twin bed and wonder if I was having a flashback or if she was.

All three Great Aunts were adamant that they never go to a nursing home. They had all worked in the service industry and so had first-hand knowledge of the depravity to which humans will sink and the horrors they will gleefully inflict upon one another. Especially over cold french fries. When Aunt Izzy died suddenly, I had little choice but to move in. So I packed up my first wife, who was only a girlfriend at the time, and moved in.

The plan was to keep Leona well fed and happy until she

died peacefully in her sleep. I had the hazy idea that this would happen "before too long." I remember thinking the phrase clearly. It just sounded right in my head. Even thinking *a month or two* would make me feel churlish and mean, but thinking *a year or two... three? Really? Shit!* would cause hopelessness and angst. But *"before too long"* was just the kind of linear ambiguity that makes loyalty possible. I felt bad for even thinking in terms of how long it might take before she died, but at that point Leona was long gone. All that was left now that her conscious personality was gone, was a lifetimes' worth of frustration, confusion and cursing which would explode to the surface like Alka-Seltzer dropped in a glass of Irish dementia.

Leona would throw things at us, push food onto the floor, and curse us out in two languages. Three if you count the pig-Latin she spoke fluently. She'd been soft and weak before we moved in, barely eating or leaving her bedroom. We arrived and fed her pasta and meat every day, took her for walks, and encouraged her to move about. After a few months of eating well and getting plenty of exercise, she grew stronger and more confident, much like a prison inmate. She grew cunning and dangerous. She continued to horde perishables and possessions she considered valuable: costume jewelry, soiled underwear, and ever-increasing stashes of toilet paper and Kleenex which held secret stashes of even more Kleenex. But after regaining her strength, she also took to stockpiling weapons or objects that she deemed capable of causing harm: knives, nail files, a screwdriver, a bottle opener with a particularly lethal Eiffel Tower. This caused obvious concern and I took to hiding these things, the way you might when living with a toddler or an alcoholic, brain damaged ex-boxer.

She'd throw things out of her third-story window into the small yard below. She'd occasionally call me "dad" and if we were out for a doctor's appointment she might complain feebly that "this ugly place" was not her house when we returned home. She'd beg me to take her home. Within ten minutes though, she was back in bed. Even with the idea that

she'd die "before too long" I wanted to do right by her. So we cooked, and fed her three healthy meals a day, made sure she drank plenty of water and took her for two walks a day, to keep her newfound strength. I also worked with her memory, asking her questions and encouraging her to do word puzzles and motor skills training tests. A few months into this routine and she did get stronger. Scary, stupid, stronger. Frighteningly stronger. She started moving furniture around in her room, pulling drawers out for better scavenging and hiding. She'd sneak down in the middle of the night and steal frozen meat, hiding it under her pillow. Bigger things flew out her window: books, a lamp, a radio, her porta potty bucket. When a thirty pound nightstand made its way down three stories to crash into the yard below, I decided to drill screws so that the window couldn't be opened more than two inches. All the while my anxiety was growing, making me feel like a chick about to break out of its shell. Only in my case, the shell was my sanity and the cracks were beginning to appear.

Behind her thick, round glasses her magnified eyes shone with the same slight confusion she'd shown for the last decade. Now there was something new as well. She had an unmistakable look of nefarious planning and steely resolve. She didn't know what she wanted to do, but she wanted to do something and she wanted to do it fast and violently.

Two or three times a week she refused to come back during our evening walk and I had no choice but to let her wear herself out before ushering her back home. I was terrified that she'd wander out while we were in bed so I bought small chain locks for the three doors leading outside. Still, I'd wake up and feel certain that something terrible was about to happen. So I'd get up and check on her, check the locks, and occasionally rub my hand against the light switch a few times. One night my fears were realized when Leona snuck down at two a.m. and, wanting a midnight snack, placed a Corn Flakes box on the gas stove and lit it. We woke to the fire alarm, maniacal laughter, and the astringent smell

of burnt chemicals from the flakes and burnt cardboard, probably also from the corn flakes. The burning box was almost pleasant. The kitchen was filled with smoke, and tiny cornflake embers softly glowed and floated through the air as if there were no place they'd rather be. Leona looked at me and laughed with eyes filled equally with delight and malice. The last vestiges of my tattered shell of sanity broke at that moment and the twitching, sweaty, counting, shuffling child of OCD and neurosis was born.

"One, two, three, four." A year passed before Leona was too far gone and needed a nursing home after all. She adjusted to the move with surprising alacrity. Instead of calling me father and demanding impossible things, Leona took to calling me Gunther and gossiping about her teenage sisters. She still snuck around in the middle of the night, but now she had developed a nascent generosity to balance the scales. The nurses found boxes of latex gloves, hundreds of Band-Aids, pens, and other miscellany in her drawers every morning, but her roommate would often discover a half-eaten cookie wrapped in a Kleenex, some dinner rolls, or a juice carton under her pillow as well.

I did not adjust nearly so well. During the day I was myself. While far from normal, it was the strange me I was used to. I could live with that me. As night fell, however, a nebulous unease would morph into an ineffable anxiety. I didn't know what was wrong or out of place, only that something was seriously wrong and every cell in my body felt out of place. We had stayed in the Aunts' house—an enormous, poorly-made centurion located in a neighborhood that was likely to fuck up your five-year plan. It had an attic and unfinished basement that ran the length of the house, three bedrooms upstairs, three rooms downstairs, a long hallway that ran the length of both, and possible disaster... everywhere. The electrical outlets were on the floor, (ON THE FLOOR, how dangerous is that?) the only bathroom was in the basement, and the crackheads of the '90s were wandering around

outside like extras in a zombie/gangsta movie that George Romero and John Singleton co-wrote and would pretty much be the greatest. Movie. EVER! As dusk approached my nerves would tangle themselves in my brain and begin to shoot little sparks down the length of my body and back up through my cerebral cortex and into my frontal lobe where they'd collide with each other and explode in a supernova of furious anti-orgasm.

I made the mistake of believing I could mitigate the tension by doing a quick run-through of the house, assuring myself it was safe. I'd think, "Oh fuck," or something equally eloquent and the next moment I found myself peeking under the bed in the attic. I started with a back corner of the room, looking under, over, and beside every piece of life debris that had accumulated over a century of low purchasing power. It was nothing neurotic, I just had to make sure that no one had snuck in and was hiding until we went to bed so he could murder and dismember us at his leisure. I also needed to assure myself that nothing was on fire or could catch fire. An unlikely event, sure, but fire is a funny thing. A funny, evil thing with the sole intent of destroying me and everything I hold dear. Burning to death has always been my biggest fear. I know what it felt like when I grabbed a cookie sheet out of the oven because I was too ~~drunk~~ lazy to find a mitt. That, all over your body? With no cookie at the end? Hells no.

I could too easily imagine the setting sun magnifying through a pair of old reading glasses and igniting the box of photo albums in the corner. Or a piece of lint finding its way into an electrical outlet, catching, and landing in the box of babushkas by the dresser. But what if a light-footed midget had stepped into that very dresser while my back was turned? So I'd turn, hold my breath and spin, trying to look everywhere at once while furiously counting to four.

Like this I made my way, backwards, through the room and finally down the attic stairs. While checking one of the bedrooms I would become convinced an evil troglodyte could have (and the mere possibility was enough) slipped into

the attic. So I bought latch locks for every door in the house. A reasonable solution, I thought. This freed up just enough time and mental anguish to allow me the pleasure of a late-night cigarette. A small, human pleasure that I deserved. I'd smoke it standing out by the curb, so as not to set the grass on fire. I stood so I could see both the front and side doors, assuring myself that no burglar/rapist/murderer could slip by my watchful eyes. *Unless they happen to be ninjas,* I thought and immediately hated my despicable imagination.

After going back inside I would sometimes, though not always, find myself searching for ninjas or ninja-like assassins. This task was pointless since ninjas would never allow themselves to be seen. One thing I had to do, though, was peek out the window an hour later to ensure that the area where I had stood smoking was not aflame. Following this the window would have to be rechecked as well as every door and outlet on my way back to the bedroom. I also became increasingly convinced that an ember had stowed away on my person, perhaps on the bottom of my shoe or even on my pant leg and that it had leapt off while I was checking something else. If I gave in and left the sanctuary of the bedroom to make sure I couldn't smell smoke, I had to start the entire process over, just in case I'd bumped into a lock or kicked a stray paperclip in an outlet. Eventually this got to be too much hassle.

I thought I found a solution: drive around while I smoke my last cigarette. If I knew I was leaving, I wouldn't have to do ANYTHING until I got back because what would be the point? Now, I could stay relaxed until nine or ten, take a nice drive, enjoy myself some American tobacco, come back, lock up and go the fuck to bed. *Brilliant,* I thought.

The OCD did not agree. I stayed cool as a kitty until my drive. I soon found that I spent just as much time locking up, holding my breath, twitching and sweating as I had before. Now, instead of backing myself to bed at eleven or twelve, I was unhappily moonwalking into the bedroom at one or two a.m. Soon I began a very dangerous game of drive-time

LOST IN SPAIN

hokey-pokey as my fear of hidden embers was rekindled.

After I'd extinguished my last cigarette, I would begin sticking various parts of my body out the window. I'd stick my left arm out the window first. The car had to be going at least 25 miles per hour and I had to hold it for two counts of four. It was possible, almost even easy, to perform this trick with both arms, my head and even my torso. My left leg was doable, but only up to the calf. People in other cars or on the street would often notice and point. To this I would wave happily and pretend I was just having fun and catching some fresh air, like a dog, say. I'd imagine them wanting to be just like me. Tapping their friend on the shoulder and saying, "Now there's a guy who knows how to let loose!"

I'd stop a mile from home and get out of the car. Knowing that my right leg might still be holding an ember I'd shake it vigorously while brushing my pants like they were full of ants. Fire ants. It was at this exact point that I realized I needed professional help.

So I moved.

We bought a place out in the suburbs. A newer, solid, brick house well clear of the roving bands of psychotic crackheads, murderous gang-bangers, and, though I could never prove it, the hordes of ninjas that roamed my old hood. The house was fresh and clean and free of the darkness and fear that hung over the old one like a manic-depressive thunderstorm.

It worked for a while; I only spent twenty or thirty minutes locking up. For me that was amazing. Before long however, my imagination did what it did best and ran wild with insane possibilities. Now that I had a garage I was convinced my car was running, even after I checked. So I slept with both sets of car keys on my bedside cabinet, waking up repeatedly to reach over and touch them. I found myself vacuuming around the dryer and water heater to prevent any lint from floating into the pilot light and burning me alive in the night. And so it went.

When my life fell apart, I was fine. I mean, aside from the

89

whole life falling apart thing. "When you got nothing, you got nothing to lose," a woman who had a whole lot once sang, and it's true. No house that might burn down. No car that might explode. No family left to get kidnapped or murdered. Plus, I was always drunk and alcohol works on anxiety the way that a pair of pliers works on a toothache.

Three tumultuous years later and I found myself with a new girlfriend, a new house, and a new, used car. These all came with new keys as well as new sets of OC's in my D. Still, I kept it down to twenty minutes a night, but I dreaded those minutes all day. Not only was it the same sweaty, anxious nightmare, but now I had a new partner, Karen, to notice and get all "What the fuck-y."

When we made the decision to live in Spain, I hoped that the Old World would bring out a New Me. And it did, eventually. Just not in the ways I imagined.

The Spanish house was a lot like The Aunts' house only five hundred years older. I was freaked out from the moment I walked in the door. The fact that it was built of stone and did not have central heating made me feel a little better. The fact that we now had to use propane tanks for everything and a fireplace for heat made me feel a whole lot worse, almost violently nervous. From the first night, life over there was so utterly foreign that my anxiety didn't know where to start and my OCD didn't know where to stop.

I'd never had a fireplace before and if I had I would have used it to store extra fire extinguishers and smoke detectors. Living through winter in a stone house, having to go outside to shower, and having no other way to warm up and dry off, we had no choice. Plus, I had no choice because Karen didn't give me a choice, she just lit it. I admit that I did enjoy the comforting warmth the fire provided, at least until bedtime. At that point I had two options: go to my death trapped in a fiery inferno or sit awake in the living room where I might have a fighting chance but would, still, most likely get roasted like a human chestnut. I chose the former because I'm too

LOST IN SPAIN

old to stay awake all night and because, again, Karen did not give me a choice. I eventually learned to relax a bit and enjoy the cozy succor of the monster that wanted to destroy me. I think I may have had Stockholm Syndrome only with fire instead of kidnappers and in Spain instead of Sweden.

Well if the fire is going to kill me, I'm at least going to make its job harder, I thought. This pleased my passive-aggressive nature and made it smile in an ambiguous way that nobody would be able to interpret as either happy or mad. I started off with small stuff that was closest to the fireplace and moved it into the bedroom. Eventually the circle spread out, like a ripple in a pond or a white man's money in a strip club. Throw pillows, dog toys, books and magazines, lamps and small furniture all moved into the bedroom for the night in this way.

It was the embers, you see; I was still afraid of hidden embers. At least if the stuff was in the bedroom with me, I might see it catching and have time to take a Valium before I died. Firewood and anything Karen vetoed went outside on the terrace. If a piece of wood felt warm to the touch due to its proximity to the fireplace, I'd make sure I wasn't being watched and spit at it. Not like a redneck with a chest infection mind you, but in the manner that a gentleman might spit sunflower seeds at a Southern wedding. I thought it was very dignified, but Karen said that it reminded her of a black snake arguing with feral cats over the last piece of meth.

There were, of course, the dreadful propane tanks to deal with. One on the kitchen stove and one on the outside water heater. A few plastic knobs and two flimsy hoses were all that separated me from exploding, burning death. I couldn't help but feel compelled (sorry, OCD) to disconnect both tanks and carry them outside, where they no doubt used the cover of darkness to plot my destruction. In a perfect world they would have been kept separated like Guantamono Bay prisoners or Tom Cruise and his sexuality, but my world is far from perfect. Besides, those tanks were too heavy to move any farther.

"What are you doing?" a neighbor would occasionally ask.

"It smells bad." I'd say, holding my hand over my nose because I wasn't responsible enough to warn them that it was about to spontaneously combust. I worried about gas trapped in the tubing so I blew into it. A quick, little staccato burst - one, two, three, four - in perfect harmony. I started over and did it again.

My only other major concern about the house was the terrace, where we took showers and shits. My concern was that it might fall down. Unlike my other preoccupations, this one was legitimate. They were all legitimate, at least to me, but this one was a cause of concern for sane people as well. Our bathroom/terrace looked, for the entire world, like it was falling down.

The terrace was built over what used to be a barn. The first time we unlocked the barn door we found old hay, a few dead rats, and large, important looking chucks of concrete. The roof had even more important chunks of cement hanging precariously over our heads. When I went to nudge one with a broom handle, Karen asked if I were stupid or just mental. I didn't know for sure so I didn't respond, just dropped the broom. You could clearly see pinpricks of daylight coming through and that seemed like a bad sign.

I needed a plan. The first phase was to begin peeing into an empty water bottle. The second phase was to call a contractor. When he showed up two days later, I still hadn't set foot on the terrace. My plan had worked. When I had to really go to the bathroom I walked up to the nearest bar, otherwise, I peed in plastic bottles, like the Moors used to do. I grew to enjoy the sound it made landing against the plastic. A sound like that makes you feel as if you're accomplishing something of significance. Pouring the vile fluid out—especially if I waited a few hours between trips—was a wholly unpleasant affair.

The contractor told us that we were all going to die horrible, naked deaths. He said I would fall through while showering and then get pummelled by concrete and slate,

before finally being finished off by the porcelain toilet that would crack my skull. I'd always assumed that I'd die like Elvis, but always thought it would be the drugs, not the toilet itself. That's what I heard the contractor say. Karen heard him say it would be forty grand to move the bathroom or redo it. Either that or we could rent a dozen floor jacks and, hopefully, be fine.

We rented the jacks—tall steel tools that crank up and are used to bear tremendous weight. They are just like car jacks, only taller and much rustier. With the help of our friendly contractor, we installed them, placing them every two feet from the barn going up to support the floor of the terrace.

"The trick," he told me, "is to crank them up enough that they're stable, but not so much that they crack the structure further. Otherwise the whole thing will fall on top of us."

"I'll let you do that part," I said, and I did.

We (he) got them up safely and as far as I know they're still up to this day.

I never could take a shower without seeing a vivid mental picture of my naked, shriveled (shrinkage) body half buried beneath stone and porcelain. I couldn't take a shit without thinking of Elvis. I still carried the tanks out every night, but now set them down with a delicacy usually reserved for bomb making or Jenga. I still used the water bottle in a way it was never intended, but only after bedtime.

I've never been a germaphobe. I pitied the poor souls who had to suffer through that aspect of OCD. For me it was almost the opposite. I was deathly afraid of the chemicals used to kill germs, as well as almost anything that's use requires it to be sprayed, shot, rubbed, or dabbed. Even perfumes and powders cause me to run out of the room with my shirt over my face. It always felt like I was being poisoned.

When I sat in a bar and someone sprayed insect killer, or insect repellent, or burned incense, or used hair spray, I'd cover my drink and disappear like a neurotic ghost for at least

ten minutes. When we did our laundry on the terrace and used powder detergent, I held my breath and closed my eyes. When my air ran out, I'd get as far away as I could, cover my mouth with my shirt and gasp. Before re-entering the house I shook off my clothes vigorously—like before with the smoking—went inside, washed my hands, brushed out my hair, washed my hands again, brushed my teeth and gargled.

For some strange reason, I wasn't bothered in the least by some forms of powder, however. White, whitish-yellow, gray, or brown—those powders that contained God knows what and definitely at least a little actual poison—I invited into my body through every available orifice. Just hand me a straw, spoon, or pair of rubber gloves and it was on like Donkey Kong and Pete Doherty at a Miami nightclub. I guess it goes to show that we are all hypocrites when it comes to our poison of choice.

I've never been much of a germaphobe, as I was saying before I got side-tracked, but the butcher shop of Javaron made me a little nervous. And by "a little nervous" I mean "blindly panicked." It wasn't that the display didn't look particularly refrigerated. It wasn't that the butchers used the same knife to cut chicken, pork, beef, and rabbit on the same bare counter. It wasn't even the blood they tracked back and forth from storeroom to everywhere else. It wasn't that they never wore gloves and never, ever seemed to wash their hands. All of those things were bad enough on their own, but what finally got to me was the money. Right after cutting and pulling and slicing all that meat, he'd casually toss the bloody flesh into a shopping bag, take my money with dripping fingers, make change, and hand the pink, wet money back to me.

The money, my hands, the bag, I thought. *Botulism, E. coli, Salmonella, Sleeping Sickness, the Black Death, The Red Scourge, Swine Flu, Bird Flu, Zombie Apocalypse, Oh My… Fucking God.*

The only power greater than my OCD was my fear of embarrassment, and that's probably the only thing that kept me in the general vicinity of normal.

LOST IN SPAIN

The walk home was a long one. Even if I stopped in a bar to wash my hands, I still had the tainted money burning a hole in my pocket, and I still had to carry the bag home. I carried the bag out, away from my body and was hyper-vigilant not to touch my face.

The first thing that happens when you are conscious of not wanting to touch your face is an overwhelming desire to touch your face. It usually starts in the psychosomatic form of an itch, but quickly progresses to believing your face is actually on fire. I'd walk faster and faster, beginning to sweat and itch, burn and melt, all the while feeling like my head was about to explode at any second. Wearing long sleeves or a coat was fine; I could just use the crook of my arm to rub my face. But short sleeves? I could not do a thing. Not when I could see, in vivid detail, the brain eating, gut melting bacteria marching up my flesh like an organized, angry funeral procession.

When my arms were bare, and the itch became too great to bear, I had only one solution. I'd have to angle my head down while lifting my knee up, giving the appearance of kicking myself in the face, to alleviate the bastardly itch. Once home, I washed the money in the sink with liquid detergent. I was usually able to avoid a shower, when the fear of falling through the bathroom naked was greater than the fear of infectious death, but I did scrub my hands and arms like a pre-operative surgeon.

The buying of the chicken became less painful once I learned how to prepare for the experience. Always carrying enough change to be exact with the bill helped. As did carrying an extra bag to transfer the tainted poultry bag into once I was safely out of sight. The process still made me nervous in a vague way—like the feeling you might get when you hear chanting in the distance, say, or right before a blind date you found on Craigslist. I dealt with this anxiety the way I dealt with all the others: not well.

I'll count my steps home, I thought. *This'll take my mind off my weirdness.*

95

I walked fast, wanting to get my meat home. I ran into a problem when I found that my house was approximately 640 to 680 steps from the shops. During the first attempt, I realized that I could see my house and was on step number six hundred and thirty. Knowing I was in serious trouble I walked past my house and up the hill.

I noticed that a few neighbors were out, so I squinted my eyes as I walked past to make it appear that I was curious about something just ahead and had to check it out. I couldn't turn around on any number in the six-hundreds, so I stopped, looked off into the distance, shook my head, shielded my eyes against the sun, held the pose for a moment as if waiting for a theme song to wrap up, and walked away shaking my head like I was disappointed by what I saw. *The old men will surely think some damn kids are up to no good*, I thought. But I knew I was lying to myself. I knew that they knew I was crazy, but damn it if I was going to make it easier to prove.

I knew the danger after my second trip and because I feared the neighbors were talking amongst themselves— maybe even taking notes—I tried my best to be discreet. I thought I could make it home under the six-hundred mark, so when I knew I had the street to myself, I took long, leaping strides. I was doing well, until people kept, just, BEING there. Sweeping their steps, looking out their windows, standing in small groups and pointing. Staring at me. Infringing upon my privacy. At that moment I hated them for their atomic structure. *Why can't they just float the fuck away*, I thought.

Once I knew that I wasn't going to make it, I had to change my strategy on the fly. At five-hundred-and-something, and within a few blocks of my house, I started taking tiny, shuffling, baby-steps. And since I had to get the chicken home before the E. coli spread up my arm, I took these tiny, shuffling, baby-steps as fast as I could manage. If you've never tried to speed walk while only taking ten inch strides—and I assume that you have not—you might be

surprised how hard it is to look graceful. The activity made me look like an anxious penguin that mistook blue meth for blue mackerel and was now tweaking his penguin balls off.

When people would come along, I'd stop dead, so as to not embarrass myself, and pretend to talk on a cellphone. If the people were stranding around or loitering about in front of their house, I'd continue, but with the same disabled stride. I'd still take those baby steps but now much slower, like I was deeply concerned with something my stockbroker, or, even better, my editor at the New York Times, was telling me. These people didn't know who I was. I could pretend to be, and pretend to be talking to, anybody I damn well pleased.

At any rate, I found I was up into the seven hundreds before I knew it. The baby steps had paid off! Still, from there I decided that counting steps was probably not the distraction for me. Too much stress and athleticism for daily food shopping.

Just after I quit drinking—by reading a book—I went on a self-help book binge. I took seven steps to become a more effective me. I harnessed the power of my subconscious mind. I learned how to pretend I was rich and happy and healthy and wealthy and loved and thick haired. I immersed myself so well in these delusional worlds that when I came back to the real one it was a jolt, like coming out of Avatar in IMAX 3D to the streets of Detroit. I found how to love God as an atheist and how to agree with myself four (!) times.

These self-help books love their numbers, but they were always good, happy numbers. Achieve anything in One Year! *Finally I'll understand Twitter and how to conjugate Spanish verbs*, I thought. Two Minute Meditations didn't work because I was too worried about running out of time to relax. Four Agreements. Five Prayers. Seven Habits, Seven Secrets, Seven Laws of Success and so on.

There were only a few books with three in the title and none with six. I assume that The Six Ways to Cause Catastrophe, Destroy Humanity, and Wreck the World didn't

have a market for mass production.

Although I hadn't yet acquired a fortune by working four hours a week or attracted myself a hot air balloon stocked with Swedish massage therapists and lunchmeat, the books were helping me tremendously. It helped that I'm easily influenced, gullible, and have low expectations. Nevertheless, they gave me a positive outlook and made my eccentricities seem almost normal again. Instead of stressing or counting as I walked home I would mouth little mantras. I allowed them to dance from my lips the way drunken angels might fall from the head of a pin.

"I am happy, healthy, wealthy and free!" I'd whisper four times.

"I am the master of my mind, thoughts, and emotions." Times four.

"I am a being of energy and light and I exude peace and love."

"I am a powerful overlord presiding over this plane of reality and I am feared and loved by all. But mostly loved. But also definitely feared."

"I have a fully stocked hot air balloon. Back rubs and sandwiches await me!"

These last I tended to say with guilt, wearing a nefarious smile and rubbing my hands together. Not because I was finally a super villain, but because I was still afraid of chicken germs.

I was soon repeating these phrases and many more, four times each, three times a day—an exercise that took up a fair amount of time. I felt I had to walk while I accomplished this, and when I paced the house muttering under my breath I felt self-conscious. So I took the dog for three walks a day. I was careful not to be interrupted or distracted, so I kept my head down and walked fast. I'm sure that people thought I was an asshole at best, but I was secure in the knowledge that I was preforming an essential function. The chanting kept my mind occupied and I was quite happy in a delusional, zealot-y way. I'd say my last chants during the dog-walk right before

bedtime and stand on the bridge over the river, releasing any negative energy and doubts from my infinite and loving consciousness.

All of these mantras and books didn't cut down on the things I checked, or the time I spent checking them, but they did ease my overall anxiety. I had a positive outlook and amazing chakra energy while I sweated and swore and backed away from appliances that I was positive were trying to kill me.

"One, two, three, four." I finally came up with an idea to end the checking all together. It didn't stem from anything I read in those books, but rather from the new, magical way my brain had re-wired itself as the result of reading the books. Whether it was the Power of my Subconscious Mind, The Universe, or The Power of Now coming to Four Agreements with the Universal Life Force I'll never know, but only because I just wrote "I'll never know." If I'd instead written "I know" then I would know. Oh yeah, my idea: simply write a list of everything I did and have Karen do it for me.

Downstairs door locked, latched, and pulled on four times.

Now look at it four times.

Downstairs window latched and pulled on four times.

Now look at it four times.

Downstairs light fixture off and not shooting sparks.

And so it went.

It took up two full pages of standard notebook paper. At the bottom of the last page I wrote:

Are you sure?

Are you POSITIVE?

Times Four?

When Karen returned to the bedroom and handed me the list I was twitching, sweat rolling down my back.

"It only took you seven minutes and twenty seconds?" I asked.

"Everything is done," she said.

"But even when I'm efficient it takes me twenty-seven minutes, I don't see…"

"Everything is done," she said.

"Did you blow on the stove?"

"Yes."

"Did you touch the light switch four times?"

"Everything is done now just read your book," she said with a finality that couldn't be questioned.

I lasted a few minutes.

"Are you sure you locked the door?"

"YES."

"And you tugged it?"

"YES."

"Are you sure everything's safe?"

"YES."

"Positive?"

"YES. Now chill out and go the fuck to sleep."

I stopped bothering her, but I did not chill out and I definitely did not go the fuck to sleep. I tried to read, but mostly just twitched and sweated. I tried to sleep, but I felt nauseated. Every cell in my body wanted to jump out of my skin and pull on doors and blow on propane tanks. But I resisted my baser urges and eventually fell into fitful napping. When I got up the next morning, I resisted the urge to try and find something she missed, knowing that it would ruin my plan. The next night it was a tiny bit easier and within a week it was nothing.

Two weeks later I abandoned the list and just asked her if she checked everything. Was she sure?

Positively sure? That I kept up.

A few months later, Karen went to visit her family in London. I was understandably worried that in her absence I'd revert back to my inglorious compulsions. I decided to make a list—just as I'd made for Karen. I promised myself that I'd only check everything once. The miracle happened and I stuck to it. I did count to four with each thing, but then I took (four) nervous steps back, turned around in a military

LOST IN SPAIN

about-face, and was on my weird little way.

These days, I'm much more relaxed. I still stick to a schedule, and if I'm not watching my shows by 7:30 p.m. (*Jeopardy's* definitely on, definitely going to miss *Jeopardy!*) I start to freak out a little inside. But if something major is going on, a death in the family or a hurricane, say, or a death because of a hurricane, I have the ability to get over it. Valium helps.

When I'm walking my dog, I still find myself mouthing chants. "I have a fully stocked hot air balloon. Back rubs and sandwiches await me." And, "I am happy, healthy, wealthy and free." But it's not because I have to. I do it mostly unconsciously; the way a banker whistles while he sets about destroying the worldwide economy.

There are still stressful moments. When I hear of a house fire or break in, when I've had way too much coffee, or when I see a stray piece of lint floating near the water heater and assign it nefarious intent I feel a strong urge to pull on doors or blow on fuse boxes, maybe even pull out the vacuum, but my heart's just not in it anymore. I know I could revert back to full blown crazy if I really wanted to, but I'd rather sit back and comb my fingers through my full head of lustrous hair. I have Karen to thank for that and maybe, just maybe, she'll surprise me with a hot air balloon one day.

6

KASPER AND NOTHING MORE

KASPER

I was spectacularly drunk the first time I met Kaspar. He was attractive, in shape, and well put together in that classic German man mold. I made this appraisal without having to question my sexuality in any way. Although he did cause me to break out in song. I sang "Cry Me a River" and "Bringing Sexy Back" into a beer bottle and danced around in front of him. This wasn't because I was gay for him (I wasn't) or because I was an obnoxious drunk (I was) but because Kaspar looked exactly like Justin Timberlake. His hair was prone to tight Timberlake curls, and when he hacked at it close with clippers he had a Timberlake shaped skull. His eyes were Timberlake-like and his skin was Timberlake white.

Kaspar listened to German rap that sounded a lot like Linkin Park or Limp Bizkit, only a lot angrier and in German. Which is redundant, I suppose. It sounded like the noise that would ensue if you gave an angry white man steroids and PCP for a year and then tied him up in a studio and beat him with a microphone attached to a chain link fence. His music

LOST IN SPAIN

sounded to me like a fire alarm sounded to Rainman.

I knew from the moment I met him that Kaspar was a good kid, likeable with a big heart. I liked him because he was a shuffling contradiction. He fluently spoke three languages but had almost no common sense. He was a street kid but polite as any suburban Protestant. He was a German, from Germany, who had a great sense of humor.

The thing I liked best about Kaspar, the thing that made him almost too good to be true, was that he had his very own catchphrase. I never knew whether it was a neurotic tic or if he'd meant it as a kind of punctuation.

"And nothing more" Kaspar would say. He'd say it following any statement of significance and with much more regularity when excited. At times the phrase was uttered in perfect context. "This ugly girl was throwing herself all over me so I allowed her to do me the oral sex, a blowjob, yes? And nothing more."

Other times it made little or no sense. "The porn collection that is only in my mind grows every day and nothing more." This wasn't as over the top as my eclectic group of friends' eccentricities went, but it was enough to make me love him.

When I first met Kaspar, he was living in a group home for delinquent boys. The facility was up in the highest elevation of the Sierra Nevada. The German government is sensible and efficient in how they deal with their errant youth. They send them to another country. Spain doesn't mind because they receive a stipend every month for every child they hide in the mountains. The kids don't mind because sunny Spain is better than habitual rape in a German prison. Most of the kids were young; they just got mixed up with the wrong crowd, strung out on drugs, made a few too many dumb mistakes and got caught up in the system. The year Karen and I moved to Javaron, there were eight boys in the group home. All of them were interchangeable blonds with filthy mouths and immaculate soccer jerseys. They were all between twelve and eighteen years old.

103

Two of the older delinquents—Kasper and a kid I was introduced to as Gustav—were sitting at the bar when I staggered in. I was two days into a two-week binge. The kind I used to have where I just drank, forgoing food, showers, dignity, and sanity for a blood alcohol content that never dropped below .35. Gustav was Kaspar's evil twin. He had black, straight hair to Kaspar's soft, curly blond. His skin was sickly and infested with hostile looking acne. His face was ugly and cruel, prone to sneering. It was a face that you wanted to punch, but only after putting on a glove. This was an urge that many found irresistible, even if there were no gloves handy. Gustav was Kaspar's exact size, hence the evil twin, but came across much smaller. He was an insolent, evil-looking, blustery young punk. Gustav spoke some English, poorly. It was just enough to make you wish you couldn't understand him at all. He also was in the habit of stalking a local English girl who he referred to as "my bitch"—this he had done for years until one day it came to an ugly confrontation with the local police and the girl's mother.

"My bitch went asleep early yesterday and did not walk by the window at all, that lazy bitch," he'd say in the way others would talk of dinner and a movie. "Some dickhead has been calling my bitch, I see her on the phone. This makes me mad as fuck."

"Why don't you leave her alone?" Kaspar would ask.

To which, Gustav would invariably invoke the universal gesture of male masturbation and say, "Fuck that, fuck you, she is my bitch." Gustav liked to draw out the vowel in fuck, sounding not unlike a root canal patient in a dentist's chair or a broken vacuum.

"But she doesn't like you dude," I said.

"Fuck that she wants my cock."

The girl was oblivious to his intense ideas of their relationship, only choosing to include him in her circle of friends because circles of friends are very limited in an isolated mountain village—especially for those not born there. It did not take a gypsy seer—or, as I called them,

neighbors—to predict prison in Gustav's immediate future.

"You are going to get in trouble," Kaspar said. "locked up because you are crazy and stupid and nothing more."

"Fuck you cocksucker."

"They are going to have your small German ass and eat their cake too."

"Fu...."

I gravitated towards a younger crowd in Spain because of my immaturity. I have never felt like a real adult. I find real adults to be off-putting and scary. Plus, Javaron was so small that everyone had to hang out with everyone else. I happened to be in the bar at eleven a.m. when the adults were working or shopping or growing weed on their cortijos, so I saw the kids more than I saw the real adults.

Another major factor was that they looked up to me. They saw me as an American outlaw, a counterculture bad ass. This was a perception I did my best to cultivate. Everybody wants to feel admired or respected, but I need it, desperately. It's not that I'm insecure—I am—it's that I can't help falling into a role that people expect me to play. When I know people think I'm funny, I'm hilarious. When people think I am an asshole, I frown and complain and gossip and interrupt their conversations to showcase my knowledge of useless trivia. The inner asshole inside me grows until it encompasses my entire persona. When I even suspect someone believes I'm stupid, I find myself at a loss for words unable to describe simple concepts like the finale of *Lost* or what it is I do for a living. Next thing I know I'm sitting in my underwear, smoking a bong, watching *Jersey Shore* and struggling with the TV guide crossword. I look around at the scene, not knowing how it came to this, but knowing very much who to blame— the person who thought I was stupid and, also, Obama.

No one has ever thought me gay and I am not sure how I feel about that. I guess it depends on how you perceive me. Knowing that the younger crowd in Javaron thought highly of me allowed me to be the hilarious, charming, brilliant, totally confident man that comprised the real me. As long as

you agree.

FREDRICK

I met Freddy on the first Fourth of July I spent in Spain. I'd cognitively known that they wouldn't celebrate the day, but I still felt slighted. I mean sure, the banks would be open and the kids would be in school, but for no one to be grilling burgers and hot dogs, for the night sky to be as dark and silent as a biology class at a Christian college, was insulting. These are people who blow up dynamite, real dynamite, to frighten away evil spirits, who set things on fire to celebrate Easter, and they have the audacity to ignore the greatest holiday the human race has ever known? I decided to show my disapproval by pouting. I became bored with that though and went to Blues Brothers and ordered a burger.

"Don't have what you want Scott," Frank said. "Only real hamburgers, ground pig burgers."

"I hate those," I said because I hated those. They were chewy and pink and very much Not. Hamburgers. Even though that's exactly what they were: ham-burgers.

"I know, sorry. I ordered beef the last time I was in Granada, but they was out again. The cows keep escaping this year, I guess."

I could have ordered a chicken sandwich, but I preferred to feel slighted. This allowed me to drink with impunity. That was my subconscious plan from the beginning, looking back.

"Never mind," I said. "Just get me a beer, Frank."

"You American then?" A guy asked from a few stools over. I hadn't really noticed him before, being too preoccupied with finding an excuse to get drunk.

"Freddy," he said and shook my hand with gusto. "They got no decent nosh in this shithole country do they?"

"I'm Scott. And no, not unless you like pork fat and fried butter," I said.

"Ahh, good one, mate."

Freddy was a square-headed man of twenty-two, good-looking in a sly, crafty way. That square head with a big, oval face. A small mouth but large ears. You'd think those features would merge to create an ogre, but somehow they worked on him. It was like a blind watchmaker put together, if not a Rolex, at least a decent Citizen or Movado out of Timex parts while drunk. An unlikely win, but still a win.

He looked like a giant toddler, but one who would try to sell you crack and steal your car.

"Look at this," he said shoving his phone into my hand. "These are your boys, over there in Iraq. Watch them dust up some dickhead terrorists." His phone showed a grainy video taken from a helicopter. There was an insurgent on the ground firing up at the copter with what looked like a .22 revolver. You could barely make out the raucous voices of the men, but could definitely hear their excitement. Boys, really, about the same age as my new acquaintance.

"Wait, wait, this is where it gets good," Freddy said.

"Watch this fucking shit," said a Marine in the video.

"Watch this fucking shit," said Freddy.

Suddenly there was a loud burst of staccato fire and the video shook. The guy on the ground all but disappeared in a puff of red mist and brown dust. This brought to mind the days of my youth, trying to catch crawfish and salamanders in the creek by my house. As soon as I gently moved a rock they were gone in the same kind of cloud. A cloud of gone, I used to call it. The unfortunate man had disappeared in a cloud of gone.

"Ommahgod, bad ass!" said Freddy.

"Hahaha fucking awesome!" said a Marine.

"A cloud of gone," said I.

"That's good mate, a cloud of gone, I like that." Freddy flicked through his phone looking for more videos of death and destruction. I was happy when he got distracted by pictures of his girlfriend and kids, until he wanted to show them to me.

"Ah look, this is my girl, Bev." He sidled up next to me so

107

we could both see.

"Look, my kids, too." The first screen was of a pretty blond girl of about twenty. She was soaking wet and had a hand up trying to block the shot. She looked a little pissed off, but that was only because she had shampoo in her eyes and hated having her picture taken when she was in the shower, as Freddy explained. Before I could say anything he flipped on.

Here was Bev lying in the bed—naked. Here was Bev on the couch wearing a pair of red panties and lace gloves.

"You should really buy this poor girl some clothes," I said.

"Never. If I could keep her naked all the time I would." A frown crossed his expressive baby face.

"Actually, I'm lying. I'm just really happy right now. It's been two months since I've seen her and I'm as randy as a goat. She always gets dressed in company. I just took these so I'd have something to wank to."

"That's nice," I said because I really did think it was sweet. Sweeter than bondage or group sex, I thought. I mean, it's not something I'd ever do. The internet is too full of good porn.

"My kids again." He flicked much faster through these. I saw flashing glimpses of a cute little girl and an extraordinarily large headed toddler.

"They're adorable," I said, because that's what I say about people's kids.

"They're all coming in a week."

"Cool, can't wait to meet them."

"I'ma superglue her to the bed and blow her back out."

"Er… cool."

Freddy then went on to describe in detail the finer points of his girl's anatomy and sexual prowess. I also came to learn that Fred had left his birth country of Wales in a hurry. He'd been stopped for speeding on his crotch rocket motorcycle and police had found his backpack filled with the European Trifecta: coke, ecstasy, hash. Freddy made bail, filled his bike with stolen gas, and took the ferry to Spain.

LOST IN SPAIN

Little did I realize that Freddy's bike would become the Chekhov's Gun of this story.

Freddy was street smart, a natural born hustler and I genuinely liked him. He also had the annoying habit of one-upsmanship. He was a big fish who grew up in little tank and had the luxury of having his fish food dropped in by a doting grandmother.

He had done everything. He was the best at everything. If you told him that you surfed he would tell you he surfed Hawaii and won an amateur championship. If you told him you'd slept with two strippers during a coke-fueled night in NYC, he'd tell you he murdered four hookers while on a crack binge in Bangkok. The kid was only twenty-two, but had already worked as a mechanic, a master plumber, dental assistant, ocean canoe instructor, scuba instructor, undersea treasure hunter, photographer, cement finisher, D.J., long-haul trucker, and paramedic. I've forgotten at least a dozen more.

His accomplishments, awards, degrees, and Boy Scout badges were impressive. Also, obviously, he was the best drug dealer.

"I didn't step on that shit, I danced the motherfucking jig on it," he said often.

By the time Freddy came to town, Gustav had gotten kicked out of the boys' home. Apparently Gustav refused to get a job and kept stealing from the younger kids. Three of the thirteen year olds had enough and cornered him in the bathroom.

"Gustav was crying and bleeding when I got home and nothing more," Kaspar reported the next day. The man who ran the home, Frank, had taken one look at Gustav, his bloody nose, torn shirt, and pathetic grimace and told him to leave.

"Then Gustav was whining that he was assaulted and Frank pretended as he would slap him. Gustav jumped a meter and left! He is out of sight now, but is planning revenge and nothing more."

SCOTT OGLESBY

Shortly after, Kaspar also moved out of the home and into the village. The two ended up sharing an apartment together despite a mutual hatred because it saved on rent money and having to smoke pot alone. As much as they hated each other, they, like most married couples I know, would rather have someone to argue with, someone to steal drugs and porn from, than to be faced with solitude.

Their sad filthy cohabitation lasted for two months, after which Gustav would check into a Spanish prison for a long, long time.

Freddy was over at my place drinking beer when Bev called saying there was trouble. He wanted me to come with him so I rode on the back of the bike. An experience as thrilling as it was emasculating. We got to his motel room apartment and saw four pedal bikes parked outside his door. Freddy led the way in and we found Gustav standing in the middle of the room with three elementary school kids sitting on the floor. They looked petrified. Gustav scowled, winced, and whatever else it was he did with his face.

Bev was high-strung with a love for cocaine that I'd describe as terminal. She jumped up and explained the situation and gave her ideas for conflict resolution.

"This lil' shit won' pay. He needs his ugly head broke." As if to illustrate her point she realized she was holding a water bottle and flung it at his head.

Gustav ducked, but it hit his shoulder and soaked the front of his white shirt, revealing a galaxy of red pimples beneath.

"Bev stop!" Freddy said, holding her back. "Calm the fuck down and tell me what happened."

Gustav grabbed at his crotch and said, "Fuck, that cunt she…" But before he could finish I pushed him against the door.

"That's not nice, be nice," I said. He knelt down on the floor, sobbing. It was unexpected and quelled even Bev.

"Why are there small children here?" I asked.

110

LOST IN SPAIN

Freddy looked as if he only now noticed the three adolescents on his carpet.

"What the fuck Bev?"

"They came with tha' ugly shitter," she said.

"Why did you let them in?"

"Cause they knocked."

"Jesus Christ Bev!" Freddy said then turned to the kids "Why are you here?".

The three of them looked at each other as if they shared a brain and were not sure who had it last.

"They came with him!" Bev said pointing. "I gave that wanker an ounce of hash and he said he'd be back tonight with da dosh. He came back with des babies an' only forty Euros."

"That's all we had," one of the carpet kids spoke at last.

"I am going to kill you Bev, I swear to bloody hell," Freddy said.

"No you need to kill Gustav now. There's witnesses though."

"I think I should go," I said because I was pretty drunk and killing Gustav actually seemed like a decent idea.

"Here I got twenty more," Gustav said between gulps of air. "That's sixty, what can we get for sixty?"

"You've got to be kidding me!" Freddy sighed.

Bev tried to kick Gustav. I checked the fridge and found a beer. Now that I had another beer I was more than content to ride this out. No matter what happened.

"Can we get a quarter then?" the boldest of the carpet kids asked. Freddy threw their money at them and told them to get out and never come back.

"You still have my money," Gustav squeaked.

Freddy answered with a resounding slap. Gustav started sobbing again as the four made their way out the door.

"Bev don't let anyone in this fucking place again, I mean it!"

"Can we get some blow?" she asked.

"Tomorrow, Bev."

111

SCOTT OGLESBY

"But I wan' some now."

"Don't let anybody in and you'll get yours tomorrow."

"Stop squeezing my stomach mate." Freddy said on the way back to my house.

"Hey if you wanted to kill Gustav you know I would have had your back," I said.

"Maybe tomorrow," he said. "But no kids, I don't kill kids."

I'd said it as a joke, as I rode bitch and hung on for dear life. "What do you mean, you don't kill kids?" I asked.

"What do you mean what do I mean," Freddy said. "It's a good principle. Do you kill kids?"

"No, not really," I said. Mostly because I don't kill anybody.

The way it turned out, no one had to do anything about Gustav. That night was only the beginning of his humiliating two-week descent into a personal, self-destructive Armageddon. Shortly after this incident, he ripped off another teenager. This one was bigger and decidedly less patient than Freddy. After the kid broke Gustav's nose and knocked out a few teeth, Gustav went on a drinking/idiocy binge. First, he stood outside his stalkee's mother's house breaking windows until the police arrived. Before the cops could take him to jail though, they had to stop off at the hospital to get him stitched up. Everywhere. He'd been breaking windows with his bare hands and, apparently bored with that, his head and face. He got out of jail two days later and effectively ended his chances of ever having an unscumbaggy life by kidnapping the girl of his obsession and holding her hostage. Luckily the girl made it out without a scratch, but as far as I know, Gustav is still in a Spanish prison, learning the virtues of humility and servitude. Given his small size and horrific personality, it's not been a pleasant stay.

Unfortunately, these events sparked another series of events that would almost destroy Kaspar as well.

112

"Now, because stupid asshole is being the dick-sucker of prison and is maybe dead and nothing more, I cannot pay my rent. My job is no longer working and I'm to be sleeping in the street like a homeless vagrant tramp gypsy mongrel dog. And nothing more," Kaspar confided in me one night.

"How much money do you need to cover your rent?" I asked.

"Almost one hundred Euros and nothing more."

"I'll lend it to you, don't worry."

"No this will not do. I will never pay you back because I am like a dog now."

"Don't say that man. You're a good kid, let me help you out," I said.

"No. I am not a charity ward of the state. I will maybe sell you things you would otherwise buy and nothing more."

"Deal," I agreed.

I bought movies and books for a twenty and he insisted I take a few wide brimmed hats that look ridiculous on anybody over eighteen years old. Or white. Especially both. The major purchase to make up his rent money was his weight bench and weights. They were still at the youth home where he'd lived until two months previous. All we had to do was go pick the stuff up.

The real roads, the ones with asphalt and a yellow line down the center—purely for decoration—were scary enough. The road leading to the youth house was a donkey trail. The donkey trail had foot-high grass growing up the center and was running along the side of a rocky mountain with four-hundred-foot-plus drops onto sharper, angrier rocks.

"Yes, turn here. I tell you now," Kaspar told me for the fifth time.

"Where?" I asked.

"Right here. Make a left right here and nothing more."

"But that's not a road, that's a dirt bike track for mice."

"You are big pussy, yes?"

"That road is the sweaty upper lip of a fat man," I retorted.

"You are sweaty upper lip of vagina."

"What?"

"Turn here and nothing more."

"Shit," I said making the turn.

"Your vagina shits."

"Dude. Stop."

I made my way slowly, winding around and around the mountain tightrope, each turn revealing another drop dead gorgeous view of the panorama.

"Wait, what happens if another car comes?" I asked.

"You show him your vagina and nothing more."

"Be serious goddamnit."

"There is only the German's home back here so this should not happen. If it did somebody would back up until there was room for passing."

At this I stepped on the gas a little. "How much further?"

"Fifteen or twenty kilometers and nothing more," he said with a mocking tone.

I drove faster still. It was getting close to sunset and I was sure that if I was on this road at night, I'd never see the dawn.

Five uneventful minutes passed until I heard a very large, very angry snake spitting at me.

"WPPTTSSS," the snake screamed at us.

"What was that?" I asked, screaming a little myself. "I think there's a fucking snake."

"That was your tire," Kaspar said.

"My tire ran over a snake?" I pictured a cartoonish boa constrictor with tread marks across his angry belly.

"That was your tire being flat and nothing more," he said, exasperated.

I stopped the car, opened door, and leaned out, checking for snakes. I could hear the last of the air abandoning its home.

"So there was no snake. Damn. I really thought it was a snake," I said.

"Your tire has exploded and nothing more. I have told you this," Kaspar said. "May I change the tire? This is

something I very much enjoy."

Theoretically I knew how to change a tire, but it had been years and I'd never done it on a snake-filled donkey trail so I acquiesced. "Knock yourself out mate," I said.

I walked back to where I'd heard the snake and found the culprit immediately: a Chinese throwing star-shaped rock with razor sharp points on three sides. I picked it up, intent on carrying it home in case Karen had any doubts about my culpability.

By the time Kaspar was done changing the tire, darkness was approaching because darkness didn't have anything better to do at the time than to make my life harder. To add to my stress level, the spare tire was a donut, which is like a regular tire only much smaller and covered with delicious glaze. Our only option was to continue forward until we found a spot to turn around and inch our way back home.

"Hopefully we don't run into any more snakes," I said because if we lost another tire we were going to die.

"I once was bitten by a snake, and it made me very sick," Kaspar said because he felt like being overly dramatic. "I will call Frank and he will bring to you the bench and nothing more."

"I need the weights as well," I said.

"This is obvious," he replied.

A few days later the equipment was delivered as promised. Kaspar had the rest of his rent money. It was money that would prove to be wasted.

The next week, Karen's parents came to visit. Her father Max is a people person. He loves watching them and listening to them and being around them. The weirder they are, the happier he is. The man loves colorful characters and they gravitate to him the way plants bend to sunlight. Max has an innate talent of bringing out the crazy in people. He should have been a psychologist or talk show host. He loved Florida for the psychopaths and our remote Spanish village didn't disappoint him either.

Karen's parents stayed in the same hotel that Freddy called home because it was reasonably priced and clean. It was the only hotel in town. Karen and I both saw the danger in this but were powerless to avoid it. The most we could hope for was Freddy to join a cult for the week.

The night Max and Karen's mother Jillian arrived, we took them to the Blues Brothers for dinner (for them) and drinks (for me). Kaspar and Freddy were sitting at the bar loudly discussing stealing cars or the best ways to escape prison—I don't actually know what they were discussing but it couldn't be far off—and I glanced warily in their direction. They mistook my grimace for hospitality and came over to join us. Within minutes they were both pouring their dark hearts out to my father-in-law.

"And they pulled me over with a backpack fulla drugs, I was shitting myself mate," Fred said to Max.

Karen's mother Jillian kept fiddling with the shots the boys had bought her.

"Was it the wacky backy?" Max asked.

"Just a handful," Freddy answered. "Mostly it was blow, ecstasy, and pure Moroccan hash."

"My word," Max said.

"If this were Germany he'd be sent straight to prison for the raping and nothing more," Kaspar said.

"Or, he'd be sent over to sunny Spain and we'd still be having this conversation right now, unfortunately," I threw in.

"The Germans send their bad boys to Spain?" Max asked.

"They sent him," I said, pointing at Kaspar.

"Yes, this is true," Kaspar said. "They nicked me for possession, vandalism, petty theft, and a few minor things and nothing more. I was a stupid child."

"This is very interesting," Max said. "I must soon visit Germany and commit a crime."

"And they'll send you on holiday to Spain," Freddy finished.

"I must find a policeman and punch him on the nose

immediately," Max said joking.

"I fought a cop," Freddy said because he had to throw some testosterone around. "They nicked me for aggravated assault and resisting arrest."

Karen's father has an amazing ability to never show disapproval. He never even squinted. "With my luck they'd throw me in the prison for life," he said. "They'd say, 'I don't like the look of you young man' and throw away the key."

"Oh shut up Max," Jillian said, trying to pass her shot to Karen.

"If it was a young policewoman she might show me some mercy and sneak me out to marry her." Max said antagonizing his wife.

"If it was a young policewoman," Jillian said, "she'd execute you herself."

"Only if it were an English woman. I should have stayed in Jamaica," Max retorted.

"You're Jamaican?" Kaspar asked. "You must have smoked your weight in ganja!"

"What?" Max asked.

"I had a baby with a black girl," Kaspar added. "I love that girl and I love my baby girl and nothing more. I also love the reggae! Did you ever grow dreadlocks?"

"What is that?" Max asked.

"The hair. The long hair that is braided and nothing more."

"Oh I don't think I have the head for that. Besides my English wife would chop it all off the moment I fell asleep."

"She probably would too." Karen added.

"I would not," Jillian said. "I'm not bothered."

Freddy and Kaspar told Max about their parents, their kids, their criminal histories, anything and everything while Max nodded, smiled, and kept them talking. He remembers everything as well. Everything. He could have made a fortune by selling information to the authorities or working as a debt collector, but he used his talents for entertainment purposes only.

"After he threw a fried chicken at the waiter, he punched a policeman right on the nose," he'd say years later at a Christmas dinner. "Can you imagine such a thing? I can't imagine doing such a thing."

Later that night, Freddy and Kaspar decided to drive down to the coast. A trip that took forty five minutes. Freddy claimed he could make in twenty. Karen and I tried to convince them that it was a horrible idea—on par with electric blankets for cats or fat free cheese—but Freddy was young, cocky and Welsh. To his credit, Freddy wasn't nearly as drunk as Kaspar and proved it by doing wheelies up and down the street before they took off for good.

The next morning, I parked in front of the hotel and we met Max and Jillian on the patio for coffee. Max was still buzzing on the insane stories of the night before. He had many questions that were hard to answer.

"Do you think they are telling me fibs? Is that German boy going to go back to his family? Do you suppose that Freddy boy is a fugitive then? He must be if he's not telling fibs."

Freddy surprised us all by appearing from nowhere and walking up to our table.

"Havin a cuppa eh?"

"Join us young man," Max said.

"You might as well sit down," I agreed.

"You must tell us more of all this madness!" Max said.

"Uh yeah, ok. But Scott, Kaspar is sitting in your car. He wants a ride to the clinic. Just to get stitched up a bit."

"What?" I asked.

"Eh, he's just being a pussy, go talk to him," Freddy said while Max, Jillian, and Karen did their best to not hear anything offensive.

"He's in my car?"

"He's in your car."

"Did you punch him in the nose?" Max asked.

"Nah, he just took a spill off my bike," Freddy explained.

I got up and walked around the patio not knowing what to expect. Turning the corner I could see him sitting in my car, staring straight ahead and rocking in the way people do when they're either coming off of heroin or waiting for more heroin. I opened the driver's side door and the first thing that struck me was the multi-layered, richly textured smell. It came in waves, like an Italian dinner or Italian rage. It was almost artful in its complexity. There was the more recognizable scent of body odor, the coppery smell that makes you taste blood, the astringent, penetrating odor of fear, brought together by the all-encompassing, unmistakable scent of urine. I reluctantly got behind the wheel, imaging myself sinking into a cesspool.

"I need a cigarette and nothing more," Kaspar said.

I took a good look at him, stuck a Pall Mall in his mouth, and lit it. There was a bloody t-shirt wrapped around his head, tied like a bandana. He was wearing a button down shirt, opened in the front and stuck to his back in large bloody patches. Every time he leaned back he caused himself considerable pain, hence the unconscious rocking. It only got worse from there. His left arm was wrapped in the remains of the shirt he was wearing the night before. It was soaked through, dripping with blood. His bare left arm looked like ground sirloin that had been rolled in dirt and gravel then reshaped into a human-like appendage. I saw that he was sitting on a hotel towel and was grateful because there wasn't much left of his pants and what was left was covered in materials better left unknown. He had one shoe on, but his other foot was wrapped in yet another hotel towel. This one cut and held in place by duct tape. I was inappropriately impressed with the medical use of duct tape, because I react to stress in strange ways.

The scene was incongruous. Out the window the sky was perfect blue, the hotel looked warm and welcoming, Spanish, clean. A perfect day in a happy country. Inside the car was a scene from a Vietnam War movie. I could hear the soundtrack from *Apocalypse Now* blasting in my head. I even

heard chopper blades beating the air, but it turned out to be a skateboarder.

I was worried about my car's interior, what with the various and unidentifiable bodily fluids leaking willy-nilly, but I also felt an instinctive protectiveness towards the boy. The way you might feel for a beloved child or an injured squirrel. Sure, I might have to clean out my car and bleach the upholstery, but I was determined to help.

"Could you just open your window?" I asked him.

He smoked his cigarette and rocked back and forth by way of acknowledgment.

"The window, dude. You stink."

"I. Can. Not. Do. Anything. And. Nothing. More."

"Fine. Forget it."

"That stupid fucking Jagermeister."

"Jagermeister did this to you?"

"Jagermeister made me drunk to fall off of the motorcycle and Jagermeister made Freddy drunk to not know I fell off the motorcycle," he said, pointing at Freddy's bike. He might have placed primary blame on the German liquor, but was angry at the motorcycle as well.

"Oh Timberlake," I said pulling out of the lot. "What happened?"

"One minute, I was having a nice ride and the next I am rolling and bouncing all over the road like a bouncy ball or yoyo."

"What exactly happened?" I said. "Like, how did you fall off?"

"I did not wish to hold onto his stomach and look like a woman so I squeezed with my legs and nothing more."

"You have to hold on. I held on just going through Javaron."

"I know this because he complained saying that you squeezed tight like the bitch you are. So I did not wish to."

"Well you should have."

"And nothing more," he agreed. "He went around a bend and went real fast and I fell off and I screamed and I rolled

LOST IN SPAIN

and I bounced and I hit myself into a ditch. I would have gone right off the mountain if the bend were facing the other way. You should know. I'd be dead and nothing more."

We arrived at the clinic and I carried/walked him inside. The place served as the town's doctor offices, utility payment center, daycare, and emergency room. We signed him in and after some citizenship confusion, were led into a waiting room adjacent to the daycare. Small children played and Kaspar bled, stunk, and cursed under his breath. One of the nurses came in to bring an electricity payment receipt to a waiting customer and Kaspar motioned her over.

"May I have something for my pain and nothing more?"

She looked at him with mild disgust. "No, that's not the way we do things here. We must examine you."

"He wants to be seen. He was just hoping for some pain medicine, maybe ibuprofen or something?" I explained.

"And nothing more," Kaspar said.

"Shut up for a minute," I said.

The nurse looked at us both, shook her head, and started to walk away. She turned back to him and explained, "You will be seen soon, you will wait."

"Freddy kept making me drink his whiskey but everything is pain, still," he said.

"So how did he get you home?" I asked.

"He did not. He did not even stop. Fredders told me he did not even know I was gone for ten minutes. Another car came along and saw me crawling out of the ditch. They were wanting to call for the ambulance but I was wanting only to go home. Fredders only came back when they were helping me into their car. I was throwing up."

"Holy shit. You should be dead."

"And nothing more."

The good Samaritans had followed Freddy back to the hotel and helped Kaspar inside. There, Freddy and Bev "looked out for him" all night. Freddy was obviously feeling guilty for having horse-powered the kid off his bike and failing to notice. They looked after him by shoving liquor

down his throat and weed in his lungs.

"And then he gave to me a coffee cup filled with his Irish whisky and tells me, 'drink up.' I finish it like he says and he pours more and says, 'drink up.' They keep lighting joints for me to smoke. They were trying to kill me to murder the evidence and nothing more."

The same grimacing nurse wheeled him away and a few minutes later came back to tell me to go home. They had to transport him to Granada for x-rays.

I went in to tell him I was leaving and he looked at me with huge, frightened eyes. "If I am stranded I will be for calling you. You and Karen will come and retrieve me. Yes?" he asked.

"And nothing more," I assured him. I gave him cigarettes and left.

When I got back to the hotel, Freddy was still at the table with Karen and her parents. Now he was drinking beer.

"How is our delinquent, German friend?" Max asked as I sat down.

"They're taking him to Granada for x-rays. He'll live."

"What a dumb fucking twat," Freddy said diplomatically.

"Freddy here was just telling us that after he joins the Royal Air Force he's going to open up an amusement park in New Zealand," Max said, looking as happy as a psychiatrist who found a brand new disorder.

"Not just coasters and shit neither. I'ma have zip lines shooting into the sea, indoor surfing, paintball stadiums. All kinds a shit that'll blow your doors off."

"It's a quiet country, Fred. Small population. Not... I don't think..." I said.

"That's what will make it successful. There ain't shit in New Zealand. Just goats and goat farmers and more goats. Those people'll go mad for some fun."

"Goat farmers?" I said.

"No, jackass. The normal people. The goat farmers have kids and the kids want fun. I'ma enroll in the RAF first and..."

LOST IN SPAIN

The hospital in Granada sent Kaspar back in an ambulance. Not because he needed it (he did) but because it's what they do. It's like a taxi service. A really, really expensive, taxpayer funded taxi service. But if misallocation of resources was a big problem in Spain, I'm sure somebody would have fixed it by now. It's not like the country's bankrupt.

The ambulance dropped Kaspar off at Freddy's hotel. A nurse had told him that he shouldn't be alone, and in true passive-aggressive flair he gave Freddy's address as his own. Freddy's underdeveloped sense of guilt combined with a nascent but dwindling empathy and he surprised everyone by agreeing. He was happy to help out. Karen's parents were safely back in London and the hotel was all but empty.

Kaspar was blessed, lucky beyond belief. He'd suffered a slight concussion—the effects of which were apparent for weeks following the accident—a sprained ankle—and some serious road rash.

"The doctor said you will be having to rub ointment onto my wounds twice a day and nothing more," he'd told Freddy that night.

His one serious injury was his left wrist, hand, and thumb. The doctors had taken x-rays but either didn't understand them, didn't care, or didn't explain them to Kaspar. They simply slapped a cast on up to his mid forearm and hoped for the best. Blind optimism is good for the patient, but this was the first I'd heard it practiced by the medical community.

Kaspar explained, "They tell me it will be ok."

"Is it broken?" I asked.

"I am wanting to know that more even than you," Kaspar said. "I ask them what is broken and why I cannot move my thumb. They tell me they do not understand to know. They tell me I will be ok and to hang in there and nothing more."

We were sitting in the bar in Freddy's hotel, both drinking coffee. It was empty other than three old ladies. They sat at the next table and folded napkins, polished silverware and gave us reproachful, angry looks. I made a show of drinking

my coffee as if to emphasize how normal we were.

"So how long are you staying with Freddy and Bev?" I asked.

"As long as it takes and nothing more."

"As long as it takes for what?"

I'm not sure if it was the pain meds, the stress, or if Freddy was feeding him coke but he became *more*. More nervous, more excitable, more amplified, more insane than I had ever seen him.

"As long as it takes to heal my fucker body you son of a bitch. I cannot even use my own fucker thumb. I cannot work and will be thrown from my fucker apartment. I cannot even care for myself and I am stupid invalid now and nothing more," he screamed, close to tears. I couldn't help notice that in his agitation he was losing his command of English. This outburst seemed to please the old ladies. It convinced them that they were right about foreigners, that the world was still predictable.

"Alright, simmer down," I said. "You do need a backup plan."

"What is this for?" Kaspar asked.

"Freddy is in there with a wife and two little kids. Besides, he's not the most... maybe you should call that group home guy and see..."

"Fucker no you son of a bitch. They are not for wanting me. I will suck dirty balls in my mouth before I do that. If Fredders evictions me then I will sleep on the street and become murdered and no bastard will be for caring and nothing more."

The three ladies got up with glee and tittered into the kitchen. I saw a middle-aged cook stick his head out a minute later. He was smiling, delighted.

He went on like this—rather melodramatically, I thought—for longer than I expected. I kept pushing his buttons. Partly because I wanted him to see the light and have a plan, and partly because I can be sadistic and found this the most entertaining conversation I'd had in ages.

LOST IN SPAIN

"Maybe your baby momma will take you in. Unless she found somebody else."

"No, she will NOT," he shouted. "She will more want to be stabbing me than giving me love when she is finding my stupid. I am supposed to be sending her monies not falling all over the road and for broking my body."

"Whoa, why's the little fella getting so worked up?" Freddy came in and sat down, rubbing the top of Kaspar's head affectionately.

"I am not for working. I can NOT work for nothing more. He is telling me," Kaspar said pointing at me in the way a witness for the prosecution would, "that you will eviction me and I will be stabbed in the street and be dying like the dog."

"I was just saying that you need a long term plan here, Timberlake. You are kinda fucked," I said, turning the knife one last time.

"Let's drink some beers and you can worry later. I ain't gonna evict ya just yet mate," Freddy said.

So we drank.

"He's gotta go. I can't take it anymore Scott," Freddy said two weeks later.

Kaspar was no longer on crutches and the bandage was gone from his ankle, leaving a pasty, white leg that stunk and was riddled with sores. The road rash was healing, but he most definitely did not look better. He still had the cast on his arm and still couldn't move his thumb. More than that though, he had somehow deflated like a birthday balloon found in the game room a month after a kid's party where someone had died. He looked withered and ill. Kaspar had stopped going outside and his skin took on a waxy, yellow tone. He hadn't showered since the accident and when Freddy took me into their room, the smell took my breath away. Then it took my breath to a pawn shop and sold it to get money for crack. The smell in the room was like despair, like hatred turned inward and left to fester in a corner and

rot.

Kaspar was sitting on the couch with his feet up on a coffee table. Although it was a big couch, and otherwise empty, Bev and the kids sat on the floor. Kaspar looked gloomy, Bev looked angry, and the kids looked confused when we walked in.

"Hey Timberlake," I said out of habit. He no longer resembled the all singing, all dancing man-child. Now he looked more like a stray cat that had grown ugly, lazy. A pet that had lost favor and learned to bite. Now he was Kevin Federline.

"Take a fucking shower, mate." Freddy said.

"I cannot get my cast wet," he said raising his hand instead of his eyes.

"I told you to just cover it with a plastic bag."

"I will wash up in the sink," Kaspar replied. "Later."

"You smell like a shithouse. Scott, tell 'em, please. Tell him he smells like a box of assholes marinated in cat piss and sautéed in garlic," Freddy pleaded.

"He's right," I said. "You do stink. You smell like something Chris Farley just shat out. And he's been dead a long time."

"You can both suck my balls," Kaspar said, without looking up.

"Your balls are likely to rot off, you don't wash them soon," I said.

"Fuck you two both, twice," Kaspar said, finally showing life.

"My fucking kids are here asshole," Freddy said with zero irony, "watch your mouth dickhead."

I knew that Freddy's patience had run out, so I went down to the front desk and got a trash bag and rubber bands. I had to promise Kaspar that I'd buy him beer, but I finally coaxed him to shower. He even shaved, although he missed entire strips of facial hair since he had to do it all with his left hand.

"At least you know he's not jerking off on your couch," I said later, at the bar.

LOST IN SPAIN

"He'd probably break his cock, knowing the clumsy wanker," Freddy agreed.

"You are both so very funny," Kaspar said joining us at the bar in Blues Brothers. "You should be a comedian team. Go to Las Vegas and hit people with hammers and make fun of them for bleeding." Kaspar had a few beers and was feeling happy for once.

Kaspar started getting out again, but showering was still not a top priority. He showed up at our house every afternoon around two or three.

"Freddy has no food and he does not share," Kaspar complained.

"So you're hungry?" I asked.

"Yes please. And I could have a few cigarettes and nothing more."

I'd heat up leftovers or boil hot dogs for him. He was grateful and appreciative. I made him sandwiches for later and gave him a pack of smokes almost every day. I didn't do all this out of pure altruism, but because it was the only way I could get him to leave.

"This is all very good but do you maybe have cheese?" Kaspar asked and that was how it started.

"This is needing hot sauce and I would like a soda…mmph, lots of ice, please," he said through a mouthful of chicken and brown rice, gesturing with his fork.

"Do you not have potatoes?"

"You are needing a convection oven."

"I borrowed some sausages from the butcher. Could you fry these up for fast? With peppers and onions if they are available."

"Borrowed?" I asked.

"He said that one of us could pay him tomorrow."

"Which one of us?" I said.

"This is needing more cheese," he answered.

"I can't take it anymore," I told Freddy as we sat in the bar.

127

SCOTT OGLESBY

Kaspar was busy napping back in Freddy's room.

"Ha, I told you his shit gets old."

"The kid eats like a cancer," I said.

"He eats like that plant. The Little Shop of Horrors. The one that says 'FEED ME' all day," Freddy said. "Wait, when do you feed him?"

"Every afternoon. Between two and four. I pack him a snack for later as well. Try to help you guys out with the workload."

"Bloody hell," Freddy said. "We feed him three meals a day. And Frank just told me he comes begging here every night. He makes him a hamburger and fries. Every night."

"Jesus. Timberlake really is like a cancer."

"Or that 'FEED ME' plant."

"Seymour, I think?" I said.

"That's it. Timberlake is Seymour." Freddy said.

"He's eating six, seven meals a day."

"No wonder he's so lazy."

"Doesn't even have the pep to shower," I agreed.

"This has got to stop."

"It does," I said. "For his own good."

Not long after our conversation, Kaspar finally got his cast taken off. He was still unable to use his thumb though.

"It is just hanging there and hurting and getting in the way. I cannot even work," he complained.

After a barrage of nagging and insults from all concerned he agreed that he had to do something. "Something" involved coming to our house at all hours to use the internet. "Something" also needed more calories, nicotine, and alcohol. He'd show up, eat, smoke, and drink beer while checking prices for flights to Germany, calling old friends, messaging Facebook friends, playing Farmville, reading online employment pages and apartment listings and applying for government assistance, all while angry, German hip hop played out of our tortured speakers.

After dozens of lunches and hundreds of hours I'll never get back, he got it all sorted out. He'd found a sixty euro red-

128

eye from Malaga to Berlin, a friend's couch to stay on until he got on his feet, and even an appointment with a hand surgeon to repair his thumb. Our little Timberlake was growing up! All he needed was the sixty euro and Freddy and I obliged with relief. Freddy offered to drive Kaspar to the airport on his bike and he, unbelievably, accepted. We all prayed he wouldn't fall off again.

A few days later we exchanged tearful goodbyes. We were all just so damn happy to say goodbye. A moment later they were off; the annoying, adolescent growl of the motorcycle fading into the night. Karen and I had lunch with Freddy the next day. He was Poland the day the German occupation ended. He was Jonah after the whale puked him out. He was a Red Sox fan when they finally beat The Curse in '06. Freddy was as happy as I'd ever seen any human being.

"I let him off in front of his gate and the little nob ask me for ten euros. I gave him a twenty, wished him luck, and nothing more."

And nothing more was our new punch line. An inside joke that burned like indigestion.

"He sure did turn into a walking hemorrhoid…" Freddy started.

"And nothing more," I finished.

"If he'd just taken a shower…" Freddy said.

"And nothing more," I said.

"Brush his teeth…"

"And nothing more."

"Clean up after himself…"

"And nothing more."

"Timberlake had everything going for him…" I said.

"And nothing more," Freddy continued.

"But he cried himself a river…."

"And nothing more."

We were just having fun. Letting off a little pent-up frustration at the helplessness and guilt of the whole situation. We both loved him and hoped he'd bounce back and have a happy life now that he was getting the help he needed.

"I have been walking for ten hours and am needing a cigarette and also some food and something for drinking and nothing more," Kaspar said. Three days had passed and I had just woken to a whiny, insistent pounding at my door.

"But... what... owwww.... Fuck... what....?" I said because my brain had imploded. I made room for him to come in. I was helpless to do otherwise; he was as obdurate as approaching death.

"Freddy has not been home or unlocking his door," he explained, explaining nothing.

"Why are you not in Germany?" I asked, trying valiantly to hide my insensitivity lest I seem insensitive. Sometimes however, I am insensitive and selfish and resentful and those parts of me just refuse to hide, much like an angry pimple that pushes its way out from behind cover-up.

"My flight was delayed. Those fuckers evicted me from the airport and said that I was not permitted to stay asleep outside. So I went walking to a near park. There were nothing but angry and crazy and junky people in Granada and nothing more. There were drinking and smoking the cocaine and sucking the heroin and nothing more. I was very much nervous to be for sleeping and did not fall asleep until the daylight and when I woke up I missed the plane," Kaspar spit out in one breath.

"You. Missed. Your. Fucking. Plane?"

"And nothing more," Kaspar said, nodding with comic panache. "I hitchhiked to Adra and was walking home from there. Ten hours. Yes?"

"Walked home?" I asked.

"To the Fredders and my room. But he is not for answering."

"Oh. Let's give him a call," I said.

"First I need food for eating please. Something good."

I fed him, I gave him water. I gave him coffee and beer and cigarettes and a few euros. I might not have felt like it, but it was my responsibility. Once you take in a stray, even a

German Timberlake, he's your responsibility. Try as you might to drive it hours away and dump it by the side of the road—assuming it doesn't get run over or picked up or re-adopted—it will eventually make its way back to you, scraggly, hungry, a little worse for wear, but just as loyal and stupid as ever.

One month later, Kaspar did make it back to Germany. He was adopted by a loving family: a black girl and their mutual offspring. He had his hand repaired. The process involved two lengthy surgeries. He called me once from his new home, said he had a minute before his girlfriend got home with his dinner. He told me about how well she cares for him, how she brushes his blond curls and helps him shave. I told him how happy I was for him. I told him that he was a good boy, such a good boy. And nothing more.

7

KILLING TIME

When I used to think of Spain, I thought of bulls, of soccer, of sexy flamenco dancers and beautiful men. I thought of topless beaches and tapas bars. I thought of cultured urbanites and rugged villagers. I thought of Don Quixote and lost glory. After having lived there that's all changed. Now when I think of Spain the first thing that comes to mind is flies. Houseflies, black flies, blowflies; loud, disgusting, buzzing balls of pure evil. They're everywhere, prolific and eternal.

Flies are a part of Spanish life, like mosquitos in Florida or Mormons in Utah. If you live there you're expected to deal with it. Dealing with life on its own terms has never been my strong suit. I have a tendency to fixate on one annoyance and blow it up in my mind until it occupies the entirety of creation; until there's nothing else but me and It. I know from personal experience these things usually end in tears, duct tape, and a restraining order or two. But this was a new kind of problem, unlike the last one I'd solved: Maria.

The Spanish have infinite patience. They learned to live with the flies. They never even bothered inventing screen

LOST IN SPAIN

doors. Instead, they hang beads in their doorframes as a deterrent. This leaves the impression of a happy, hippy village where there are hash brownies baking behind every door while the inhabitants nap to the soothing tunes of Bob Marley or the Dead. That impression is wrong. I found out the hard way.

Left with no other option, we hung our own beads. A shiny, multi-colored collection that I felt reflected our personality as well as our inability to find any other style. The beads looked nice and did a surprisingly effective job. Even with them, however, dozens of flies still managed to make their way inside every day. They landed on my food, dive-bombed my head, buzzed my ear just as I was drifting off to sleep, and tried to reproduce in my mouth. I think that's what they were doing. It's hard to tell with flies. At first I tried to ignore them or gently shoo them out. After a few solid hours of exemplary Liberal behavior, I turned murderous with rage. I wanted them dead like I've never wanted anything. My being ached for it. Their death was my *raison d'etre* and I wouldn't rest until they rotted.

I needed them dead like breath. Like oxygen. I wanted them to suffer. While an unruly mass invaded the house, an infinite army was just outside our doors. The pool, the parks, anywhere and everywhere. They planned and plotted and swarmed. They bided their time and marshaled their forces. Within a half mile of our house there were sties with pigs, pens with chickens, pastures with goats and horses and donkeys and mules. These same animals walked our streets every day leaving their business as they went about their business. It was a fly assembly line and they were incentivized workers.

Our terrace was reached through the kitchen door. It was the only outside space we had with a modicum of privacy. The terrace was my sanctuary, the only place I could bask in the sun. Once they'd learned my weakness, they congregated, attacked. We did all of our laundry by hand because we wanted to live like pilgrims for a year. I'm just kidding; we did

133

it because Spain hasn't invented washers and dryers yet. We washed laundry in our bathroom—also on the terrace—and hung it outside to dry. Hundreds of the hateful beasts would swarm onto our fresh and sweet smelling garments within minutes. There, they'd mate, fight, love, form governments, revolt with coups, slaughter the old despots and prop up new dictators, create new religions, plunder, pillage and rape, raise children and eat some of them and they did it all on a pair of freshly washed boxer shorts. That wasn't enough for them. Every time I'd start to relax they'd attempt to colonize me as well. I'd drift off to sleep and wake up with flies on my bottom lip. I could too easily picture where they'd spent their morning and the experience gave me a bad taste, feeling dirty and wanting to drink hand sanitizer and bleach. I felt woozy and sick, as if I'd just drank hand sanitizer and bleach.

My revulsion and hatred only grew, like a river fire in Cleveland or a fly civilization on the shit-smeared streets of a rural village.

Inside, we hung fly traps. They were gross, terrible devices before they'd even completed their obscene work. After two days, with forty or fifty dead black bodies stuck rotting and melting, the sight was revolting. The hour after one would land on a trap was torturous. Realizing it was stuck, it would proceed to make a sound which would turn your very soul black. It sounded like a tiny weed whacker. A possessed, demon weed whacker that knew it was doomed and screamed revenge. The sound would go up and down in pitch and intensity, like a car alarm or a teething baby. Just when you thought it over, it redoubled its effort with inhuman rage.

The flies were a presence all year. They'd disappear during bad weather, but give them one seventy degree day and they'd be back like obnoxious tourists. Only instead of throwing around money they'd try to inseminate your epidermis… not unlike tourists. When we lit the fireplace in the winter, the flytraps would slowly melt. After an hour the traps would uncurl and drip glue covered corpses onto our floor.

I'd often lose my temper and stalk them with rolled up newspapers. When I had the chance I'd swing with aggression. This left black, white, and red stains on our walls, and I had to abandon the practice after Karen made me abandon the practice. I bought flyswatters often. They were flimsy plastic toys, no match for my strength. No match for the flies' speed or sturdiness. Besides, even when I got lucky, there was a grisly mess to clean up. We were sitting on the terrace one day when Kasper—Our German, Timberlake-like/pet/friend—witnessed one of my fly-induced rages.

"No, you do not need to work yourself up into such a crazy person," he said with a calm grin.

"Ugh. Grr. Ummmmph. Shit!" I replied, having knocked over a flower pot with an errant swing.

"Sit down and watch me and nothing more," he said.

I sat down opposite him and watched. My pride might otherwise protest, but I was humble in my pursuit of fly killing perfection.

A fly landed on his knee and I held my breath.

"You do not attempt to hit the fly," he said, becoming the sensei. "The fly is too smart, too fast for this. It feels the air movement before you can strike. It escapes and nothing more, yes? So you clap your hands above, like this, and nothing more."

Kasper brought his hands swiftly together in a manner reminiscent of a toddler with excellent motor control or the old lady in the Clapper commercial. "An inch above where it sits. This, the fly does not suspect. You see it feels the air flow but because we are smarter, we anticipate where the fly will flee. Always they fly up and nothing more."

The fly bounced off his knee and fell to the ground dead. I was impressed.

"Wow, you're good at creating a systematic procedure for mass murder. I mean, for a German." I said ironically, because I tend to say really offensive and inappropriate things when I'm high on caffeine and bloodlust. Karen looked at me with the big, strained eyes she gets when she's trying to tell

me not to say something I've already said because she doesn't understand the linear nature of time, but Kasper didn't notice. The younger generation seems to be free from the national guilt that burdened their parents.

"Thank you very much," he said, "but I saw another do this. It is not my invention. Now it is your turn to learn."

An obese fly landed on my knee, I clapped above it and it fell out of the air like a stroked-out bird—dead. I was hooked. The three of us spent the rest of the afternoon drinking coffee and massacring the multitudes. By sunset there must have been a thousand dead.

Clap too hard and you pop it, ending up with fly blood and guts on your hands, literally. Clap too gently and you only daze it. After lying still (playing dead?) for a few moments it will twitch and come back to life. After a few adjustments I learned the perfect form. Sometimes, I'd purposely daze one, picking it up before it gained consciousness, to throw it into a spider web. Your enemy's enemy is, indeed, your friend. I began feeding the terrace spiders with the zest and flair of an Italian grandmother. I threw food at them until they collapsed in their webs satiated, exhausted.

I knew it was disgusting, but I was powerless to stop myself. I knew it was sadistic and ultimately pointless, but the knowing did nothing to slow my descent into madness. Now that I had the weapon, I found it impossible to allow any fly to stay alive anywhere at any time. The situation or occasion made no difference. I should say the occasion *makes* no difference because, still, I cannot stop. I'll be watching a football game at a friend's house, having drinks at a restaurant, celebrating a graduation, or mourning at a funeral. A loud, jarring clap echoes across the venue and everyone turns to look at me. My expression glazed, my head bowed in concentration, eyes fixed on my knees. The small black corpses pile up around me like so many victories. "I am more intelligent than you, yes?" I mumble.

8

BROKEN BAD

I sit on the pleather couch dry heaving into a bucket already half filled with the culmination of my life's poor decisions. And vomit. Lots and lots of vomit. Vomit, bile and chyme laced with bloody threads. Also in the bucket are a few cigarette butts, many tears, and one contact lens. I'm also missing a favorite pen, but I'm not putting my hand in there to search. I'm wrapped in a giant yellow parka looking very much like Big Bird when he's kicking Sesame Street heroin.

Despite the coat, I'm shivering. It's been raining for over a week. The freezing cold, constant downpours of hell. It's the kind of rain that makes one contemplate a move to the Middle East or even Phoenix, Arizona. All that water—an eternity of water—and we don't have any tap water. A week of rainfall has melted the snow from the surrounding mountains and brought mud and stones and trees and fence posts and tires and dead animals down upon our hapless little village, flooding over the banks of the river, knocking out the electricity, and destroying the water main into the town. Our streets have become raging rapids. The four and five hundred year old homes of Javaron are flooded from both the leaking

roofs and from under doors. The houses are taking it in both ends and I'm giving it from both ends.

I can hear indignant outrage from goats, chickens, donkeys, and dogs as they are forced from the first floor, where most farmers keep their animals in makeshift barns, up into the house where angry Spanish women are screaming at them to stop being so animal-like. It's now illegal to keep working animals in the village, but our neighbors have an almost violent aversion to authority. Tell them they can't dance and they'll bring in Kevin Bacon to get footloose on your ass.

Our house is not only leaking in several places, it's also freezing. I can still see steam rising from my sick bucket. Our fireplace doesn't work because the storms have destroyed part of the chimney. Even if we don't mind dying of carbon dioxide poisoning, and I don't presently, it's hard to light a fire when water is pouring into the fireplace. It's the amount of water that comes when you flush a toilet. Only there's no toilet. Just gallons and gallons of black water and a cement floor to welcome it. We put buckets and towels down, but it's like trying to soak up the Red Sea with a Tampax: a good idea in theory, woefully inadequate in practice. We do have a small space heater that runs on propane, but we only have one mostly empty tank that we shuffle between the stove and the heater. The propane man hasn't come because there are no roads that haven't been converted to rivers.

The pain is unbearable when I sit. It's excruciating to stand or walk. I feel nauseated when I lay down, which is just as well, because lying is almost as painful as standing. See, I broke my ass last week. I fell down wet cement stairs while holding a drink and rather than sacrifice my vodka I shattered my coccyx.

Karen threatened to leave long before this. She should have left. She didn't. If she had I would have gotten my way and been long dead. She's kept me here. I did not understand love like that. I'd learn to understand it well.

Karen leaves to fill up another water bottle from a

fountain a quarter of a mile away. The fountain was originally a horse trough, but through it runs clean mountain water from an underground reservoir, or so we were told. You quickly learn the value of water when you only have a few gallons a day at your disposal. Water is liquid gold. This whole situation makes me want to watch *Waterworld* again, but with a new appreciation. I won't though because that film is, at best, a marginal, overwrought abortion of cinematic excess and creative bile. It's worse than having no water. Besides, we have no power for the DVD player.

I throw up everything I consume, be it food, drink, or cigarette smoke. Vomiting smoke and small pieces of nicotine stained bile is even less fun that it sounds. I can't go to the bathroom. My body has forgotten how to urinate, defecate. My body wants to use my mouth as a kind of all-purpose pipeline, but I'm not okay with that, so I try to sit on the toilet anyway. I try to retrain my digestive track, so I sit and rock back and forth and squeeze, tears coming to my eyes from the pain of my quivering tailbone pieces. Nothing is coming out, but I feel something starting to come up, again, so I try to calm down by sitting still and breathing slowly. This isn't easy considering that the bathroom is outside on the terrace. The bathroom has a roof—leaking—and walls— mostly—but a large empty doorway that was built too wide to put an actual door on is open to the elements. I rectified the situation in a burst of male fortitude by tacking a piece of burlap to the top of the doorway. To close the canvas door one only had to push the fabric over one of the many nail heads imbedded on the side of the frame. Over a period of weeks, the burlap has ripped and shredded and now has all the stability of an addict working nights in a hospital. It always seems to know the precise moment when to give out and blow up and out, much like Marilyn Monroe's dress when it sensed a camera nearby. This usually happens while one of us is showering. While I'm scrubbing one of those "hard to reach" areas or while my wife has shampoo in her eyes. This is the reason the old men gather on neighboring

rooftops and balconies. They pretend to tinker with an antenna or feed the pigeons, but their lawn chairs and binoculars give them away.

Due to the horrific weather that week, no one was outside when the privacy curtain walked off the job and committed suicide by diving off of the balcony and allowing the wind to take it away to paradise. About the same time that icy rain water blew in on me at twenty miles per hour, I also noticed a new drip, strategically placed so as to fall on the back of my neck and slowly roll down my spine.

"What the hell did I do to deserve this?" I thought to myself, but I knew what I'd done.

One month earlier I'd been sober for one year. I told my wife and friends that I was going to quit drinking for one year after one particularly bad binge. That binge had been on the back of two previous binges and I was losing hearts and minds in this ground war. So I did what I said I would do—against all odds—and became proud, haughty. "One year and I can drink again." I'd told myself at the beginning. Near the end I ignored the fact that I was happier and less breakable the more I abstained. BUT NOW, now, I could go out and enjoy an alcoholic beverage like the responsible adult I was.

I was surprised and indignant—righteously so—that my wife wasn't nearly as exuberant about my return to glory as I was. I honestly felt a little sorry for her that she seemed to have forgotten how much fun I was when I drank. My only concern was that I'd begin smoking again after being free of that noxious poison for the last nine months. I reassured Karen and myself that I'd constantly, consciously, analyze myself and keep a firm grasp on my version of sanity. I totally knew what I was doing. Karen totally knew what was coming.

With a spring in my step and love in my liver, I headed up to the quiet Spanish bar where we'd had our first meal in Javaron. I thought that this would allow me to pace myself and accustom my mind and body to drinking like the Spanish. They drank the same amount and got just as drunk, but

LOST IN SPAIN

somehow did it with more dignity. I knew I had to avoid Blues Brothers. That place and the shifty characters that frequented it only brought calamity.

I sat down at the bar and ordered myself an ice-cold beer. The bartender poured a warmish and slightly stale *cerveza* and added two ice cubes. I smiled at him as if to say, "I wish I knew your language well enough to make you cry," but I think he took it to mean, "That'll work." He smiled right back at me and went off to play the slot machine. Now I had to practically chug the beer to get it down before the ice melted and watered my reward. After a few gulps, my mind developed the strange urge for a shot of tequila and another beer. I observed the thought—just like I said I'd do—and found it reasonable.

"A little of what you fancy does you good," I said aloud, and the bartender begrudgingly left the slots to ask what I wanted. I guess he was used to foreigners with impulse control issues and had heard the phrase. While he poured, I ran across the street to buy a carton of Pall Mall Menthols from the store because I don't do anything half-assed and because they don't sell Newports in Spain. That first cigarette tasted like death, but a pleasant sort of death, like having sex with a beautiful woman while overdosing from morphine on a bed made out of luxurious Asian hair. Still analyzing my thoughts and actions at every turn, I decided that I was showing impeccable self-control and should go mingle with the heavyweights from the United Kingdom.

Walking in Blues Brothers I was surprised to see only Frank, Kappi, and a trio of town drunks. I didn't know any of their names, but remembered one because he had pulled out his penis in another bar and urinated on the floor. For a moment I questioned my decision to begin my drinking career anew on a Tuesday night, but quickly regained my composure by remembering that I was the fucking champion of a year spent abstinent, and I deserved this shit whether anyone was there to celebrate with me or not. I ordered my strong, English beer and after a second of introspection, a

shot of Absinthe. Frank did a worried-looking double take and Kappi beamed at me with pure adulation.

"You are for the drinking now, yes?" Kappi said. "I shall be for the drinking too!"

"No," Frank and I both said simultaneously. Kappi's face darkened for a split second before he had an idea.

"Give to me the marry wanna?" he asked with renewed hope. Frank gave Kappi another joint and I ordered him a coffee.

"Give to me café con brandy," he pleaded.

"Café solo," Frank corrected.

Frank gave me my drinks and said, "Haven't seen you in ages mate."

"It's been a year, haven't had a drop in a year. I also quit smoking nine months ago," I said, lighting up.

"What changed your mind then?"

"I promised the wife I'd quit for a year. And I did. So I'm all good."

"You're good?"

"I'm great, brother."

"Fuck it then. Let's party."

By "party" Frank meant shooting pool all night while drinking copious amounts of alcohol and smoking pot with Kappi. My last memory before blacking out was of having an intense conversation with Kappi about demons inhabiting our lower levels of consciousness.

I woke up at four or five the next morning still sitting up on the couch with a beer between my legs and cigarette burns on my shirt. I had a splitting headache and my mouth felt like an ashtray that a fat man had shit in and then blow-dried. I staggered to the kitchen and found beer in the fridge. I felt more than relief at seeing those bright green bottles, I felt salvation, rapture.

I drank all morning, all afternoon, and all night, but only because it was my re-inauguration... um, week. Karen showed her love by not beating me up or stabbing me. When I ran out of beer, I went to the neighbor's for some

142

homemade wine. It was a service he provided. You just brought an empty one and a half liter water bottle and he'd fill it up for five euros. By nine p.m. I was all tuckered out and went to bed. I was able to leave it at that, just Tuesday night and all day Wednesday. I'd shown more restraint than most homeless people, hell, more than most Kennedys, and for that I was proud.

I explained to my concerned but still not stabby wife that I simply had to get that out of my system and now that I had, I'd be a shining example of someone who was not at all alcoholic. I'd be just like the blonde Coors twins, only less tall and bouncy. I'd drink responsibly. Or, better yet, I'd be just like The Most Interesting Man in the World and only drink Dos Equis when I drank beer and spend the rest of my time swirling single malt scotch in a crystal tumbler, fighting mountain lions, and doing lines of blow off of various supermodels' ass cheeks. She told me she'd be happy if I just stuck to drinking once a week and never doing shots. She didn't mention supermodels or coke so I assumed I had carte blanche in that regard.

I lasted a few weeks of sticking to the plan. I only drank on weekends and only did shots when I secretly gave someone money to buy them for me. This happened more than you'd think. I didn't do coke off of any supermodels, mostly due to the annoying lack of supermodels. Two weeks before Christmas, though, I went all *Leaving Las Vegas* again. After a Friday night in which everybody seemed to be buying me shots with my own money, I woke up at five a.m. on a Saturday morning and with "Roadhouse Blues" playing convincingly in my head, I got myself a beer. Because that worked out so well for Jim Morrison.

By nine a.m. I was in front of the *supermarcado* waiting to buy vodka and pacing, wondering why the Spanish never, ever seem to open on time when you really want them to. By noon I had ceased to exist in any real sense. I was a mindless robot capable of only drinking vodka, smoking cigarettes, watching *The Departed* over and over again, and passing out all

over the place. I don't remember any of it, but my lovely wife was thoughtful enough to take pictures. She also made a video. The pictures were mostly of me passed out in different spots. On the couch, the cement floor, with my body on the couch and knees on the floor, with my legs on the stairs and my head on the floor, and—my personal favorite—me wrapped around the toilet on the terrace with my pants around my ankles and my head mostly in a laundry bucket. The video was just a monotonous ten minutes of me trying to crawl up the three stairs into the kitchen and failing repeatedly.

Despite all the hard evidence, I found it impossible to accept that this is who I was when drunk because I couldn't remember even a minute of it. I put the experience in the same category as racism or the success of Stephenie Meyer as an author—real, but too painful to accept. I drank for nine straight days. A fifth of vodka every morning, and if I woke up again before midnight, another water bottle of highly combustible wine from the neighbor. The wine wasn't really that bad once you got used to the chunks of whatever and didn't mind a purplish stain on your lips, teeth, tongue, and, inevitably in such endeavors, every inch of your body. I walked around looking like I'd just given Barney the Dino the blowjob of a lifetime. The only thing I ate during that vacation from sanity was chunks of wine flotsam and jetsam.

This wasn't the first time I'd Left Las Vegas. I'd had bursts of binges sporadically over the previous ten years resulting in all sorts of unpleasantness. In the three years before moving to Spain, I was kind of okay. By okay I mean not falling through a black hole and waking up with vomit on my shirt and blood on my pants. By okay I do not mean a glass of wine with dinner or sociable drinks with friends. After the move, though, I adapted to what I perceived the Spanish lifestyle to be, and fell through that hole and was very much not okay. I'd just endured three horrific binges in two short months and promised myself that I would not touch a drink for one full year. I also promised this to Karen as well

because she couldn't hear the voices in my head.

I had tried AA in the past and knew it wasn't for me. It may be a life-saver for countless others, but almost every aspect of the program is anathema to me. The foundation itself—the first step—is impossible for me to grasp intellectually. "We admitted that we were powerless over (alcohol, drugs, vaginas, scratch-off lottery tickets, double bacon-burgers, jumping off of roofs naked: pick your poison) and that our lives had become unmanageable." I can accept the unmanageable part; at its worst my life was like a convenience store being run by an ADD-addled circus bear addicted to meth, but how can anyone be powerless over an inanimate object? Excluding the vagina, I mean, because most that I've met were nothing if not overly animate.

Even if George W. Bush held a Leviticus-inscribed machete to my throat while making me smoke amphetamine out of a phallic-shaped meth pipe, I wouldn't be powerless over the speed. I'd be powerless over W, because he gets crazy violent after a few hits, but even then, I'd have the option of not smoking and letting him do whatever Jesus whispers in his ear. On the other hand, if I have an overwhelming compulsion to drink, even when part of me doesn't want to drink, I'm not powerless over the vodka; I'm powerless over my mind and am, at that moment, certifiably schizophrenic. Which is often exactly what happens with alcoholics and addicts. But to say that anyone at any time is powerless over a substance is crazier than anything Bush would do to me. That's not just semantics, it's the difference between having to sit and drink coffee with cantankerous old men every night and being able to just stop, move on with your life, and do something more worthwhile with your time, like watching YouTube videos of LOL cats or scrapbooking or trying to write a book, say.

I found the second step just as absurd. "We came to believe that a power greater than ourselves could restore us to sanity." I have no problem with people believing in God, but

to expect him to just drop everything he's got going—
preventing the slaughter of innocents in Somalia and Darfur,
feeding the starving kids in Haiti, stopping the gay marriage
initiative in Iowa and helping Tebow beat the spread against
the Pats—all to make sure you don't fill that next prescription
of Vicodin, that's just magical thinking. He's God, not Dr.
Phil for heaven's sake. On one hand, they say that your
higher power doesn't have to be God, it can be the group, an
apple tree, or a Harley Davidson. Personally I preferred the
Chuck Palahniuk literary collection, but the idea never caught
on. I think Chuck's work is too nihilistic of a spiritual
principal for that crowd. If only they were as open-minded as
the Testicular Cancer Support Group my experience may
have been different.

It only gets worse from there. Step 4 wants you to take a
moral inventory of yourself and step 5 wants you to tell your
higher power and someone else all about it. Even if I knew
what a moral inventory was and how to take it, I'm sure I'd
have to order a carton of fresh morals from the moral
superstore. And since my supplier of these things was Mr.
Fight Club, a man who has more issues out than *Playboy*, I
was screwed. It would be nice to get some things off my
chest, like the time I convinced a Bud Light girl to help me
use ecstasy as a suppository, and then returned the favor. I'm
sure Chuck could relate, but I think most other people would
get more than a little freaked out. The rest of the steps
involve a lot of list-making and do-gooding until you are
finally asked to begin evangelizing. If I wanted to proselytize
I'd do it in a cool way by wearing a badass hat and telling
people that the end is nigh.

These programs reminded me of a cult or the Wal-Mart
Corporation, where they break you down, or more accurately,
get you to break yourself down, so that you can be
reprogrammed to suit their nefarious purposes. Their own
sayings only reinforce this notion. "Take the cotton out of
your ears and stick it in your mouth," "Keep it simple,
stupid," and "Your best thinking got you here." They want

you to get a sponsor right away to be your personal Yoda who is there to give you profound insights like "don't drink" and "take the cotton out of your ears and stick it in your mouth." I could go on and on, but if I wanted you to be brainwashed by anti-intellectual propaganda I'd tell you to go to a creation museum or join Weight Watchers.

The whole scene was like a depressing soap opera where the cast were adequate—if a little homely—the writing was clichéd, the set was a church basement, the props were peoples' souls, and the swag was a fucking key chain or metal coin. The parts I did enjoy were the war stories, which, if delivered with decent comedic timing, were quite good fun. I loved hearing how Bob G. got drunk and married a Russian hooker or about the time that Amanda M. smoked something she'd picked out of her cat's ass hoping it was crack. (It wasn't). DUI's, stealing steaks, dining and dashing, bar fights, orgies, hallucinations, mental breakdowns, emergency room visits, doctor shopping, ambulance stealing, breaking into a DARE car just to get the briefcase with the samples, coke swallowing, heroin smuggling by way of the colon, jailhouse hooch made in the toilet of a cell, halfway house assault, cocaine psychosis, meth-mouth, Grand mal seizures, and more blowjobs than you could shake a phallic-shaped stick at. I couldn't wait to get my chance at the podium.

These wonderful tales of adventure were always somewhat sullied by the endings. By the second half they would only be saying things like, "And now when I feel like snorting coke off a midget's tits, I get myself right to a meeting." or, "If it weren't for my higher power, whom I choose to call Jesus Christ (Or Harley Davidson, depending) I'd still be drinking mouthwash in the bathroom of the grocery store." Sure, it's uplifting in the overly sappy last minutes of Modern Family kind of way, and I'm glad that Fred A. finally got a bus pass and his own apartment at 45, but that's just not the way I would have written it. Please don't get me wrong, there were plenty of highly successful people 12-stepping as well, I just don't remember their stories. If I didn't hear the words

criminal conspiracy, RICO, or blowtorch in the first ten minutes they'd already lost me.

AA and NA work for a lot of people but never had a chance with me. Most of it was probably due to my inability to tolerate most human beings for longer than five or ten minutes, especially people who feel it is their solemn moral responsibility to get all up in my business and save my liver from my mind. I don't know if a psychiatrist would call my condition social anxiety disorder or just call me an asshole, but it's one of those two diagnoses. Maybe both.

I was doomed from birth. The gene that tells a person's brain to get as far away from reality as possible, as quickly as possible, by any means necessary, was passed down through my family's generations like blue eyes or a silver coke spoon. My father and as many of his male ancestors as could be traced all died of alcoholism in one way or another. If my lineage could be traced back to the Paleolithic Era, you'd find a guy who looks like me, without the receding hairline presumably, lying facedown in a puddle of fermented fruit with a loose gaggle of females standing around weeping and yelling at each other.

That gene—let's call it GFU'D—first reared its tipsy head when I was a toddler. I remember spinning in circles just to get dizzy. Every kid does that, sure, but I wouldn't stop until I slammed into a wall or fell down some stairs. Then I'd get up and do it again until I got yelled at or hurt badly enough to yell at myself. You eventually do yell at yourself when you're five years old and all hopped up on Cocoa Puffs and spinning and have blood coming out of both ears. When I was eleven, I had to undergo a tonsillectomy. I kept trying to escape the hospital until they shot me full of Valium. As a result I had the most profoundly meaningful conversation with an orderly in the history of philosophy or pediatric medicine. I remember ruminating on the meaning of life, death, and all the things and finding The Answer. It had something to do with the way energy effects matter... and hamburgers, but I

LOST IN SPAIN

never could remember the totality of it.

I awoke moaning and sick. The nurse came over and turned a knob on a bag hanging above my bed.

"Do you feel a little better now sweetie?" she asked, brushing my bangs back.

"OHMYFUCKINGGODYES," I thought, but "mmnnggger" was all I said. I suddenly knew where I wanted to have my next birthday party. Cake and ice-cream and pretty nurses and magical dripping bags of liquid heaven for everyone. We could even have wheelchair races so long as they didn't interfere with our IV's.

I didn't experience that feeling again until I got my first real alcohol buzz. My mother took me to a Christmas party and allowed me to drink rum and Cokes. Why she chose to let a thirteen year old boy from a long line of unapologetic alcoholics drink is a question for the ages. It's right up there with "Is there a God" and "Are eggs good for you?" Whatever the reason, she did let me drink and I loved her for it. The transcendental elixir transformed me from an awkward boy into a charming sophisticate, confidently telling boob jokes to MILFs before MILFs were even a thing or I even knew why I wanted their attention. They laughed and punched my arm and tousled my hair and said things like, "Oh, you're just too much fun," "I bet you grow up and become a comedian," and "Where is your mother?" I was a hit, a social butterfly with wings of Bacardi. I felt validated for the first time in my short life. When we arrived home, Donna—I had taken to calling her that after my second drink—explained what were, and what were not, appropriate conversational topics at adult gatherings.

"Donna, honey," I purred, "You just need to loosen up a bit. Maybe next week we'll breeze by Rachael Hoffman's anniversary shindig, knock back a few stiff ones and find you a man."

We never made it to Rachael Hoffman's anniversary party, for whatever reason. The next event that we did attend was a family reunion for my mother's side of the family. Like my

149

father, my mother didn't have any real blood family left, but because my grandmother had remarried when my mother was only sixteen, she threw herself into the in-law fray and I was helplessly dragged along due to my lack of debate experience or firepower.

When we arrived at the picnic pavilion, I learned that German Protestants really enjoy picnic pavilions. They expressed their pleasure by ho-humming, scowling and being unsure what to do with their hands.

"If I'm half Irish and half Italian why am I here?" I asked my mother who had already looked uncomfortable in an effort to better blend in.

"Just go be quiet and have fun somewhere," she said.

So I sidled my way over to the cooler and took a beer. I had no idea she could move so fast because before the bottle even left the ice she ripped it out of my hand with no small effort.

"Christmas Eve was a special occasion," she scolded with her finger wagging in my face, "and I said you could have one. Had I known that you would sneak behind the bar and tell people that you were making me drinks all night I never would have agreed." She was really blending in now, having given the Germans something else to frown at.

"You're not getting another sip until you have a degree and an ex-wife."

"But I hate these people," I said because I hated those people. "You just want to act all strict now because you're all weird."

She was clearly all weird. I spent the afternoon not drinking and not telling boob jokes. In fact I barely spoke at all, expecting a groveling apology from her and non-blood relative concern frowns from the others. I got neither, probably because I fit in quite nicely brooding with this particular brood.

Beginning at this ruse of a reunion, this gimmick of a gathering, this farce of a festivity, and lasting the better part of thirty years, I noticed an uncanny coincidence: the parties

where I drank and the booze was flowing freely were all glamorous affairs attended by gorgeous debutantes, telling amusingly delightful anecdotes, laughing coquettishly and all finding themselves overcome with a pulsing and vibrant amity towards me, the simmering star of the eternal night. The gatherings where I couldn't drink were violently boring, filled with dull, petulant and miserly prisoners of a reprobate universe. They spoke with clipped bursts of what looked like pain, as if afraid that a grotesque bug would dart into their mouth if they relaxed their face even for an instant. They moved like they had something angular and unwieldy lodged into their digestive tract yet were terrified of it falling out. The latter were a cruel, self-loathing crowd who clearly needed some liquor. The few times that I dared to mention this fact, I was met with recriminations.

"You're that Oglesby boy aren't you?" they'd say. Or, "This is a wedding. There'll be drinks at the reception. In a half hour...?"

When I was fifteen, my father came out of an eleven year blackout, and after introductions and a few pleasantries, went right back in. Only this time he brought me with him as claimed baggage. He said that I could visit him on weekends and drink as much as I liked. All he wanted in return was a devoted disciple and all the money I could beg, borrow, or blackmail. Within ten minutes of me arriving we'd always go buy more beer. He loved bringing me along so he could show off to his beer selling friends at the store and so that I could carry the beer home. It wasn't that he was lazy, it was that I was young and strong. Also, because he couldn't walk while carrying anything without spontaneously falling down. Even with his hands free he sometimes fell down. Usually though he'd manage to violently bounce off of stuff. Walls, cars, houses, street signs, garbage cans and the occasional puddle would often initiate hostilities with him.

I had a vivid imagination as a child, but I never imagined myself escaping a tragic, self-destructive fate. I never even tried. It was as unavoidable as taxes or being robbed by a

hooker in my eyes. I still had fantasies about it, but they all ended the same way: my good-looking corpse and a heartbroken public.

It didn't matter who I was or how I died, really, only that I was memorable. And dead. And that it was the most incredibly tragic event in the national consciousness for at least a decade and that the world was inexorably changed and profoundly heartbroken by the void my passing had created. That was the important part. I had dozens of these fantasies and I would flip through them like the kids today with an iPod.

Looking back on it, I realize that I subconsciously accepted that I was going to die young and of addiction. I accepted it the way an Arts and Humanities major accepts that he's never going to make money. I romanticized the notion because I never saw a way out. It just seemed like a good idea at the time. I wanted to at least make a mark on the world before I left, I just didn't know how much work mark-making required.

In the years after school, I grew older and more pathetic. I felt irritated at first, then irate, at my continued existence and lack of wealth or notoriety. I was outraged that fame and fortune never threw themselves at my feet like a horde of Vietnamese pedicurists at the mall. I had, after all, done my part. Lots and lots of heavy drinking and drugging and very little else. It may have helped if I'd learned to act, or paint, or box, or sing, but I was too busy practicing the partying part. I should have had a fallback plan, but who needed to complete college or search for a real job when planning to die young, rich and idolized anyway?

After all that, a lifetime of *that*, I finally quit. First for a year, and finally for good. I did it with Karen's help and encouragement and by reading a book—*The Easy Way to Stop Drinking* by Allen Carr. As soon as I read the title I knew it was for me. I don't want to give away the ending (Aunt Mable kills Uncle Ted with Bacardi 151 and a well-placed birthday candle) but the book changed my life by changing

the way I thought about alcohol. Instead of seeing booze as my BFF, or even a frenemy, I started to see it as the kind of creepy stalker who slips you a roofie. You wake up dressed as a Boy Scout and chained to a radiator in a hotel room that hasn't been serviced. I saw that my addiction didn't want me dead, like they say in those alphabet meetings—it was Switzerland on that—but it did want a loyal supplicant for life. I had enjoyed picturing myself a tragic figure, a martyr. But a slave for life? No, that wouldn't do at all.

Anytime I had the slightest urge to drink I only had to look at that yellow parka hanging in our hallway. With one glance I could bring up—in excruciating detail—the horrors and pain and sickness that alcohol brought me. That coat came became a talisman of sorts, a doorway between worlds. One world I loved and cherished filled with life and fun and food and sex and the world I'd kill myself to avoid.

One of the biggest surprises I had about quitting was when I spent time around drinkers and addicts. AA says that you should avoid these situations like an evangelical brother in law. They want you to think of alcoholism like an airborne virus and you to behave like a Japanese tourist. I found the situation to be the exact opposite. Watching other people drink has been one of my best reminders to stay sober. Even better than the coat. Watching people who are normal drinkers become obnoxious and caustic shows you exactly what alcohol does. To see my friend who had a diet water and three watermelon seeds for lunch every day for a month shove deep fried mayonnaise sticks down her throat, watching happy people turn mad, mad people turning sad, and sad people turn homicidal, was all so predictable. Even those that don't get hammered seem to regress in maturity and age with every drink. Ever see a middle-aged woman flash her middle-aged breasts at a bar full of men? That would be alcohol.

I'd always thought I was introverted and awkward when I was sober and that drinking morphed me into a dynamic, funny, interesting, and enigmatic showstopper. What I found

by talking to friends from back home after I quit was that alcohol turned me into an arrogant, obnoxious jackass that they could only barely tolerate. They only liked me when I was sober, the opposite of what I'd thought. Now that I quit I'm still introverted and socially awkward, but now I don't piss my pants or throw up on strangers. Sometimes in life, that's the best you can hope for.

Despite the positives, Spain did not take the news well. My neighbors could not comprehend the fact that I quit, that anyone would quit drinking for longer than a few hours. These people saw me at my worst—staggering around at four a.m., knocking on their door at seven a.m. and asking for wine, buying vodka at nine a.m. sharp and drinking it out of the bottle on my way home. They were happy that I took a break, sure. But to simply stop drinking, that was anathema. It was a personal affront, a slap in the face to their very culture.

"It would be better to spit on the grave of my mother," Kappi told me during a lucid moment. It would be no worse had I slapped a bullfighter with a white glove, sodomized Rafael Nadal with Roger Federer's racket, and used the Spanish flag to burn down Madrid. In Spain you aren't regarded as an alcoholic until you're living in a cave and drinking anti-freeze from a puddle on the street. Even then, it's nothing that a decent meal, a glass of good wine, and a few hours of sleep won't cure.

For months after I quit, the townspeople would try to get me to drink at fiestas or drag me by my arm into a bar. I'd go in, and when I ordered coffee they'd throw up their arms in comic surrender. Each time they realized I wasn't going to relent they made the same throaty grunt of disapproval. "Aaugh," they'd say. It was the sort of sound you might expect someone to make after they accidentally stepped on a dead kitten. It was the sound an Italian grandmother makes when their *nipote* refuses to eat.

A year and three days after I'd quit for good, my neighbor

LOST IN SPAIN

Paco—of the homemade wine—showed up at my door.

"Un ano Felicidades!" he said as I opened the heavy wooden door.

"Gracias."

"You are better now, yes?" Paco said as he pushed what had to be a five gallon jug of wine into my stomach.

"No gracias." I said trying my hand at the Spanish finger wagging fun.

"But it is one year. *Un ano*...?

"Si, si, but this time it is forever. *Para siempre.*"

"No no no no," he argued. "It's is time for you to stop this silliness and become a man again."

"Never again. *Nunca Mas.* I do not wish," I explained eloquently.

"But this is a gift! For you!"

When I stopped trying to argue and just shook my head he gave up.

"Aaugh."

That summer—a full year and a half after I'd taken my last drink—the annual Fountain of Wine Fiesta started and dozens of people brought me dozens of plastic cups.

"For you," they'd say.

"No thank you."

"It is complimentary. For you. Free for you!"

"No, but thank you."

"Vino. Here. You take this now please?" Literally pleading.

"It's like this town is trying to kill me," I said.

"Que?"

"Thank you, no." I said.

"Aaugh."

I'm surprised that I didn't get assaulted, honestly. If it had been 60 years ago they would have shot me as a fascist or as a revolutionary, any excuse they could find, they just would have shot me. I could see it in their eyes.

Weddings, funerals, christenings, fiestas, market days were all seen as opportunities to bring me back into the fold. One day when I was sick I went to the pharmacy to get some

antibiotics. The pharmacist was about my age and spoke perfect English. The place was always packed given the village's elderly population. They all had a violent aversion to doctors, but the Spanish love and cherish their pharmacists.

After she'd filled my prescription she said—loudly enough for all to hear—"I think it is very good that you are no longer drunk."

"Aaugh," came the chorus of opinions.

"No, no, you should all be happy. This is good. Very good. Many more peoples should be doing this. This man is healthy and looking for good now," she said as I hacked up something green into a tissue.

"Aaugh," I said trying to avoid a full blown hacking fit.

As the pharmacist goes, so goes Spain. Word spread fast as it does in small towns and prisons—anywhere people get stuck, really—and eventually the people stopped trying to force wine on me.

Before we left for good I knocked on Paco's door. He opened it and I saw a glint of hope in his eye.

"Vino?" he said, before noticing the giant yellow parka bundled in my arms.

"No vino." He answered himself with resignation. "Que es esto? What is this?"

"A present. For you. I don't need it anymore."

9

POLITICAL DISCOURSE

PART ONE

My first experience with politics was strange. I remember standing in The Great Aunts' living room and pronouncing that Jimmy Carter was a donkey-toothed carpet bagger and a poopy head as well. Considering that I was only six years old at the time, I'm assuming that I picked up the first half of the insult at the bar my father took me to daily. The second half came from the playground, since FOX News hadn't been invented yet. It wasn't that my dad was a terrible father—he was—but I wasn't the only child wasting away days at the bar. There were usually at least three kids between toddler and beard huddled in the back corner. These were the places where the neighborhood drunks could get a break from 'the brats' and find temporary solace in polite, political discourse and Iron City Beer. The bar corner kids and I were quick to pick up on the vernacular and used it any chance we got. A few weeks earlier I had gotten the wooden spoon for remarking that my mom's iced tea tasted "like warm piss on sauerkraut." I was plagiarizing unemployed alcoholics, but

157

mom must have thought I was creatively gifted.

Before I could start in on Carter's foreign policy, Isabel—one of The Great Aunts—flung herself at me and clasped her hand over my mouth while Leona—another Great Aunt—hurried to close the blinds, and Aunt Bea—the third, and favorite Great Aunt—gaped at me. I'll never forget the smell of BenGay, the taste of greasy cold cream, or the look of abject horror on all three of their faces as I struggled to free myself from Isabel's Irish fist. These three old women had all grown up together in this old, wooden, plaster house. They had buried four siblings young and had stayed to care for their ailing parents, and eventually, each other. Only one of them—Aunt Bea—had ever had a boyfriend and none of them had ever had sex. At least, that's what I prefer to believe. The Great Aunts were from another era, one where totalitarianism and brutal fascism were flourishing in large parts of the world. The fact that those parts of the world were thousands of miles away did nothing to diminish their fears. At any rate, they had lived tough lives and I could not blame them for their eccentricities. I'd learned my lesson and after the Jimmy Carter kerfuffle of '78, I only discussed politics with my bar friends.

I was riding my Big Wheel through the halls of our apartment building when Hinckley tried to assassinate Reagan. My mother was single by then and worked a full time job, leaving my Great Uncle Willie (married to yet another Great Aunt) to babysit until she got home every night. Willie was a great man who became more of a father to me than my own father was to his young girlfriend, much less me. Uncle Willie taught me to ride a bike, roller skate, and take off my glasses before I was about to get beat up by bigger kids. Willie taught me to love nature, sports, and dogs, especially dogs. Willie had a big heart and meant well. He also had, not so much a sadistic streak, but more a deep-seated belief that you had to scare a child into behaving responsibly and staying safe. Simple sadism probably would have been easier to deal with.

LOST IN SPAIN

As soon as I got home from school Willie would make me a PB&J with sliced bananas and chocolate milk. He set them up for me at the tiny kitchen table of mom's apartment. Once I sat down he'd pour himself a beer, only one, and sit down with his papers. He had sections of three or four papers folded open to articles he'd circled. This was Uncle Willie's favorite part of the day. He became visibly excited and his eyes shone with that particular glint of adrenaline that only releases when one believes they are fulfilling their destiny or when one finds Jesus in prison. Just as I dug into my sandwich he'd begin reading aloud news stories all about misbehaving or careless children who met an ill fate. Some, I'll never forget. I still carry them with me like baggage that you no longer need but are afraid to put down because you can't just leave baggage lying around these days, somebody would report you as a terrorist. One little boy—about my age—was playing with firecrackers and "he blew his whole face clean off." I have a feeling that Uncle Willie may have improvised the vernacular. One girl, who shared my birthday, ran away from home after getting in a fight with her parents. Three weeks passed before a search party found her decomposing corpse. "The wolves were still fighting over her left ankle before the police shooed them off," he'd said. "See this picture of her? Hard to believe she's all dead and wolf food huh?" I remember an article about a man who'd hung himself in his garage. "He was a teacher, see, and his students were always being little smart alecs," Willie said, "drove him to it."

Uncle Willie did more than just stay informed, he also knew people from every walk of life. When we were out walking and I'd scamper up onto a railing he'd relate a story about a boy—about my age he guessed—who'd tried to tightrope walk a fence, fell, and cut his balls "clean" off. He knew a lot of kids. One had to have his finger cut off because "he was screwing around with nuts and bolts and got one stuck." Another kid he knew stole a cigarette from his father and "when he tried to light it something or other went wrong

and his tongue caught fire. It had to be cut clean off."

Contrary to his overly cautious nature, he did encourage me to play sports, hard, and even to fight when it came down to it. His one warning was to take off my glasses first because he knew a boy who had been blinded in both eyes, apparently from a single punch. But that's what you got when you screwed around with your glasses on. He even showed me how to fight one day. He stood with his fists turned in and his forearms up in a pose that looked like the Notre Dame Fighting Irish mascot and brought to mind phrases like "Put your dukes up!" and "You'll be sorry you rapscallion." The Greatest Generation seems to have more panache and pizazz than we do today.

When Uncle Willie came rushing up to my Big Wheel, his whole body vibrating with the excitement of unfolding tragedy, I knew something big was up. "Quit screwin' around and come quick," he said. "Wait till you see what's on the Zenith!" I rode like the wind back to the apartment expecting to hear about some little shit that fell down a well, a kid that drowned herself in a bucket, a boy who had fried his brains screwing around with the outlets, or some little imp who'd burnt herself up playing with the stove. But when I heard the hushed tones of Dan Rather turned up to "excited old people" volume from other apartments as well, I knew it was something bigger than that.

The grainy video played over and over again on an endless loop, only interrupted when there was breaking news. *He must have done something really bad*, I thought. I waited patiently for him to tell me that the president had stolen a candy bar or called somebody a bad name or screwed around with the wrong fella, but my Uncle Willie just stood there in front of the TV, rubbing his chin and shaking his head. "Did the president say something about that man's mom?" I finally asked.

"What?"

"He must have done something real bad to make that man want to shoot him," I said.

LOST IN SPAIN

"What the hell is wrong with you? Don't be a damn jerk!" was all he said, but I knew he was keeping secrets because presidents have people that can hear you and watch you through blinds. *They're like Santa, only angrier and more mysterious. They probably don't even like cookies,* I thought.

Time passed and I asked every adult I saw to explain what had happened. I came to understand that Ronald Reagan hadn't done anything wrong after all, Jodie Foster had. The clip was still constantly playing on every channel and my focus shifted to Secret Service agent Timothy McCarthy. A man so brave as to use himself as a human shield. From there, my imagination did what it does.

I began fantasizing about Reagan's daughter. Not in the way a normal person might, but in the way a clown would masturbate: colorfully and over the top. I thought she was around my age because I thought that the human population consisted of great aunts, great uncles, parents, or children of around my age. I didn't know her name so I thought of her as Constance. Constance Reagan came to our municipal swimming pool for a birthday party because they were having pizza and ice cream and also because it was at a pool. The kid trifecta of awesome. Constance Reagan was bad because she had pizza and ice-cream and didn't wait forty-five minutes before swimming and everybody knows that if you don't wait exactly forty-five minutes you'll get a cramp and drown and the lifeguards will have to dig you out of the filter the next day. Not only that, but Constance Reagan was screwing around on the diving board, so when she fell in and began to die it came as a surprise to no one. Everyone else got all scared when they saw her drowning, just laid down on the ground and cried, but I heroically dove in to save her. By then she had sunk to the bottom and her swimming cap was stuck in the grate. Well I ripped that cap off her pretty little head and swept her to the surface like Superman or one of the CHIPS policemen. She cried for a while and then kissed me on the cheek. I shuddered because I thought that was gross. Ronald and Constance Reagan and all the people took me to

161

a big town where people clapped for me and cut ribbons and gave me a gold medal while the National Anthem played and airplanes flew by really fast.

I did not pay attention to politics in high school or college. My only political cause was the legalization of marijuana and I became an outspoken activist. I smoked bowls at home and had a Grateful Dead bumper sticker on my car. I'd pick up ounces for friends and preach to the choir on the industrial, economic, and environmental benefits of hemp. "It makes an awesome rope," I'd say. My compatriots would nod and ho-hum while I outlined how much better weed was for the human body than alcohol, and the likely progression of societal and spiritual evolution if the human race would only stop what they were doing and get stoned. None of us seemed to notice the hypocrisy of doing shots of Jim Beam and slamming back Milwaukee's Best during our one-sided non-debates. I didn't know which party supported legalization, but I was all for that party.

Then a strange thing happened. Through my knack for exuberant laziness and lack of moral compass, I became better than other people. I became a Republican. I'd been busy in my shiftless lifestyle selling weed to my friends, taking bets for a local bookie, and running a lowbrow Ponzi scheme involving poker machines and beepers when I heard about the longest-running caper in history. No, not prostitution, that's legitimate and burdensome work. The oldest hustle is government work, and a few friends told me how to pull it off.

The incumbent State Representative for our district was in the midst of a hotly-contested reelection campaign and was desperate for support. When I heard his opponent's allegations of embezzlement, bribery, adultery, and dwarf tossing, I knew that this was somebody I could work with. I don't want to give his real name here, because I don't want to get sued so I'll call him Wasp. Not because he was a white Anglo-Saxon Protestant, which he was, but because he was

LOST IN SPAIN

long, skinny, and annoying. All I had to do to get in with Wasp was pretend to be a right winger. The neighborhood I grew up in was not exactly a bastion of conservative values so I had no idea what that looked like. It was easy to imagine old men in golf pants smoking cigars, drinking scotch, hating "the gays" and "the ethnics" and lamenting the loss of pure blood lines and the end of the robber baron era. To do a quick study I listened to Rush Limbaugh while I was in the car since he was the only right winger I knew of. I was often driving around, carrying out my various interests. It turns out, that for once, my imagination was not that far off. Once I had the buzzwords and catchphrases down and knew the right people to pretend to hate—it turns out the list was much more complicated, and extensive, than gays and ethnic groups—I put on my best suit and went to Wasp's office.

Having grown up mostly outside in a mostly Italian neighborhood my style was, perhaps, overly familiar. His secretary showed me in and when Wasp shook my hand I clapped his shoulder and said, "Hey, how you doin' brother?"

Wasp looked reticent at first, but warmed right up after I talked about how Clinton and his murderous cronies were ruining the country and how funny it was that so many important people were "mysteriously dying all over the place." He stood up and unbuttoned his suit jacket which I took as a sign of a Republican getting comfortable.

The Wasp was well over six foot three and couldn't have weighed more than an average sized golden retriever. He had the fine brown hair and beige complexion usually found in middle management of the banking industry or ads for erectile dysfunction and he permanently smelled of cinnamon. I assumed it was gum or breath-mints, but it could have been anything.

My first impression was not good. He had that shallow kind of depthless intelligence, a large, somewhat clumsy vocabulary, and all the right complaints regarding pop culture. He lacked the intellectual curiosity, however, to be anything but a vacuous tool. So I did what I've always done and tried

163

to fit in.

"I think it's time to get down to brass tacks," I said because I thought it sounded businesslike.

"What can I do for you?" Wasp said.

"The question is, my friend, what I can do for you," I said, pointing at him. "See, I know a lot of people in the area here, important people and non-important people. Union people and working stiffs. Strip club owners and, well, strippers."

"Er…" Wasp said.

"The thing is, I can help you get reelected. I can talk to people, make phone calls. Hell, I'll even put a sign on my front porch. A thing like that, it goes a long way. I'll do anything short of what 'our' president would do to anything with a pulse." Then, on cue, I offered him a cigar.

"I see," said Wasp. "I certainly appreciate your help and support." A moment later I saw that my joke had finally registered when a deep pink had crept into his cheeks.

Wasp took the cigar and put it in a drawer. "It's too bad we can't smoke that in here. The ordinances prohibit it," he said, officiously.

"No problem, I don't really smoke cigars anyway. So, my point was, I can help you. And maybe you can help me? I'm doing okay for myself you know? But I'm getting older and have a kid on the way, need something stable, something responsible, benefits and all that. Do you think we could help each other here?"

"Just leave your pertinentables with my secretary and we'll see what we can do."

I then alluded to the fact that if he ever needed anything stronger to smoke or felt the need to put a few hundred on Monday Night Football, he should give me a call. I left knowing full well that a man who made up a word as lame as pertinentables was not a man who smoked weed. Maybe a man like that kills prostitutes or saves his fingernail clippings in a bell jar, but he definitely does not get high.

The following week I took the initiative and met him at a local high school's homecoming game. I smoked a bowl in

164

the car and met him at his kiosk by the bleachers with a six-pack of Molson. "You gotta love NAFTA," I said by way of a greeting, holding up the beer.

"Indeededo," Wasp said. "Just pour them into these nifty mugs and we'll be all set." He handed me two plastic cups with snap-on lids and a built-in sippy straw. They were emblazoned with his name, district and capital (R) above a blob of smeared ink that was recognizable as a badger only because of the setting—Badger Field, home of the Bitin' Badgers.

"See, we're not allowed to sponsor or have any official affiliation with the schools but this is a neat little loophole I came up with a few years back."

"Neat," I said.

"It's a badger," Wasp explained.

"Looks great, really."

We passed out bumper stickers and pens and magnets and key chains and every other form of politi-junk he thought to attach his name to. He talked to anyone stupid enough to slow down within ten feet of him about the evils of redistricting and property tax reassessments while I took greedy gulps of beer.

A few weeks later I got an application in the mail. A month after that I went to Harrisburg for paid training that taught me how to make change, issue receipts, and replace ticket rolls as a toll collector for the Pennsylvania Turnpike Commission. This was an unreasonably high paying job that a trained monkey could do even if it was less than a year from monkey retirement and had a crippling addiction to methamphetamine. I found that the vast majority of my coworkers were dumber than a box of penises left out in the sun all day. Even so, I settled into the job and made the most of it.

The turnpike booths only had AM radios and after two weeks of all sports all the time, I went back to the man who had helped bring me here: Rush Limbaugh. A lot of what he said was outrageous and ridiculous and would make me

visibly angry, but it gave me a surge of adrenaline, not unlike being unexpectedly punched in the face by a semi-retired, meth-addicted turnpike monkey. Drivers would pull up and ask what was wrong. "Oh, it's nothing," I'd reply. "I just don't understand why people have to be so mean."

As the months went by, something began to happen, a sort of talk radio Stockholm Syndrome. I looked around my life, saw that I had a beautiful wife and daughter, a nice car, I'd bought a house in the suburbs, and was, for the first time in my life, filing tax returns. I had crawled out of the gutter and made something of myself and I found less and less of what my new friend El Rushbo said outrageous. I still became visibly upset daily. When a driver would ask what was wrong I'd say, "I'll tell you what's wrong, the goddamned ACLU filed another frivolous lawsuit and activist judges are giving this country away." But only after I was sure the car wasn't a Subaru or Prius and the driver didn't have dreadlocks or leather necklaces. If the driver was over fifty and white, he usually agreed. If not, well, I couldn't hear that well anyway. Not with the traffic noise and conservative angst coming at me from a tiny AM radio in the back of a glorified metal closet. It didn't matter that I still took bets and moved around a little grass, or that most of my friends were mobbed up; I had pulled myself up by my Timberland bootstraps and saw myself as "all respectable and shit." Why couldn't all the welfare queens do the same? Why couldn't all the poor people hustle enough to buy a suit and go make nice with some piece of shit politician? "They could even get after school jobs and go to college or something!" I said to the radio one day and knew that I was losing it.

After a few months though I got bored of it and found this new ideology to be unsustainable. It was exhausting being indignant and angry all the time and I thought I noticed frown lines forming. Besides, I was soft on crime, loved rap music, porn, drugs and gambling and was always more Buddhist than Christian in disposition. I had to admit to being a poser. It might have been a slow evolution becoming

a Republican, but I snapped out of it with the speed it took to turn a radio dial back to sports. As soon as I made the decision I felt better, as if a heavy cigar-smoking douchebag had been lifted from my shoulders. I went right back to being non-political. I still went to the Wasp's fundraisers and parties, but only for the free drinks and because half of his staff were placing bets with me every weekend by then. I'd never even registered to vote so the RNC couldn't stalk me like a jilted lover. Or denounce me. Or hang me. Or whatever it is they do to turncoats.

A few years later, I screwed up my life in the grand Oglesby tradition: alcohol, drugs, depression, toying with the idea of suicide. Not in the way a boy plays with action figures but the way an old man might tinker with a fuse box—with haste and confusion. I'd lost everything. My family, job, house, my will to live. It was then that I looked inside and realized that I was actually a hard core liberal. Thank god for the social programs that were out there, but there needed to be more. People like me need help every so often, serious, expensive, all-inclusive help, and all the nice people turned out to be to my left. I made some stupid mistakes, acted irresponsibly and dug my own grave. While everybody else in my life was trying to push me in and cover me with dirt, the dirty hippies threw me a hemp ladder.

I left Pittsburgh and started over in Florida. Armed robberies at churches, floating homeless encampments, vending machines that sold beer, bookmobiles turned into mobile pawnshops, RV casinos, pill mills, crooked cops, corrupt judges, a girls home run by a misogynist pedophile, restaurants that only cooked meth, churches that served beer, hospitals that dispensed methadone, booze cruises, crack motels, hooker hotels, nudist resorts, alligator parks, murder, mayhem, and a born-again Christian governor. In hindsight, maybe Florida was not the ideal place to get straightened out. But I did, mostly. I pulled the ragged tatters of my life around me and wore it with pride, like Rocky Balboa's robe. The one in the first Rocky, the one with the meat packing ad. I got a

SCOTT OGLESBY

job, met my current wife, and went about not killing myself like a goddamned champion. I was once again apolitical in the same way that Lady Gaga is asexual; I had a team, but nobody but me knew which one.

PART TWO

I knew that Europeans did not like Bush and I shared their opinion. It was only after we moved to Spain in '07 that I found out how despised he actually was. The fact that I couldn't understand most of what they said didn't matter in the least. The head shaking, finger wagging, and awesomely expressive tongue clicking was all I needed to cement our ideological kinship. "The Bush es muy malo," the butcher would say every time I came in.

"Si claro," I agreed. "The Bush is malo grande."

The Spanish followed American politics with zeal. When an Iraqi journalist took off his shoe and threw it at President Bush, it caused a lot of excitement in the village. It was all anyone wanted to talk about. With me at least. As soon as they saw me they'd pull me aside and pantomime the scene—beginning with the reporter whipping off the shoe and whipping it at Bush in the smooth, gunslinger style that brought to mind Eddie Murphy's routine in *Delirious*—and ending with Bush's duck and shocked facial expression. "El Presidente es stupido, si?" the butcher asked.

"Si claro, presidente mucho stupido grande." I answered, happy to add to the depth of the conversation.

"What do you need today?" he asked.

"Dos pechuga de polo," I said confidently now that we had a rapport.

"No, no, no, no, no. You want *pechuga de pollo*. Pooh-yo. You ask me for two breast of penis."

"Pooh-yo, si si," I said. "Bush es mas moronico."

The happiest I've ever seen the people of Spain was when

168

they won the World Cup in 2010. A distant second was when Obama won the election in '08. We got the news in the morning and by the time I walked into town there was a fiesta-like atmosphere. When I passed someone on the other side of the street they'd raise their fist in solidarity, giving a little pre-*Jersey Shore* fist pump. Or they'd raise both arms in the air as if to say, "GOALLLLLLL!!!" If I passed men they'd shake my hand vigorously. When I walked by a woman she'd grace me with the hallowed fake double kiss and smile as if to say, "I admire and respect you and your great country. If I were sixty years younger I might take you to bed this instant."

Some clapped, others cheered, but they all looked at me with sparkling, shiny eyes and the kind of appreciation that's usually reserved for prostitutes who unexpectedly quote Whitman. I wanted to ride this wave of admiration by association for all it was worth and went for a coffee at Blues Brothers. The usual crowd of British morning drinkers were ambivalent. A few patrons were cautiously optimistic and said things like, "Yeah, well, we'll see," and "That's all right that the black fella won. You reckon he'll get himself assassinated?"

That mood wouldn't do at all. I was feeling optimistic, exhilarated. Anything was possible for me in that moment. The world's first official mulligan had just been called. We could all start over from scratch. I had a new lease on life and I wasn't going waste my day with realists.

I finished my coffee and went to a Spanish bar where I would be properly appreciated for having the good sense to have my mom spit me out of her vagina in such an enlightened country. It was there—where many of the Spanish spoke English—that I was able to have a conversation with the interested townsfolk and got a clearer perspective of why they were so moved by the election.

"This is very good, yes?" said Hollywood Jose the ambulance driver, as I sat down at the bar. "Your people, they are not for racist any longer. *Muy Beuno!*"

"Well…" I said to explain the complexities.

"A humble African man is now Prime Minister. This is only for the good."

"It's very good, yes," I said. "There are still a few racists. You should see some of the protesters and their signs."

"Yes, of course," Jose said. "But now they will surely be sent away."

"Well, no."

"Ha!" he answered with a booming laugh reserved for drunks or imbeciles.

"Racism still exists in large pockets of America, mostly in the undereducated and rural communities. And maybe the super-rich. But yeah, we've come a long way." I said.

"Martin King and Kennedy and the baseball Robinson and Sammy Davis and Denzel are very happy now, yes?"

"Yes, yes," I agreed, "would be and are. Very happy."

Another customer said something to the bartender in guttural Spanish, who then asked me, "A poor goat farmer, how does he do this?"

"Obama? He... er... he was never a goat farmer." I said.

"Oh yes, yes," the bartender argued. "These Africans, always with the goat farming."

"He's not African, he's American. He has family in Kenya I guess, but he's American. Wait, do you get Fox News on the satellite?" I asked.

"A fox ate his goat?"

"No, no, no goats. Never mind." I should have known better.

"So he does not even own goats?"

"NO. HE HAS NEVER OWNED GOATS."

"Ok, so how does this humble man who is too poor to even own goats, how does he do this?"

"Most people don't own goats in my country," I said, exasperated.

"So the US is more poor than we were to know?" the bartender asked.

"Goats just aren't a thing in America," I said. "People don't like to own goats. When Americans have extra money

they like to buy another car or get a tattoo or adopt a baby, they just don't buy goats."

"I can see why your America is going poor, with all bad choices. So, your Prime Minister, he was a traveling merchant?" Jose interjected.

I began to realize that the only experience these villagers had with people of color consisted of their interactions with the Moroccans who came to this part of Spain for work. The only blacks they met WERE goat farmers or traveling merchants. They came to sell trinkets or work the land, sometimes with their own goats, sometimes goat-sitting other people's goats. There were usually goats involved. Their cultural ignorance went deeper than that though, much deeper. Most of these people were born in this small, rural town. Most would live their whole lives here. Most would die here and be buried here, next to dozens of tombstones of past generations bearing their names. Very few of them owned televisions, or even watched TV. If a soccer match was on they might walk up to one of the bars or listen on the radio. They might catch glimpses of life in Madrid or Barcelona, maybe even London or Paris, but they simply could not comprehend it. They couldn't see what that life would look like any more than Native Americans could see how someone could own land or kill them for it.

Even the college educated people from our village were unable to grasp the subtleties and nuances of 21st century life anywhere outside of rural Spain.

"No," I finally answered. "He was never a merchant."

"Americans do not yet trust Africans with their goods and monies?" Jose asked.

"What? No, no. I mean, yeah. They are trusted. They own their own businesses and sit at the helm of corporations. Black people are exactly the same as white people. Some sell things and some do not."

"I was hearing that they do not wish to be named black but are preferring to be called Africans," The bartender said.

"African Americans, I guess."

"But you are for calling black?"

"I grew up when they were just black. Plus, I'm from the city. I have many black friends," I said, not liking the way I sounded. "I would only use African American in a formal setting. Otherwise, black is fine."

Jose grew excited and began tapping my shoulder. "If Mr. Denzel Washington or even Will Smith comes to Javaron, what will I be calling them?" He asked.

"Sir, I'd guess."

"Yes, yes. Of course. Very formal!"

The bartender said, "This new Prime Minister then…"

"President," I corrected.

"This president, is he African American or black?"

Jose was happy to answer this for me, proud of his new knowledge. "It is depending on the formal or the informal. Like Spanish, yes?" He glanced at me sideways.

"Pretty much," I answered. "Let's go with that."

"This is all very complicated," said the bartender. "Obama was nothing with goats or farming, he was not for selling. Tell me, what did he do?"

"Well," I said, "he went to Harvard, became an attorney."

"Harvard is university?" the bartender asked.

"Big, good. Grande university. Very prestigious," I explained.

"Like *Good Will Hunting* went to?" Jose asked.

"That was MIT but yeah. Just like that. Then he became a community organizer." I said.

"Like Che Guevara? Viva la revolution?" the bartender asked.

"Are you sure you haven't been watching Fox News?" I asked again.

"What is this fox?" Jose and the bartender both perked up at the mention of an animal.

"Nothing. He just helped people fix their neighborhoods and get involved and go back to school. That kind of thing," I said.

"This is very good. And he made the wealth like this?"

asked the bartender.

"No, not really. He's also an attorney. That made him wealth... made him wealthy, I guess." I answered.

At this point Jose and the bartender looked at each other up and down. It was a look that said, "Oh, yeah, we wrecked that car," or "the prostitute, she is dead." It turns out that the Spanish have a profound distrust of lawyers and judges, even surpassing that of doctors and police. In truth, the Spanish really don't trust anybody but priests. And that may not be the best idea either. This distrust, this hatred, was something that no one spoke of, like miscarriage or the Basque uprising.

"It's okay," I said. "Obama is a good man I think. He'll do good things."

Jose looked at me with guarded optimism. "We'll see. I am for hoping."

We were all for hoping. As America erupted into the most contentious, angry, bitter politics I'd seen in my lifetime, Spain prepared for their own elections.

Politics in Spain were totally unlike anything I'd ever experienced in America. It could be because I've never lived in a rural community in America. More likely though, there were parts of Spanish culture that were just better. Certainly more entertaining. Spanish politicians are proud, cocky. Instead of hiding their corruption like their American and British counterparts, they flaunt it. There were no photo ops with pols kissing babies. Rather they'd pose shaking the hand of a feudal lord, or as they're known in Andalusia, a real estate developer. The "gift" of a 10K Rolex was prominently displayed on the pols' wrist like a badge of courage.

Local officials would loudly brag in bars about scams where they rezoned condemned land so it could be sold to unwitting foreigners. When the property sunk into a sinkhole they would gather around, hum, haw, and promise to resolve the situation. Then they'd get back into their German sedans and, I assume, cackle like movie villains. Politicians sold construction rights to the highest briber and traded in favors

like old time mafia dons. At one point in '08, something like thirty percent of municipal officials were serving sentences in prison. This place made Illinois's politics look like a bastion of ethics.

The last two weeks of December '09 it did nothing but rain, and it rained in biblical proportions. The higher altitudes got as much snow as we got rain. Then it warmed up by twenty-some degrees overnight. This melted all the snow above us and sent a waterfall rivaling Niagara down upon us all. The massive flooding destroyed roads, took out electric and phone lines, and even knocked the underground water pipes loose. The town was without electricity, phone, cable, and water for weeks. Strangely, only one block was spared from nightmare; the block that our new mayor called home. The old mayor was friendly, down to earth. After he retired, Javaron elected the Spanish Blagojevich.

It seems the city was given grant money to repair and fortify its infrastructure. The contractors hired to do the work labored from ten until two and from five until seven - barring cigarette breaks and phone calls—in the usual Spanish manner. They started with Calle Royal, which translated means Royal Street. I'm not sure if they renamed it after the mayor moved onto it or if the mayor moved there because of its name. Two months later Calle Royal was done. New electric and phone lines, new water and sewage pipes and sidewalks done in what for all the world appeared to be actual marble. It was pretty but not particularly practical in the rain. The contractors moved on, digging random holes and knocking various objects over on the next block, Calle Real. Then, as the local legend goes, the money ran out. Out of the public coffers and into the mayor's pocket. The construction crew packed and left and the mayor followed suit. Three weeks later he returned with a glowing tan, singing the virtues of the Canary Islands and his new BMW. "For the official business of the city," he told his neighbors as he re-packed his car with wife and wine for a weekend getaway in Madrid.

The townspeople took these things in stride. It was what

they'd come to expect after all, and the little matter of embezzlement was never brought up again until the town had no electric or water for two solid weeks. The fact that the town could see the glowing lights of the mayor's manor every night proved to be more salt than the city's wound would tolerate. The situation reached a boil when a middle aged housewife threw a cup of wine on the mayor in the bakery one morning and called him "a short willed horsetail." At least that's the translation I got. Apparently regional insults don't translate well into English, but I'm assured that the barb hit its mark. The mayor became furious and attempted to punch the woman's husband before being restrained by his cohorts.

The election process was like it is here in the U.S. in that the prospective candidates shake a lot of hands and tell a lot of lies in an attempt to coerce the citizenry to vote them into office. They also ran smear campaigns, but they tended to be even less relevant to any real issues than what we're used to.

"My challenger is nothing more than a dog," the mayor might say. "Even worse than a dog because he does not have the fine nose for hunting of a good dog." Or, "This man could not possibly manage a drawer full of socks, how could he manage our complicated and beautiful city?"

"Yes, of course he would say such stupid nonsense. A man that cannot even manage to keep his car clean. The city is kind enough to buy a BMW and he treats it worse than the dog he compared me to," his challenger responded.

As always happens in these matters, things tended to escalate to the personal level. "Let's be honest," said the mayor. "My challenger is very stupid like the donkey. Like a donkey, he is also stubborn and refuses to do what he is supposed to do. This donkey should never be trusted."

"He calls me donkey now. He called me a dog before. Our mayor is obviously desperate and falling into psychotic delusions. Maybe his precious car is leaking fumes or perhaps the man is on drugs. Hopefully he will not snap one day but...

who can predict such things?"

The majority of these attacks were purely vacuous. There must have been some kind of unwritten rule not to hurt each other by delving into reality. They never outright accused one another of corruption or hardly ever brought up policy or actual politics.

In America we talk about government waste and cutting taxes. Over there they don't seem to mind either. It's just one more annoyance they take in stride, like houseflies or the mayor's newest car. We could never remember their names so we took to calling the incumbent Blago and the challenger Traficant.

They promised the locals everything, but in a very vague, noncommittal way. Farming, for instance, will be made more profitable while, at the same time, the price of food will shoot down as if by royal decree. The people will be made happier! Tourism will boom! The town will be made most beautiful! Like America, no one seemed bothered to ask how.

There was no talk of being tough on crime, they were the only crime. They were a lot of things, but masochistic was not one of them.

Then one day it all started without warning, like an Ebola epidemic or new dance craze. Supporters hung campaign posters on every available surface. By the next morning detractors had defaced them in the most sophomoric ways. Karen and I would walk by the fountain in the town square at night and watch as they were hung with pride, working side by side with their opponents. The sides would bicker and argue, mutter and spit, shake hands and go their separate ways.

The next morning brought ruin to their work. A penis drawn onto a nose. Black eyes and missing teeth. Devils horns, comic scars, and the inevitable scrawls of insults. It would seem the work of teenagers or young children, but they didn't seem to think so. They blamed each other, publicly and loud. Hostilities continued to rise.

America has the Republican elephant and the Democratic donkey to represent the sides. Spain had red and green. There, the green represented an Andalusian party and red represented some sort of nationalistic party. The outline of the posters and other political detritus was rimmed in the representative color. The citizens would show their support by "flying flags" of the appropriate color. Being a spendthrift lot they hung whatever they had handy.

One porch might have a green shirt draped over the side, a green tarpaulin hung haphazard over the barn, a green sock on the TV antenna. Another house had red pajama bottoms hanging out on window, the pajama top out another window, and empty Coca-Cola cans strung on fishing wire hanging from the roof, clinking and glinting red in the breeze.

It was all very festive, like Christmastime in a mental hospital. Every shop had their allegiance and it caused many heated arguments. Or possibly not. They sounded like they were yelling at each other even in the most harmonious of times.

The citizens took to wearing the colors as well. The semi-professionals would don a red tie or a silk green handkerchief. The farmers and everybody else wore bandanas tied around their neck or wrist. It all became very gangland.

The reds were Blagos or Bloods and the greens were Traficant Mafia. I started looking at people differently. I'd see a bank teller wearing red cufflinks and I'd know he was the bag man, the washer. I'd see the farmers wearing green and wonder how many bodies were fertilizing their crops. I'd be very careful not to let the sun set on my white ass in the wrong part of town. When I said that exact phrase to people—because I thought it made me sound cool—they'd look at me as if I were crazy. "I saw *Colors* and *Boyz n the Hood*." I'd say with authority, "I know how gangs work."

On the morning of the election, I walked into town to buy the day's food, just like any other day. It was not anything like any other day however; I could see that from the beginning. Passing houses with red or green laundry I noticed more

windows open than usual, with old ladies leaning out on meaty forearms. They were yelling back and forth and gesturing with gusto. There was also more litter than usual with ripped campaign posters, beer bottles and the occasional sock lying forgotten in the rising sun. I thought of *Psycho*. I thought of New York tenement apartments in the '60s. I thought of drugs and wondered whether I'd forgotten that I took some.

Within a quarter of a mile, I could hear a commotion, and as I drew near the atmosphere became electric, festive with an undercurrent of impending violence. As I got to the town square, I saw that the village had, literally, divided upon itself. One side of the high street was red, the other side green. Each side had their own makeshift bar: wooden tables laden with beer, wine, vodka and whiskey. "Gratis gratis," both sides shouted continuously.

Normally I wouldn't be able to resist such temptation for long, but since this was no ordinary day I didn't even try. One side of the street looked like a St. Patrick's Day party gone horribly right. They were all dressed in green, drinking out of green plastic cups, wearing green hats, purses, shoes. I was veering in that direction when I noticed the butcher. He was standing, drinking a mug of wine. He was on the right side of the street. Team red, team Blago.

"You cannot vote of course," he said. "But you can drink."

So, I did.

He tried to explain what was going on in Spanish, but I took in less than nothing. The contender, Traficant, stood behind tables that were in a line a hundred feet long. He walked up and down shaking hands, talking to people and occasionally yelling across the street to Blago. I recognized the words "dog" and "car" but little else.

Kappi saw me the moment I noticed him, and when our eyes met I knew I was in for some confused levity. He rolled over to me, an excited ball of energy. I noticed with alarm that he had a beer in his hand and asked him about it.

LOST IN SPAIN

He explained that when it's just sitting out like that he can't be stopped. Somebody would get hurt, he said. Then he elaborated with, "Hahahaha cerveza!" Lifting his red cup and splashing a well-dressed couple that quickly and quietly moved away. Si," I said because I could see.

"Cerveza gratis todo el dia!"

"Si, cerveza. But let's not get too drunk."

He laughed louder than ever and took a gulp that emptied his cup. I had a distinct feeling that he was laughing at the implausibility of my statement on both of our accounts.

"So what is this?" I asked.

"Cerveza gratis todo el dia... but, no marry wanna?"

"I don't think so, no. So what is all this?" I tried again.

"Gratis cerveza todo el dia!" And he clapped me on the back hard enough to rattle my teeth.

Eventually Kappi wandered off twitching his nose, looking for a charitable smoker. I noticed new people arriving who were as apolitical and unaffiliated as I was. Pretty much all the Brits and Spanish teenagers fit that category. We talked, drank, smoked. Somebody lit up a hash cigarette and Kappi appeared out of nowhere like a pot genie.

I noticed Spanish who were not wearing Christmas/gang colors and realized that these were the prized undecided voters whom this entire setup was meant to woo. As one of them would approach they were met with deferential smiles, drinks, and unabashed ass-kissery by Blago or Traficant themselves.

Later, I noticed Hollywood Jose on Blago's side and knew I'd finally get the scoop.

"What's up Hollywood?"

"Ah my friend! How are the Americans today?"

"We are well," I answered for my country. "What is all this?"

"Free beer," he said. "All day."

"Motherfuck."

"What is your bother?" he asked concerned.

"Nothing, never mind. Sorry. Can you explain what going

179

on besides free beer?"

"I can absolutely. This day is of elections. Cause for celebration all around. Our fine mayor wishes to thank his loyal friends and also to convince all the crazy people who are too stupid to do the right thing."

"Looks like they both have the same idea." I said.

"Not, no. The dog fucker of the green is for bribing the ignorant pond scum. [Traficant] is a bad man, my friend. His friends are sick with brain injury. I am for telling you."

"Kappi is drinking." I said to change the subject.

"Yes. How can this be stopped? This is the fault of the father of goats. He would allow the beautiful Darryl Hannah to get drunk even when she was on a blind date with the Bruce Willis. All for voters. He is a sonofabitch, a wandering devil."

I was unnerved. The usually serene, light-hearted Jose had turned into an asshole for the afternoon. If politics could do this to him, what might it do to the less stable? I then remembered Glenn Beck and got another drink.

Promptly at six, as the church bells rang out, Blago and Traficant stepped out from behind their respective sides, met in the middle of the street and shook hands. I was excited for a second, thinking it was the beginning of a duel, but they simply walked up the street into the town hall. Some people rushed to finish their drinks, and other citizens took theirs plus a few extras with them into the hall.

Only the outsiders were left standing in front of tables stacked with booze. The English, the teenagers, Kappi and the Gypsies, a gaggle of Nordic backpackers, and me. For a moment we all looked around at each other with uncertainty. That moment passed and we continued drinking unperturbed.

A few of us, curious, took up our drinks and walked to the town hall. It was a large, impressive 18th century building of slate, marble and ancient-looking wood. The windows were all completely blacked out. I tried the heavy door and found it locked. I knocked to no avail. I put my ear against the wood,

LOST IN SPAIN

but remembered Uncle Willie warning me that a boy had gotten brain termites that way, so I put my ear against the glass. Willie had plenty of stories about glass, but I put them out of my mind to hear what was going on.

Not a sound. It was as if the building were a portal through space and time allowing voters to see the effects of their choices. Or perhaps it was a Tardis and Blago was a Time Lord. It all seemed possible given that absolute, black silence.

I wandered back down to the town square and continued drinking with the Gypsies and Brits, watching as teenagers filled up their backpacks and trunks with free/stolen beer. I asked around, but none of the outsiders knew what was going on. They were all as befuddled as I was and didn't seem to care.

Exactly three hours later at nine pm the town hall's doors opened and the crowds made their way back to the now empty tables in the town square. Blago and his people looked happy in a subdued way. Traficant and his supporters seemed disappointed in a relieved way. They all looked as if they had aged ten years. I caught sight of Hollywood Jose and asked what had gone on.

"Far too much my friend." He answered cryptically. "Our mayor is still yet our beloved mayor so there is much happiness. There is that."

"How did you vote? I mean, what is the process."

"Do you remember when the Tom Cruise was Maverick in *Top Gun* and he was talking to the pretty woman who was not Julia Roberts with the puffy hair?"

"No." I said.

"That is a shame. You really need to see that movie. It is legend. Not the Will Smith movie, it is better than that."

"I saw it; I just don't remember it all."

"I see," he said, disappointed. "Tom told Puffy Hair what I am telling you now. I will not tell you because to do that would be killing you."

"You'd tell me but you'd have to kill me?" I helped.

"Goddamnit. Why must I mess this," he said, clearly exhausted.

I could see that he'd had enough. I didn't push him any further.

Not knowing produced all sorts of eccentric fantasies fighting for attention in my brain. I wondered about human sacrifice. I wondered about Doctor Who. I wondered about Iowa Caucuses.

The next day, posters were taken down, litter was swept up, red and green laundry was taken in, folded, and put away until the next election or somebody needed their red pajama bottoms or green socks. Feuds were dismissed and friendships were remade.

It was as if nothing had happened. The town made up with itself and threw an after election party. There was tapas and churros and paella, beer and wine and music. Traficant milled about clapping shoulders and shaking hands while Mayor Blago packed up his BMW for a week in Greece.

A few days later as I was ordering my crusty bread in the bakery, I saw two little boys pointing at the mayor's autographed picture and saying "*perro* come *pene*." When a middle aged woman came rushing over to give them a playful smack, I knew that nothing will ever change in this world or the next.

These days I still identify as a liberal. For me it's not a complicated decision. I look at the craziest fringe on both sides and ask myself who I'd rather be stuck talking to at a party. It's really no contest.

Once in a while I still turn on Limbaugh or Beck just to get my adrenaline flowing again. I realize now though that they are only entertainers after all. I feel nothing but pity for the scum-sucking dog-fucking family of goats that believe all that nonsense. Nothing but pity. It is only politics after all.

10

MARKET DAY

When you live in a small community, relatively unimportant occasions take on a greater significance than rationality should allow. Look at basketball in Indiana or high school football in Ohio and Texas. Or, especially look at the Westboro Baptist Church of Topeka, Kansas. Such was the case for us. After a few short weeks in the sleepy rural village of Javaron, Spain we were ready for, desperate for, anything. So when Karen and I heard that there was a market—in which vendors would drive in from all over and the high street would be closed off to traffic—we were exuberant, exultant. I imagined a Moroccan-style scene where there were hidden treasures to be bartered for, and around every corner lurked the possibility of danger or potent hash.

The morning of our first Market Day we got up early, both showered, and both put on clean clothes. I even shaved and clipped my nails. These heretofore daily rituals were becoming more of a special occasion, like dinner out at an expensive restaurant or marital sex. It wasn't that our only bathroom was outside (it was) or that I'm inherently lazy (I am), it was because there ceased to be a point to it all. For the

183

first few weeks Karen and I both did what we've always done and presented our best sides to the village. But nobody else did. We began to look down on the great unwashed with pity and disgust. Before long the dirty scourges were following me around prancing and chanting, "Look at the fancy boy in his fancy shirt." Or maybe that only happened in a *Seinfeld* episode, but it felt real, dammit.

Now though, NOW, we had a purpose, a reason for our highfalutin' basic hygiene. We stuffed our pockets with small bills and strode with the excited confidence of hungry Midwesterners headed to a Presbyterian pancake breakfast. We walked up the ancient streets and passed elderly locals laden with bags of oranges, boxes of sardines, baskets of cherries.

"Oooh, there are deals to be had." Karen said.

"Was that a box of sardines?" I asked.

"Looked like a box of sardines to me."

"I didn't know that was a thing."

"You have a lot to learn Scotty, boxes of sardines are the new tub of mayonnaise, let's go."

From a block away we could smell the burning grease and melting chocolate of fresh churros as well as the mouthwatering aroma of meat roasting on a spit fire. There were a half dozen produce stands run by Gypsies who had— unlike our fumbling, bumbling, homegrown clan—been blessed with the gift of thievery. Hungry for a change from my daily routine I picked out a bunch of bananas, a few oranges, peaches, and one giant eggplant. I'd never cooked eggplant before but felt adventurous. It looked so pretty and purple and shiny just sitting there, I couldn't resist. I handed my bounty over to the woman who threw it upon a scale en mass. She looked me up and down as if deciding if I was suitable to enter an exclusive nightclub. She judged me unworthy and sneered "Thirteen euros." I bought the same amount of fruit from the supermercado for less than three euros.

"Es moi cairo," I snorted back with derision, waving my

LOST IN SPAIN

index finger back and forth and shaking my head like a French waiter turning away a poorly dressed tourist who'd asked to use the restroom.

"Why would it be 130 percent more from a produce stand?" Karen asked because she doesn't understand how percentages work.

"You buy or you leave," the Gypsy vendor said.

"We're still deciding," I said.

"Can you tell us more about the fruit?" Karen chimed in. "Are these the Mercedes of oranges?"

"Oooh, maybe they're magical oranges?"

"Don't be stupid, everybody knows beans are the only magical fruit," Karen argued.

"The more you eat the more you toot?"

"What? No. That's not magic. The complex sugars found in beans pass all the way into the large intestine before they are finally broken down. Hence…. Flatulence." Then a small rainbow appeared over Karen's head and she said, "The more you know! I meant beans like Jack and the Beanstalk beans. Real magic."

"That wasn't about beans." I said. "Everybody knows that was about drugs. Beans are a euphemism for ecstasy."

"You had a terrible childhood didn't you?"

"No. It. Was. MAGICAL. I could sing my happy *beans* song in peaceful ignorance."

"Do you have any magic beans?" I asked but the lady was busy ripping off other people. I noticed a white faced tourist staring at me with open mouthed curiosity and said, "What? She started it."

I stood back and watched as she charged the people she seemed to know one price and financially sodomized the tourists and British. As we moved on up the street, I noticed nearly all of the vendors were drinking beer and smoking dope. This was no different than any other day on this particular street, although they all had the shifty eyes and furtive gestures that inspired old-fashioned animosity, bringing to mind the phrases "no-good-nick" and "ne'er-do-

well."

We found one stand selling every variety of nuts imaginable. I ordered a half kilo of pistachios and the guy was kind enough to throw in a long cigarette ash with curling balls of burning hash as a bonus. I believe that's the Spanish version of adding a squirt of butter to movie theater popcorn.

"You're the worst OCD'er ever." Karen said.

"I'm the best O... what?"

"You lock doors and flip light switches forty times, you literally run away from powder laundry detergent. Now you're about to eat salmonella tartare because it comes with salt?"

"And a shell." I said.

"They sit out open in the sun all day every day. Then they sit in a closed up raper van all night being exposed to god knows what. You think a shell is going to protect you?"

"Shells are very defensive. You've obviously never seen *Teenage Mutant Ninja Turtles*." I said.

"You've obviously never seen *Outbreak*." Karen said.

"*Outbreak* was about a monkey. Monkeys will freakin' cut you man."

"A pimp monkey with a switchblade has nothing on these pistachios. I'll be fine."

"I hope your Ninja Turtles visit you in the hospital." Karen said.

"Of course they will. That's what they DO."

"Come on, I want to get churros and chocolate sauce before they run out."

"I hope the hospital offers couples' discounts." I said.

The churros were delicious and not at all poisoned. Turns out fried sugar bread dipped in melty chocolate is even better than stale, salty nuts, but they complemented each other well.

We walked on and found plastic cookware, plastic shoes, and metal toys. I saw a sippy cup emblazoned with a bright green weed leaf and imagined a precocious three year old swinging back his dreads and taking thirsty gulps of Red Bull between

LOST IN SPAIN

bong hits while Sublime leaked out from his ear buds. Then I realized how outrageous that scenario was; Sublime wasn't popular over here, the toddler would be listening to techno or house music.

Further up the street, there were rows of clothing tents. Iconic and legendary faces such as Bob Marley, Tupac, Che Guevara, and Triple H hung alongside sports jerseys. Famous soccer players were prevalent, but Pau Gasol held his own. It was unfortunate that, although the manufacturer nailed the colors of the Los Angeles Lakers, they used the initials NRA in place of NBA. While these two organizations may have some commonalities, their demographics are very, very different.

The sales of sports jerseys were so great as to prompt the entrepreneurial market to shit the bed/throw up all over itself. I was delighted to find regular shirts emblazoned with non-sports related celebrities. There was Penelope Cruz printed on the back of a polo shirt. Antonio Banderas on a V-neck. Name a celebrity, any Spanish celebrity, and you could find them on a shirt. My favorite was Sergio Garcia on what someone, somewhere, believed was a golf shirt. If the potential customer—I never saw anyone buy or wear the shirt—wanted to dress up as Sergio's caddy for Halloween, they were set. The biggest sellers were anything with Nadal printed on it. A witty Moroccan vendor could stitch Nadal onto the inseam of a Members Only jacket and it would sell like Members Only jackets at a *Sopranos* reunion party.

My favorites were the T-shirts that made a statement. Literally. I still have a photo of one featuring the supernova of celebrity, Vanilla Ice. He looked as if a rabid badger had attacked his eyebrows and had his hands twisted into the universal gang sign for Douchebag White Protestant. Below his head are the words "Steel Forgings," "Immunity," and "Tribal Forceness." Another shirt said simply, "Feel the energy nothing is too good for everybody!" I still use this as a kind of Aurelius Meditation. The only other word salad garment I remember—and only because I took a picture—

187

was "Paradise, Blue For You Can Achieve A Dreamer."

Other stalls featured knitwear with men on horses, or alligators sewn somewhere in the general vicinity of the chest, sometimes low and centered as to appear like a mutant belly button. They sold shoddily made lingerie, plastic sneakers, and faux fur vests, sunglasses with names like Rae Ban, and purses that didn't even try.

Cash money burning a hole through my pocket and disappointed in the flea market-quality merchandise, I wanted to end the experience on a positive note in the only way I knew how: eating.

"Let's go back to the spit fire chicken man!" I said to Karen.

"It's eleven a.m. and we just ate the diabetic's special."

"The chicken's for tonight. I'm going to get a coffee. I'll meet you at home."

Karen made the right decision. I waited in line for close to an hour, and then I waited in line for another hour. Small, round, elderly, but determined Spanish women kept cutting in front of me in line and I was too much of a gentleman to complain. Besides, I couldn't think of what to say. The grease smoke choked me to tears and the sun beat down on my balding head with what could only be xenophobic malice. I wanted to give up many times but it became a personal challenge, something to achieve. Some people try to win the Pulitzer or the Nobel, others championship rings and trophy wives, me: I just wanted to bring a fucking chicken home.

Karen joined me as I got near the front of the line.

"What the hell?"

"Eerrrggh" I said because I was in the zone.

Finally it was my time. I was sweaty, pouty, and weepy but I had arrived. It was my moment and I was going to shine. I ordered "una de pollo" and watched as the vendor unhooked a dark brown, crispy bird and put it in a filthy metal sectioning box. The box, like everything else, had sat in the sun for four hours. I didn't question the sanitation of the

LOST IN SPAIN

operation. I didn't complain about the line. I hadn't punched any old ladies. I was proud of myself. The chicken man placed the crushed, but now packable, meat in a cardboard takeout box and, before I could stop him, poured a ladle of hot grease over the whole thing. Now my crispy chicken was mushy chicken grease soup. He set the container down and added to the pool of grease dripping off the table and forming a lake on the ground. I'd reached my breaking point and became the ugly American stereotype I loathed.

Pointing to the cauldron of boiling oil I shrieked, "No, no, no motherfucking grease please. How the fuck do you not have a heart attack just serving this?"

"Well that escalated quickly." Karen said because the *Anchorman* line was perfect for the occasion. It was enough to restore my sanity and a second later I recovered and said, "Lo siento. Una de pollo sin grasas. Lo siento por favore."

"You want dry chicken?" he asked sardonically.

"Yes please."

The chicken man pulled another bird from the spit.

"You don't even have to section it."

"It will not fit into the box if it is not chopped." He said.

"I can carry it whole. Sorry."

"You are very strange." He said.

"Yes I am. Sorry. Really, sorry."

"It is motherfucking ok. You are very strange."

"Yes. Sorry."

He placed the chicken on top of the box. Only the bottom third fit in. It looked like a fat cat trying to sit in a jewelry box. After re-apologizing profusely I paid. It was seven euros but I gave him a ten and told him to keep the change because I'm cool like that. I had to carry it with two hands, the way you might carry a baby or an expensive bowling ball, say.

"So," Karen said. "You think you finally snapped?"

"No not yet. I was hot and frustrated and old ladies kept elbow blocking me into other old ladies who then pushed me and I was choking on grease smoke and that chicken looked so crispy and then that bad man poured melted fat all over

everything."

"That's exactly what someone who'd snapped would say. How long before you're standing on a roof naked with a blow up doll and a machete?"

"I did that last week. For our housewarming party?"

"We didn't have a housewarming party." Karen said.

"And now you know why."

"This is why we don't have nice things." she said.

"We have crispy chicken sin grasas."

The market was not what I had expected: nothing ever is when you live in my brain. It was unique for us though and became something we looked forward to twice a month for three years. They started getting better as well. New vendors came with new merchandise and foodstuffs.

A leather-monger came and brought a herb guy and a plant girl. One stand came and offered a small variety of gag gifts: fake blood pills, a fake vomit and fake poop, masks, wigs and handcuffs. I spent a lot of money there. A grilled sausage and pepper stand popped up as did a cart selling loaded baked potatoes. When I bought one Karen told me my Irish was sticking out which made me feel self-conscious.

Through it all I kept buying my chicken from my chicken man. I always apologized for the unhappy incident and I always tipped. Once every month or two he'd say, "Look, the motherfucking dry chicken man!" as a kind of witty banter.

We went when we didn't want or need anything. We went to other markets in other villages. I never understood why. I've often ruminated on what drove me there. Was it blind American consumerism, or something deeper? Did I want a sense of experiencing another culture at the microeconomic level, or was it just the dry, crispy chicken?

11

AWKWARD INSECURITY

I'm insecure around people I've just met. It's enough to cause me to forget who I am in a fundamental way. I suffer a temporary personality disorder whereby I mimic, mime and impersonate anyone unfortunate enough to be in my vicinity. I'm not always aware I'm doing it at the time. It just happens, like a tan when you live in Florida or sex when you're young and shameless enough to beg.

When I find myself in an urban setting, around the young or the black for instance, my pants tend to loosen and drop an inch or two. Not as low as some mind you—I don't have the ass or the coordination for that—just low enough to make me feel part of the community. Walking, I begin to stride my right leg slightly further than my left. Not enough to show a pronounced limp, just enough to give me a subtle gangsta shuffle. Think George Jefferson on lithium and you'll be close enough. My voice gets twangy and my vocabulary switches with the ease of a Babel Fish.

"What's crackin'?" I inquire. "Five-oh creepin' round the cut," I yell as the youngins get ghost.

"I'm one of you," I'm trying to say. Not that anyone

191

would mistake me for an undercover cop, my skull's not symmetrical enough and my posture is terrible.

I play spades, roll dice, and knock bones (dominoes) with the best of them. It's all good as long as the games involve sitting or counting and not running or jumping. And for a moment or two I DO belong. It feels authentic and warm and not at all disingenuous.

I grew up around a lot of Italians and upon entering their homes I instantly transformed into another character, one that was tactile and effusive and warm. I kissed everyone, twice. I allowed grandma—nonna—to pinch my face with the sharp, desperate fervor of love. I ate seconds or thirds as we listened to opera on AM radio. I never brought up the mafia or politics as the former would start a screaming match and the latter would end in blood and tears.

When I hung out with my Irish friends, I laughed and sulked and drank and fought and eventually went to rehab.

With one set of friends, I listened to Metallica and smoked pot and watched *Beavis and Butthead*. With another set of friends, I listened to Tupac and Public Enemy and smoked pot and watched old gangster movies. With some, I listened to the Grateful Dead and smoked pot and drank wine and created god-awful art. With others, I listened to pirate radio and discussed philosophy, the positives of communism, and the Carls: Jung and Sagan. We decried the banality of twenty-first century life while smoking pot and eating ice cream. With the jocks, I played basketball and drank beer and watched sports. With the rich kids, I pretended to know which fork to use and held it in my left hand while their parents were home. After they went out or retired to their quarters, we smoked pot and drank and stabbed each other with silver cutlery. The pot was the same quality, but the liquor was top shelf and the glasses were crystal.

Looking back now, I shouldn't blame the Irish for my stints in rehab.

I'd roam from group to group like the X in an algebra equation, hiding behind a parenthesis and praying not to be

LOST IN SPAIN

noticed by the last set.

Maybe it's not a personality disorder, maybe there is a vacuum where my soul should be. I mean a Hoover as well as a matter-less void. Once I spend a certain amount of time around people, I invariably end up sucking bits and pieces of their personality into my own. Which is only a larger collection of bits and pieces of other people's soul debris. I leave my friends spent, exhausted, empty, while myself becoming whimsical or angry or a genius Time Lord committed to saving the universe. Then, while they slouch in a corner and quietly cry, I build a scale model zombie apocalypse using prescription bottles and Smurf action figures, yell at random tourists, or travel through space and time saving the universe as non-violently as possible. Do you see how this works?

I'm a voracious reader, and my favorite authors' writing styles rub off on me almost unconsciously. After a Sedaris streak, I tend towards cultural humor and self-depreciation. After another long bout of Adams' "Hitchhiker's Guide," I use throw-aways and disinterested nuttiness with a philosophical bent. When I read my favorite blogs, I write run-on sentences and stream of consciousness-focused inanity. When I read too many political sites or YouTube comments, I give up and soak in a bleach bubble bath. When people accuse me of being unoriginal, I Google a witty Dorothy Parker comeback.

All that said, it really is unintentional and usually unconscious. I have a deep-seated desire to make people comfortable, to make them happy, and to make them tea if tea makes them happy. Since I am so influenced by other peoples' moods I need them to be comfortable, so I can be comfortable. If I'm around a calm friend, I remain calm. If I happen upon a panicked stranger, I become even more frantic myself which makes it worse for them—seeing a total stranger panic from whatever is going on in their own head probably adds to their paranoia—which makes me even

193

panic-ier still when I realize that I don't even know why I'm panicked to begin with. I'd make a terrible hostage negotiator. I'd scream into the megaphone, "Oh my god you're going to kill everybody aren't you?" I'd make a poor therapist, CIA agent, or funeral director as well. I'd fail at any profession that doesn't involve me sitting on the couch all day watching cat videos. I'm good at that as long as I don't read the comments.

The only instance where I don't camouflage myself against the cultural backdrop of my peers is when I hate my peers. When that's the case I make myself the exact opposite by default. If I find myself surrounded by rednecks, I become an intellectual elitist. Around snobs, I am proletariat. Forced to interact with right-wing evangelicals, I'm transformed into a pagan transsexual. Thankfully, I'm never forced to interact with right-wing evangelicals.

I'm a people person, though, so I usually just emulate. I went to school with some of the wealthiest kids in Pittsburgh and some of the poorest. What I thought of as my adaptability allowed me to move seamlessly between the socioeconomic mixes without ever getting too close to any of them. Looking back now I realized it wasn't adaptability. It was a social ineptitude.

Still, the ability to blend in was my superpower, and when you're blessed with a gift like that it's a sin not to use it. I'd rather have the ability to fly or breathe underwater or whatever the Green Lantern had. Even if it was just the lantern itself. You don't get to pick these things, however, they pick you.

Europe was my Kryptonite. Not only could I not speak Spanish well enough to emulate regional accents, I couldn't speak it well enough to enunciate the difference between chicken breast and penis... breast. The Spanish told me that I sounded like a Mexican. A drunk and stupid Mexican. The butcher, literally, said that. I don't know if he was prejudiced against Mexicans or prejudiced against me. The primary

LOST IN SPAIN

language was out. On top of that I wasn't even able to speak English. Not the way the English spoke it. Back home, I made people accept me as one of their own by using slight changes in inflection and vocabulary. Here, it was impossible. I'd practice Liverpool and Manchester accents only to sound drunk and angry and still it didn't work. I'd attempt a posh London accent and come off sounding like a Dickensian wretch who had wandered into a mental hospital for the chronically confused.

I couldn't dress like them either. The Spanish youth had a fashion sense that I'd call '80s Glam rock. There was a lot of white leather, high collars, and shimmery pants. They wore ankle boots and even their underwear and socks were studded. Their hair was coifed and moussed and trained like a well-loved dog or an exceptional ferret. The trend towards metrosexuality didn't miss Spain and the boys were almost prettier than the girls. Their eyebrows were as manicured as their fingernails and they all had the flawless skin of Polynesian royalty. They were all shiny and perfect and I knew I could not compete with that and, therefore, hated them bitterly. None of them drove cars, they all rode motorcycles that I prayed would tip over just once.

Most of the English seemed to put so little effort into their appearance that, paradoxically, it proved far too labor intensive for me. The lugubrious nonchalance that was required to form a respectable gaggle of dreadlocks was enough to make me crave a nap. They probably wasted a dozen pairs of perfectly good corduroys just to create one with the proper fraying and staining. The authentic hash burns looked stylish, but took years to acquire. I never had the pants commitment necessary to find out.

I knew I needed a new tack, but I didn't know what tacks were or where I might buy one in our small village. So I settled for a new strategy instead. If I couldn't talk like them or dress like them I could at least find some common interests to share. We were all human after all, I just had to find the bridges that cross all cultural boundaries. We all want

195

the best for our children, for example, and held an unexpressed desire for misfortune to befall our betters. We all dream of success, admiration, and wealth, but most of us repudiate the thought of wasting our youth in the endeavor. We all have an innate need to be noticed, to make a difference, to matter as something more than the carbon compost that is our shared destiny.

Sports! I thought. Sports had saved my formative years from social ruin; they might just save me again. I'd been amazed to find a basketball court in Javaron and more amazed to see people playing. I walked down to the court and with a series of gestures and nods joined a game. I played well, but my mannerisms were all wrong.

During free throws, I bunched my shorts into my fists resting on my knees and leaned forward as if for a colon exam. They put their hands on their heads and leaned back, skyward, as if asking God for more oxygen. I tried it once, but felt something in my back give out. After a big basket, I'd unhinge my jaw and shriek in a primal scream of victory while they turned away, embarrassed. After a late three pointer, I attempted a chest bump with a teammate who had no chest bumping experience. He turned away at the last minute causing me to look ridiculous. I can imagine the sight of my naked, white torso flying one inch off the ground toward a cringing, light brown body turning away in fear and possibly disgust.

They kept chattering in smooth, melodic Spanish while I shouted, "I'm open all day over here!" in a brash American screech.

After one of the kids made a shot at the end of the game (first to *trienta*), he produced a Spanish flag out of thin air like patriotic magic, draped it over his shoulders, and pretended to fly around the court like an airplane. *Well where the fuck am I going to find an American flag before tomorrow night's game,* I thought. The game was over and I tried to fist bump while they tried to high five; I slapped them on the ass while they

LOST IN SPAIN

looked offended.

What I'm trying to establish here is that I am not a terrible human being. I can be selfish and irritable and immature, but I'm almost never terrible. The number one rule in writing is show, don't tell, though, so I'm basically screwed.

After a lifetime of social awkwardness and conscious and unconscious mimicry, after two years of knowing I wasn't fitting in, knowing that I couldn't fit in, Karen and I took a vacation to Italy.

The awkwardity, as well as yet another public display of personal humiliation, could have been avoided entirely if only I had a filter between my brain and my face. I do not.

After a marathon night in which we drove from Javaron to Malaga, flew to Pisa, and took a train to Florence, we arrived at the hotel at four in the morning. We got up, groggy and befuddled and made our way down to the lobby of our hotel for the free breakfast buffet. After slamming back four espressos from the coffee machine, I was a little too excited at the prospect of eating. A waiter came by and I ordered freshly squeezed orange juice just as I was getting up to start the binging process. I am a true American at heart, so I piled the food high and wide upon my plates. Plates, plural. It had been two days since I'd had a real meal.

I saw the girl bringing my juice just as I was returning to my table. She looked at me in what I first assumed was either a half disgusted grimace or half really big grin out of the right side of her face. Only the right side of her face. She kind of looked like Billy Idol and The Joker had a lovechild who now worked food service in an Italian hotel. She looked like she didn't know whether to laugh hysterically or start screaming at the gluttonous American. That's all I thought it was. I thought she was simply reacting to my two plates of food heaped high with fat and sugar.

I'm not sure if it was the sleep deprivation, the meth-like espresso, the cultural guilt I felt for being such an obnoxious pig, or just my social ineptitude that made me do it, but I

smiled/grimaced right back at her. It was as if my face had a mind of its own and matched her freakish half grin molar for molar. My thoughts raced to make sense of the situation even as my face contorted. *What is going on here?* I thought. *Is she disgusted and happy at the same time? Maybe she likes me and hates me at the same time—that's a thing right? I wonder if she had a stroke while smoking crack, so instead of half of her face getting sad and droopy it got all tweak-y and hyper. Is that a thing?* I was sure I've heard of that being a thing. *She'd be really fun to party with*, I thought.

I tried to act natural and slowly even out my own smile. I tried to pretend that I was just really shocked and awed that not only did they have oranges in Northern Italy, but that they even squeezed them into a drinkable liquid and brought the delightful concoction to my very table!

I can't imagine how hideous I looked. Actually, I can because in addition to the twisted grin, I was also caught in the Fake Smile Continuum, a look that's been captured many times. When I smile unnaturally, in the presence of a camera, say, or somebody I'm supposed to like but don't, something happens to my eyes. They get weird and googley-ish and far too intense. I end up either looking a little slow or very manic in a "who can I kill next" kind of way.

The fake smile continuum loop presents itself often. I'll be at a party or at work, around people I don't necessarily not like, but don't know well enough to feel comfortable with when this sudden alien-like feeling comes over my face. I become aware that I'm smiling in a not at all convincing manner and try to overcompensate by smiling even harder, showing more teeth. And it hurts. It hurts my concentration and it hurts my face.

At this point I also become aware of my hands, as if for the first time. *It's weird that my hands are in my pockets*, I think, and remove them only to find that they have nowhere good to go. I put them on my hips and know in an instant that this is all wrong as well. I cross my arms over my chest, my hands

now clenched into fists, and now I feel like an actor playing an asshole cop on a bad procedural drama.

"Stop fidgeting," I hear my mother say from across space and time. I put my hands back into my pockets but I'm lost. Irrevocably lost. Now my hands are trying to fly away like jittery birds and my face hurts. I feel frozen, stiff, and yet fluttery at the same terrible time.

The person or people standing two feet away might be talking about the stock market or a race riot and I'm still wearing an inappropriate plastic smile. A death mask of socially awkward pain.

"Would a normal person smile at this?" I ask myself. If they're talking about the stock market I'm stuck because I don't know if the stock market is supposed to be a good or a bad thing because I don't understand how economics works. If they were talking about a race riot I'm happy because I don't have to smile anymore, but if they were talking about there not being any more race riots I'm kind of screwed.

All the while my hands are trying to escape my body and my smile is trying to chew itself off of my face, my eyes are bulging like something out of a cartoon. At least I have an explanation for this last problem.

In both my third and fourth grade school pictures my eyes were closed. I wasn't a sleepy child, I'd just been caught in the act of blinking. Two years running. These two consecutive bad luck pictures traumatized me in an unspeakable way because I can't remember any of it. Now though, when I see a camera appear my eyes get as big as my fake smile and inexplicably bulge even further. The effect is greater than the sum of its parts. The effect is staggering, hideous. I know because I catch glimpses of myself in the dilating pupils of those backing away from me in haste. This is why I should not be allowed to leave the house.

I did leave the house though. This should have been the end of it, but I am constitutionally incapable of letting things go. *It doesn't matter,* I thought. *I have to make this girl feel better.* So I

hatched a plan to make her feel better. When I saw her again I smiled/grimaced again in an attempt to make her think that this was my natural reaction to seeing people.

The Girl also performed bartending duties at night, so she was the one I had to ask for ice to take up to my room. Because I eat ice every night, this gave me ample opportunity to make amends. I knew she was watching me as I entered the room, so I always had to crazy eye smile/grimace at every tourist who was nearby in an attempt to further deceive her. They'd glance up with a "I'm on vacation let's be civil but not talk" look and I'd stretch half of my face skyward. They would look away and usher their children out of the room. I'd glance at The Girl to see if she'd seen and her back was usually turned, but I could see a satisfied set in her shoulders, a forgiving tilt to her head.

When she brought me the ice, I'd pretend that it was the most astonishing beautiful, iciest ice that I'd ever been privileged to receive and I'd show my appreciation by showing her where my upper right wisdom tooth used to live.

The morning of our last day in Florence, Karen and I went down for breakfast. Once we were settled in, The Girl walked up to our table and asked what we'd be drinking with her usual plucky Italian charm. What was not usual, what was extremely unusual, was her face. Her face was as unremarkable as an extra in a Richard Gere film about bored white people. I felt shocked, horrified, and sick to my stomach. I felt betrayed, like I'd never known her at all. The next table over must have felt my intense surprise and glanced over. I smiled the same smile I'd been forced to smile since that first morning—my sideways, crack-stroke smile of stupidity—damned if I was going to break character this late in the game. They both looked away and I put my lip back down.

The Girl asked again what we'd like and this time smiled. The smile seemed directed at me and I also thought I saw a glint of "fuck you" in her eyes, but I often imagine these things. I was stuck now, all-in, so I smiled that same screwy

LOST IN SPAIN

half smile up at her and ordered my orange juice. If what she'd had was a temporary facial tic it would be far too coincidental for mine to have disappeared at the same time. So I "smiled" again when she brought the juice. I "smiled" at the guy who brought our luggage down and I "smiled" at the front desk staff as we settled our bill.

I gave everybody their tips for the week, healthy American-sized tips, and when I got to The Girl she stopped, everything stopped, time stopped.

"Thank you, you are beautiful," I said.

"Yes," was her only answer.

I could almost hear the hotel breathe a sigh of relief as I walked out. The doors behind us whooshed shut just as one window in the lower right corner opened in a lopsided grin.

ABOUT THE AUTHOR

Scott Oglesby now lives back in sunny Florida with his wife Karen, two dogs and one very strange cat.

He is hard at work on a novel, because after careful consideration he realized that if a fictional character gets on his nerves he can kill him without going to prison. He thinks that will be sweet!

You can follow Scott Oglesby on Facebook
https://www.facebook.com/scott.oglesby.9

Stay up to date on his exploits by visiting his website at
www.ScottOglesby.com

Printed in Great Britain
by Amazon.co.uk, Ltd.,
Marston Gate.